Michael Kirst

The Governance of Teacher Education

M. L. Cushman

A Phi Delta Kappa Publication
distributed by

McCutchan Publishing Corporation
2526 Grove Street
Berkeley, California 94704

Library of Congress catalog card number 76-52063
ISBN 0-8211-0228-1

Printed in the United States of America

TO
CLIFF

Contents

Foreword

In this book Martelle Cushman copes with one of the most serious problems of a free society: the governance of teacher education. Teacher education has provided a major market for the product of higher education in the United States since colonial days. From the end of the Civil War until Pearl Harbor, at least 50 percent of all persons completing two years or more of college were destined to teach in school or college. From Pearl Harbor until the launching of Sputnik in 1957, one-third of all college students were preparing, consciously or unconsciously, to teach.

As of the fall of 1976, about 20 percent of the more than eleven million students enrolled in two- and four-year institutions of higher learning were in teacher education programs. Taking turnover into account, and including two hundred thousand estimated future college teachers, it is a fair guess that two million persons will probably attend colleges or universities in preparation to teach in schools, institutions of higher learning, or related establishments during the rest of this century. This may be considered a nearly stable situation in U.S. higher education. The costs of providing higher education year in and year out for two million future U.S. teachers in nine hundred institutions, figured conservatively, comes to about ten billion dollars a year.

With such a large number of students and so large a budget coming from federal, state, and private sources, it is no wonder that governance of teacher education has been and continues to be a serious and complicated problem.

Compounding this problem further is the fact that in the United States the schools and colleges have lay governance. Just as lay governance in the United States is unique, so the teaching profession that serves these institutions has become unique. And it follows that teacher education is unique. This makes it dangerous to make too many comparisons of teacher education with professions like law and medicine.

For several years some of us have encouraged Dean Emeritus Cushman to tackle the problem covered in this book. He is well qualified. For eighteen years he was dean of one of the colleges of education in the National Association of State Universities and Land Grant Colleges. He was chairman of the Studies Committee of the American Association of Colleges for Teacher Education in the early sixties, as well as national president of Phi Delta Kappa. These professional activities have taken him to nearly a hundred campuses. He has known and communicated with many historic figures in teacher education over a long period. Armstrong, Peik, Flowers, Hunt, Hager, Hill, Evenden, Wright, and Stinnet are to him vivid personalities who worked and sometimes struggled for their beliefs about teacher education, a struggle now continued by such newer lights as Cyphert, Davies, Denemark, Edelfelt, Haberman, Howsam, Pomeroy and Masoner.

There is in these pages a great deal of documentation of the factors affecting the control of teacher education policies from World War II through the present. Cushman's bibliography is the most comprehensive ever put together on this topic.

The data he presents and the conclusions he draws create an interesting and rather sobering picture of the forces and problems that are likely to affect classroom teachers, college teacher education faculty, deans, directors and chairmen, trustees, students, and citizens in the foreseeable future.

If one wishes to affect the governance of teacher education, one has at least four important avenues open: (1) expand the knowledge base; (2) orient the preservice and inservice personnel on control procedures; (3) suggest changes in structures and processes; and

(4) develop movements, secure coalescences of groups, and motivate them with a missionary zeal. This book is addressed to the first three. The reader must undertake the fourth.

Dean Cushman has his answers to the question, "Who should control teacher education during the next twenty-five years?" His answers are stated clearly and definitely, and it should be fascinating to read these answers now and make your own predictions, then check in 1985 or 1995 and see how it all turns out.

John E. King
Southern Illinois University

Preface

The influence of educational organization on the performance of educational functions is poorly understood and too little appreciated. There are many lay and professional people who should be interested in better understanding the complex relationships between the structures for teacher education and the governance policies that emanate from them. Four groups in particular might wish to be better informed concerning the controls over the preparation of the nation's teachers.

One group consists of those teacher educators who are devoting a lifetime to such preparation: deans of colleges of education, department chairmen and faculty members in such colleges, and supervisors of student teaching. Indeed, this study was to some extent inspired by the endorsement given it in 1972 by the executive committee of the deans in the Association of Schools and Colleges of Education in State Universities and Land Grant Colleges. (In one respect, therefore, this is a report to that association.) A second group includes other university personnel: the president, his vice-presidents, other deans, the faculty in academic and vocational specializations for teachers, and of course, the students planning to become teachers. The third group includes professionals and lay people outside the university: the governing boards of academic institutions, governmental officials, state department of education professionals, and national leaders in teacher education. At the local school level are thousands of parents and school board members who might want to know who controls the education their teachers receive. But the largest group is the million and a half local school teachers who are interested in the preparation of their successors because they supervise them in student teaching experiences, because the entrance of these students into the profession vitally affects their own welfare, and because such teachers want a post-graduate education that is meaningful in upgrading their own skills.

This is a most opportune time to improve teacher education by analyzing its controls because the emphasis of the profession is shifting from the graduating of sheer numbers, so necessary in the sixties, toward the improvement of quality. There is also a noticeable shift toward improving the local schools themselves through better preparation for all teachers and school service personnel. The modern world has grown so complex that modern man cannot be educated to cope with it, let alone guide it, unless his education is made more efficient and much more relevant. The margin between education and catastrophe as it affects civilization, noted by H. G. Wells a half century ago, grows narrower with each passing year.

The current ferment within the broad spectrum of the profession of education also makes this an opportune time for improvement. The day is past when professional educators and academicians recognized that they both had a common stake in teacher education, and the day is now at hand when the education profession itself, as represented by the National Education Association, the American Federation of Teachers, and other practitioners, recognizes its interdependence with college teachers and acknowledges the contributions each can make to wise and effective teacher education policy.

No one has in recent years digested the huge volumes of literature concerned, both directly and peripherally, with the governance of teacher education. Although I attempt to do that in this book, I still do not have all the answers. This volume is merely an introduction to a complex subject, and it is hoped that others will systematically investigate university governance to determine what is best for teacher education by on-the-scene visits that can be more evaluative. Further, it is hoped some researcher will systematically comb through the files of the National Council for the Accreditation of Teacher Education in order to sort out the influence of institutional structure on the discharge of the institution's responsibilities in teacher education. My efforts to be objective probably cannot mask my own ideas of what might be or ought to be. One cannot live with the business of education from elementary school through graduate school for over four decades and keep his prejudices from showing through. I shall have served my purpose if the reader is clear as to what are the wise observations of others and what are my own. Perhaps such observations will inspire others to expand this search for a more defensible rationale for the governance of teacher education than that which currently prevails.

Computer searches for references through Bradley University in Peoria, Illinois, and the Systems Development Corporation at Santa Monica, California, produced only a few dozen relevant sources. Consequently most of the references reviewed in the chapters that follow were developed by the usual "hand labor" procedures. This effort produced a good number of books, pamphlets, bulletins, mimeographed committee reports, and other pertinent documents. One relatively early work that assembled a list of the many influences on teacher education was written by Stiles, Bar, Douglass, and Mills, who saw more than a dozen national, regional, state, and local bodies as influential in determining teacher education policy (Stiles et al., 1960, pp. 69-95).

Naturally, I have had considerable help in compiling this report. Mere acknowledgment of such assistance is not enough, but that is all I can generate at this time. My indebtedness to Dr. Thomas J. Clifford, president of the University of North Dakota, is extensive, because leave to write on this project has been most valuable. Similar support was rendered by Dr. John Penn, dean of summer studies and assistant to the president. The year-long "professional home" made for me at the University of Illinois at Urbana by William P. McLure, David D. Henry, Harry S. Broudy, Ernest F. Anderson, J. Marlowe Slater, and the late Ray Williams made possible the first drafts of the manuscript. The second draft was made possible by spending several months with another coterie of professional colleagues in higher education at Southern Illinois University, where much encouragement was freely given by Elmer J. Clark, Arthur L. Casebeer, Jack W. Graham, John B. Hawley, Roland

Keene, and Donald J. Tolle. The chairman of this department, John E. King, must be accorded a special note of appreciation because of both material and professional help of significant proportions. Without his assistance this project would not have been completed.

The second draft of the manuscript, submitted to a number of professional colleagues in many parts of the country, elicited suggestions for new emphases, rearrangement, additional sources, and several corrections, all of which have greatly enriched the final product, although, of course, that does not relieve me from the author's usual final responsibility. These colleagues included George W. Denemark, Bill J. Fullerton, Fred F. Harcleroad, Virgil Lagomarcino, Edward C. Pomeroy, David E. Purpel, Donald W. Robinson, and Frank Steeves. Certain chapters were also reviewed by Rolf W. Larson and Roy A. Edelfelt. The most valuable assistance of my two secretaries, Donna Winczewski and Julie Fredericksen, is also gratefully acknowledged.

Finally, I must pay tribute to my daughter Marlene, whose review of syntax, grammar, and vocabulary greatly improved expression, and to my wife, Florence, whose encouragement was continuous and whose patience was greater than my own.

M. L. Cushman
University of North Dakota

There are few earthly things more beautiful than a University. It is a place where those who hate ignorance may strive to know, where those who perceive truth may strive to make others see; where seekers and learners alike, banded together in the search for knowledge, will honor thought in all its finer ways, will welcome thinkers in distress or in exile, will uphold ever the dignity of thought and learning and will exact standards in these things. They give to the young in their impressionable years the bond of a lofty purpose shared, of a great corporate life whose links will not be loosed until they die. They give young people that close companionship for which youth longs, and that chance of the endless discussion of themes which are endless—without which youth would seem a waste of time. There are few earthly things more splendid than a University. In these days of broken frontiers and collapsing values—when every future looks somewhat grim, and every ancient foothold has become something of a quagmire, wherever a University stands, it stands and shines; wherever it exists, the free minds of men, urged on to full and fair inquiry, may still bring wisdom into human affairs.

John Masefield

I

Social Change and Teacher Education—
An Introduction

The history of American education clearly reveals that the American people have had a continuing faith in the capacity of education to make each generation of citizens competent for the difficult task of self-governance so essential to a democratic society. This faith has manifested itself in many ways since schools were established on the Atlantic seaboard nearly as soon as the forests could be cleared away and log cabins and churches could be built. This faith has sustained the American public school system as one that has been free, democratic, nonpartisan, nonsectarian and public in its purposes, organization, financing, and controls for more than two centuries. Within recent years, the criticism of public education might lead one to believe that this faith is not only waning but has been seriously eroded. The perspective of history, however, indicates that criticism and suggestions for improvement have always characterized education in the United States. Indeed, this is one of the little-appreciated features of a democracy: it carries within it the freedom for critical analysis, and this in turn becomes the generating mechanism for slow but constant self-renewal.

Frequent Criticisms of American Education

In recent years, these criticisms have become so pronounced, and so magnified by radio, television, magazines, and dramatic public speakers, that the American people, perhaps more today than in the past, have become increasingly concerned with the general welfare of their school system. Much of this criticism of education is laid at the doorstep of the teachers and their administrators and is in turn directed at the teacher education institutions—schools, colleges, and departments of teacher education. The question then arises, "What if anything, is deficient, in the organization and governance of these colleges that makes it difficult for them properly to prepare teachers and administrators for the local schools?" This organization and governance is what this study is all about. Educating teachers in multipurpose state universities is more difficult than educating architects, doctors, lawyers, engineers, and other professionals, because colleges of education must tap the resources of universities wherever they may be found, while other professional schools are relatively self-contained. Some elements of teacher education specialization are found in colleges of arts and sciences in the traditional academic subjects, some in the vocational departments such as business education, agricultural education, home economics education, and industrial arts education, which may be outside of both arts and sciences colleges and colleges of education. How do colleges of education organize themselves, and how does their governance fit into the overall governance of the university? A review of how they actually do operate may throw some light on how they should operate to prepare school personnel.

During the decade of the sixties, certain specific shortcomings of the schools have been criticized with increasing frequency. These include such failures as their apparent inability to effectively teach minority groups such as Spanish-Americans, American Indians, inner-city blacks, and other culturally disadvantaged populations. The schools have also been accused of making inadequate attempts to provide vocational education opportunities, and the notion of "career education" is now one of the bywords of the day. The schools have been so concerned with the preparation of students for college that they have forgotten that 40 to 60 percent of students never attend, or, having attended, never graduate from, an academic program in higher education. The schools are caught up in the social movement toward egalitarianism and anti-intellectualism. It is said that they are staffed by personnel of second- and third-rate ability.

Critics frequently maintain that the schools fail to update their curricula in an age of science. Developments such as the "open classroom" and "free" schools are suggested as answers to the nation's current socioeconomic problems, and when the schools fail to accept these answers, then, of course, they are said to have failed society itself. The trend toward egalitarianism is discernible in the notion that our schools are staffed by lower-middle-class teachers imposing middle-class values on students in culturally deprived areas, resulting in a lack of success for the former and unhappiness for the latter. There are repeated pleas for the notion of "alternative" schools, which would allow parents, ethnic groups, religious groups, and ideological groups to promote, under the name of democracy, their own particular set of educational values.

During the sixties the social, economic, political, and international ills of American society permeated the consciousness of the American people, and the schools were made the scapegoat for failure either to recognize the problems on the horizon or to adjust school programs to them. Such social evils as poverty, racism, and environmental pollution were said to exist because of current and past failures of schools, just as limited scientific accomplishment represented failure a decade earlier to teach the fundamentals of modern science and mathematics.

These criticisms, many of which were made by responsible educators, produced little change in the schools, and the reasons for this lack of responsiveness were demanded with repeated frequency. It was explained by Harry Broudy on the grounds that schools were characterized by bureaucratic rigidity, a middle-class bias, and a lack of sensitivity and intelligence among teachers and administrators (Broudy, 1972). Silberman ascribed this lack of responsiveness by the schools to the "mindlessness of teacher education institutions and the professors of education" (Silberman, 1970).

Criticisms of Teacher Education

These criticisms were often extrapolated into criticisms of teacher education and teacher institutions, because this was where the weaknesses of the teachers and administrators were thought to have had their origins. Critics accused teacher education institutions of irrelevant curricula, of programs that were out of touch with the socioeconomic changes of the real world, of softness in their demands on scholarship and depth of subject-matter fields. It was said that their personnel lacked motivation to publish scholarly work or to involve themselves in the professional life of the public schools into which their graduates went. Colleges of education were accused of stressing pre-service training at the expense of in-service preparation for those whose education needed updating in the public schools.

Considerable criticism was leveled at education instructors in colleges, who were considered ineffective in many respects. One study concluded that those teacher education faculty members judged to be ineffective in their teaching performances were most strongly characterized as (a) lacking in knowledge of their special field and in preparation for college teaching; (b) unable to relate effectively with their colleagues and students, and emotionally un- stable; and (c) lacking in motivation, creativeness, and ability to communicate effectively, and unable to use instructional methods and materials effectively. They were also found wanting in their research activities because they lacked specific research knowledge, had little preparation for the tasks of educational research, and lacked creativeness. They were further criticized as ineffective in their service functions because of their lack of relevant professional experience, their emotional instability, their inability to relate effectively to their broader community, and again, their lack of motivation and ability to communicate effectively (King and Ellis, 1971).

The curricula of teacher education institutions were attacked because students spent seven semesters learning about teaching and only one semester teaching. Students had few professional laboratory experiences for working with children in the classrooms prior to student teaching in the typical four-year program. Additionally, colleges of education lacked effective relationships with the public schools, or so it was reported in many sources. Their preparation programs were not relevant to the day-by-day classroom problems faced by the public school teacher, nor did they effectively utilize local school personnel in these programs. Very frequently, criticism was directed at the lack of strategies for change within colleges of education. Innovation was the password to better education during the sixties, and colleges of education did not have it. Indeed, more recently they seemed unconcerned about the opportunity for more rigorous selection of candidates for training and employment offered by the end of the teacher shortage.

Changes in American Society

It is more than probable that the impetus for so much disaffection by so many malcontents was an upheaval in the fabric of American life that developed with an irresistible force following World War II. Many scholars have documented this, but few people have appreciated its dimensions and significance (Full, 1972). Edgar Morphet and his associates in the late sixties noted that since schools were a part of society, they reflected social needs and pressures. Consequently, his "Eight-State Project" summarized the changes in society and determined their implications for education and hence their implications for the preparation of school teachers and administrators. The major trends identified included (1) automation; (2) urbanization and its concomitants; (3) communication; (4) breakthroughs in biology; and (5) breakdowns in religious, ethical, and moral concepts. Other societal changes added to the list included (1) the struggle for human equality; (2) the war on poverty; (3) the changing balance in work and leisure time; and (4) the many faces of rebellion and protest. There was also a group of trends primarily concerned with international affairs: (1) the threat of nuclear warfare; (2) the emergence of many new nations; (3) the determination of minority groups to achieve their legitimate positions; (4) the population explosion and the concomitant crisis in food production; (5) the ever-increasing and more visible disparity between the "haves" and the "have nots"; (6) the ideological struggle between democratic and communistic systems; (7) the emergence of person-to-person forms of international relations; and (8) the rise of programs for international cooperation. All these developments suggest that the world was changing at an ever-accelerating rate. The implication for education was that citizens should be trained to think more clearly and to have greater adaptability to change and greater receptivity to new ideas. Morphet's committee concluded that "we are not going to develop our flexible, problem-solving, ever-learning kind of man by means of a curriculum loaded with facts and a classroom loaded with routines. *The need for a new kind of man suggests a need for a new kind of teacher"* (Morphet and Ryan, 1967, pp. 2-3).

Postwar periods are generally trouble-laden; at least they teem with problems and issues, and force upon a people new ideas and new policies. But the years after World War II had more than their share. That period saw multiplication of trade, swift alteration of monetary systems, industrialization in the undeveloped countries, the rise of international corporations, the realignment of allies and enemies, and the upsurge of minorities everywhere. Inevitably, education was caught up in these earth-shaking events—and so its critics had their day. Among these postwar developments in education were the internationalization of education, the startling growth of federal participation in education, new emphasis on content in the curriculum, rediscovery of the child by Pestalozzi and Froebel, and specialized education to meet the unique needs of the emerging minorities (Wesley, 1973).

The attitude of the public toward schools, and toward teachers, has been rather thoroughly explored by Gallup polls for several successive periods. Among the questions raised in several polls was: "In recent years has your overall attitude toward the public schools in your community become more favorable or less favorable?" The national totals on this question showed 32 percent of respondents more favorable, 36 percent less favorable, and 32 percent with no change or having no opinion. Confidence in teachers and administrators was noticeably lacking. Somewhat contrary to this attitude was the public's conception of teaching as a career. When asked, "Would you like to have a child of yours take up teaching in the public schools as a career," 67 percent said "yes," 22 percent said "no," and 11 percent did not know. This attitude did not differ materially from that of professional educators when asked the same question (Gallup, 1972). Why do Americans have these two contradictory attitudes about their schools?

Such attitudes also characterized citizens a quarter of a century ago. One of America's great historians, Henry Steele Commager, wrote in 1950 that "the American mind today seems deeply worried about its school system as it never has before. . . . There is an uneasy feeling that the schools have somehow failed to do their job . . . is education still the American religion?" Despite the many deficiencies he observed, Commager maintained that "our schools have kept us free," and he called on the nation to renew its faith in education: "No other people ever demanded so much of education as have the Americans. None other was ever served so well by its schools and educators. . . . For it is in education that we have put our faith; it is our schools and colleges that are the peculiar objects of public largess and private benefaction" (Commager, 1950).

The essence of the criticism of teacher education has been that higher education has not properly trained teachers and school service personnel to develop and maintain schools that would meet the new demands of society. Teacher training institutions were especially criticized for failure to prepare teachers to educate blacks in the inner cities, minority groups, and other culturally disadvantaged pupils. It was said that elementary teachers lacked empathy with their pupils and high school teachers were not scholars in their subjects. The American Association of Colleges for Teacher Education called the situation a *Crisis in Teacher Education* (AACTE, 1971).

Responses by Teacher Educators

The attempts to respond to these and other accusations have been many and varied. Professional teacher educators in many organizations have produced a remarkable array of innovative attempts to train better teachers. This is attested to by the publications of the Association for Student Teaching (AST) and by the American Association of Colleges for Teacher Education (AACTE) in its scores of committee reports and in its program of distinguished achievement awards (AACTE, 1965-1976).

Although few institutions have responded by reorganizing their structures to facilitate better teacher education, some have made significant changes. The University of Vermont has undertaken a reorganization based upon the need to provide for many new kinds of human services. It was recognized that community needs and community problems were not neatly sorted according to such academic disciplines as anthropology, history, and biology, but usually cut across many disciplines. Accordingly, the university proposed to combine its colleges of technology, agriculture, and a few related departments in the College of Arts and Sciences into a Division of Applied Sciences. The College of Education would become the College of Education and Human Resources, and its internal organization would be built around programs rather than departments. According to Case, this would be a matrix organization that "stresses the notion of temporary system structures that bring together interdisciplinary resources to achieve specific program objectives; it creates the opportunity for fluidity of personnel rather than rigid classification" (Case, 1972, p. 11).

Considerably less revolutionary was the program and structure for teacher education at the University of Illinois at Urbana-Champaign. Redesigned during the 1970-71 academic year, the Urbana Council on Teacher Education was founded on the belief that the planning of each teacher education curriculum should be done jointly by faculty and student representatives of the subject matter areas and by representatives of professional education. There were in that year twenty-three area committees functioning within the supervision and coordination of the Urbana Council on Teacher Education. Composed primarily of deans of the various colleges, the Illinois structure was an attempt to demonstrate that "the education of teachers is an all-university function which is under the general administrative authority of the Urbana Council on Teacher Education" (University of Illinois *Report*, 1971, p. 35). Notably absent from this governance structure was any significant representation by the practicing profession.

Somewhat similar to the Vermont proposal but with considerably less rationale was a plan proposed by the academic vice-president of the University of Montana. The university was to be organized into five colleges; arts and sciences; social and behavioral sciences; natural sciences and resources; health sciences and professions; and graduate studies. The School of Education was designated to be divided so that only elementary education would be left as an undergraduate curriculum, and it would function as a unit within the College of Social and Behavioral Sciences. Presumably, secondary-school teacher preparation would be phased out but in practice would probably have become the sole province of the College of Arts and Sciences. Everything else would function as a school within the College of Graduate Studies (Landini, 1973). After some study and discussion, both the School of Education faculty and its graduate students' council rejected the proposal (Rummel, 1973).

These three examples, and there are many others, demonstrate that there is some experimentation with new structures to facilitate teacher education in universities. Little rationale has been developed and no distinction is made between the two major areas of knowledge found in universities—the academic disciplines and the professions— but the search for such a rationale continues.

Professional teacher educators have also responded with many curricular innovations in their present teacher education structures. Concern about deficiencies in the preparation of science teachers was followed by concern about the educationally disadvantaged, the ethnic minorities, the culturally deprived, and the irrelevancy of the standard curriculum to the inner city ghetto schools. In the middle sixties the profession became more person-oriented, although this was not a reaction to the teachers' alleged lack of knowledge in science and mathematics. It was instead an addition to current programs and was evidence that the profession had an almost simultaneous concern for both people and subject matter. Both scientists and humanists had their influence.

This noticeable reorientation of the philosophy of teacher education included a broadened outlook on the mission of a college of education in a university. Professional education was coming to be regarded as something more than preparing elementary- and secondary-school teachers to teach. The comprehensive college of education was broadly based enough to include educators in fields such as higher education, the use of audio-visual media in industry, and specialists in the supporting disciplines of educational psychology, educational history, educational sociology, and educational philosophy. It was coming to include the study of recreation, consumer education, community activities, ecology, and other social service occupations to which expertise in education could make a contribution. In fact, some institutions emphasized this trend sufficiently to rename themselves a "College of Education and Human Resources," signifying the possibility of developing educational leadership in many fields. The current decade is probably the best of times to make these and other changes. The profession is no longer under the pressures of the sixties to produce sheer quantities of new teachers or to acquire funds for innovation, and it is not bombarded with indefensible public criticism. It can now emphasize logical organization instead of expediency, quality instead of quantity, and scholarly objectivity instead of political pressures.

It is now necessary to develop some answers to the problem of the future role of colleges of education in universities, because questions are being raised as to whether or not these colleges will survive. Tyson and Carroll have proposed that survival will depend upon "(a) clarification of the concept of teacher education; (b) acceptance by the school of education faculty members that they were not taught what they needed to know in order to function effectively in the profession; and (c) commitment on the part of school of education faculty members to the development and refinement of instructional theory" (Tyson and Carroll, 1972, p. 439).

A National Policy for Teacher Education

The deans of the National Association of Colleges and Schools of Education in State Universities and Land Grant Colleges several years ago commissioned Donald Cottrell at Ohio State University to write a paper proposing a national policy for the improvement of the quality of teacher education. After noting that universities were under powerful pressures from many sources, Cottrell stated that the education of teachers for schools and colleges, who were to influence the vital mainsprings of cultural life, had become confused by overpowering pressures upon universities and often tended to be submerged and left to the mercies of expediency. He urged a new appraisal of the proper use of university resources for vital teacher education and demanded an enlarged priority for it by proposing a National Teacher Education Foundation to be created and financed by the federal government (Cottrell, 1970).

Paul Masoner suggested another approach: The development of a national policy at a White House Conference on Teacher Education similar to the work of the earlier Educational Policies Commission. This could be done by securing staff support by developing a National Center for Teacher Education as a unit of the National Institute of Education. The need for such a structure and such a policy is evident from the following brief summary of Masoner's analysis:

American education is being challenged to play a key role in the improvement of a society threatened simultaneously by domestic crises and by international conflict. Critical to the ability of educational institutions to meet this new and urgent challenge is a national effort in teacher education which will prepare in adequate numbers and at a high level of quality the broad spectrum of educational workers—paraprofessionals, teachers, administrators, educational researchers, college teachers of education, and others—for the total educational system from kindergarten through college and university.

Fragmentation is an obstacle. Responsibility for teacher education rests in over a thousand higher education institutions, fifty state government education agencies, hundreds of public and private cooperating local school districts, the business sector of the nation, a number of regional and national accrediting agencies, numerous professional organizations—all operating in a relatively independent fashion with no clearly defined policies to coordinate this vast professional enterprise and to point the way to a level of quality equal to the task assigned by society to the schools.

An imperative need exists for the development of a national policy for teacher education. The policy must merit the confidence of the public and serve as a guide to federal, state, and local agencies; nongovernmental organizations and agencies; professional organizations and associations; colleges and universities; and others who make decisions concerning teacher education. Policy development should focus upon such matters as control, finance, social responsibility, partnership roles, program, accreditation, certification, new career patterns, professional competences, evaluation, technology, accountability, multi-cultural needs, the urban crisis, international understanding, experimental programs, and long range planning and educational forecasting. (Masoner, 1972, p. 31)

It is not the function of this report to evaluate, explain, or justify the shortcomings of the schools or of teacher education. The purpose of this study is to determine, through examination of the literature in the field, the extent to which colleges, schools, and departments of education are effectively organized to facilitate teacher education. It is a particularly important question in the large, complex, multipurpose universities, 210 of which are doctoral degree granting institutions (*Chronicle of Higher Education*, Feb. 19, 1974). It is of special concern to the administrative officers, the faculties, and the deans of the colleges of education in the 130 members of the National Association of State Universities and Land Grant Colleges, although it is also relevant to the 168 members of the Association of American Colleges and Universities and to many municipal universities, public and private. How, then, does or should a multipurpose state university, or a large, complex, multipurpose college, organize itself so as to facilitate its teacher education programs? The answers to that question are the essence of this study.

There are several difficulties in the study of governance structures and processes because of their indirect impact on outcomes. Does teacher education really make a measurable difference in ability to teach? How is training related to performance? How are training and performance evaluated? How are structures and processes of governance related to the quality of teacher education programs? The difficulty of measurement of these factors and the very indirect, third-echelon level of the impact, whatever it is, raises serious questions about the influence of governance of teacher education on the ultimate learning of pupils in the schools. This may account for the lack of research in the field.

Early in 1972 Frederick Cyphert presented a well-informed look into the status of research in teacher education at the beginning of the seventies and determined the prospects and possibilities for the forthcoming decade. He reviewed eighty-three recent reports of teacher education research gathered by the ERIC Clearinghouse on Teacher Education which had followed an earlier analysis he had made in 1964. Cyphert summarized his major generalizations about the status of research relating to both the pre-service and in-service education of teachers in fourteen different categories. Not one of these was related to the question of administrative organization to facilitate teacher education in multipurpose state universities (Cyphert, 1972).

The Meaning of Governance

Perhaps at this point it would be well to analyze the term *governance of teacher education* so there will be no misunderstanding of what is being studied. We define governance as a process. It is not a structure, it is not a philosophy, and it is not implementation or administration. It is a process in higher education by which decisions affecting behavior are determined. It is highly complex, dealing with both external forces and internal forces. It is also a growth process affecting the trustees, the president, university senates, and even students. It is most frequently described from a partisan point of view, because partisans, whether they are students, alumni, faculty, or newspaper editors, will want only a favorable piece of it. There is little research dealing with governance as a process in higher education and still less research in the governance of teacher education and the structure necessary to implement policy formation.

During the last decade, the governance of teacher education has been under considerable pressure because of the two-fold increase in enrollment of students in teacher education, many dramatic re-arrangements in the governance of universities as a whole, and the demands made through the public schools upon teacher education institutions for better quality.

Governance is sometimes confused with autonomy. Governance does not mean that anyone in a unit of the university can do as he wishes. There are many restrictions through financing and internal structuring of multipurpose complex institutions that limit the autonomy of the unit for teacher education. Perhaps autonomy in the sense of complete independence of colleges of education would not even be desirable. Autonomy is something that must be won and deserved.

A distinction must also be made between governance, which is policy formation, and administration, which is policy implementation. While governance is a process involving the reaching of decisions by people, structures such as departments, schools, colleges, university senates, and graduate schools are the implementing agencies for institutional governance as well as the mechanisms through which the process operates.

In his monumental volume on academic governance, in which he reviews research on institutional politics and decision-making, Baldridge has stated that there are probably three models of university governance: the bureaucratic, the collegial, and the political (Bald-ridge, 1971, pp. 1-19). Baldridge described decision-making in the bureaucratic model as rational and formal, involving the usual bureaucratic procedures. In the collegial model he considered decision-making a task to be shared among professional equals. In the political model decision-making was viewed as a negotiation or bargaining process operating as a sociological process among individuals and groups rather than as a scientific or logical process built upon the nature of the subject matter. He indicated that the political model was a more accurate description of what actually transpired in university governance than either of the other two.

According to Eugene Lee and Frank Bowen, there are three vantage points from which governance may be viewed: "(1) the environment of governance—social, economic, and political; (2) the structures of governance—governing board, administration, and faculty and student organization; and (3) the substantive processes of governance—including academic planning and the preparation and administration of the budget" (Lee and Bowen, 1973, pp. 4-5).

Harold Hodgkinson and Richard Meeth generally agreed with the definitions of governance stated by most authorities. They made a distinction between agencies having indirect controls, such as state legislatures, and four agencies having direct controls, such as (1) governing boards and presidents; (2) students and faculty; (3) government agencies and accrediting bodies; and (4) donors. They defined governance as "the process of direct control by groups or individuals over university policies" (Hodgkinson and Meeth, 1971, p. 2).

In this report we shall consider both indirect and direct controls and influences which originate both inside and outside the university and the structures through which governance operates. The governance of teacher education can therefore be defined as the political process by which decisions are reached and policy developed for the preparation of school personnel.

The structure through which governance functions would include the administrative office of the president and his staff, the deans of academic and professional schools, the department chairmen and their assistants, and the faculty members functioning as individuals or in committees or other groups. The day-by-day implementation and execution of the policies decided upon through these structures would constitute the administration of teacher education. We are here not much concerned with the techniques of administering a teacher education program but largely with the policy formation process, the political and sociological strategies involved, and the mechanisms through which these are exercised. However, administrative mechanisms are also important and are often the same structures as governance mechanisms, although administration usually is assigned to an individual rather than to a group.

The governance of teacher education is a subsystem of the governance of higher education in general. Just as the governance of the university in general has controls from within the institution as well as from outside it, so also does the governance of teacher education. There are subtle differences between governance on the one hand and influences and controls on the other.

Systems Analysis as a Point of Departure

The word *system* is used with certain limitations, and perhaps some explanation of systems analysis as a means of describing and understanding the governance of teacher education would be helpful at this point. Systems analysis as it is applicable to education has been described by Banghart. He stated that "a system is a group of interdependent elements acting together to accomplish a predetermined purpose" (Banghart, 1969, p. 25).

An excellent, very brief review of teacher education and systems has been developed by Howsam, who has stated that systems are a way of looking at things as well as a technology. Systems analysis is a most productive conceptual approach, and he felt it to be as significant with reference to planning as the scientific method is with respect to research. It is an important part of modern life and should be useful to the teacher educator as well as the teacher. We shall, therefore, quote Howsam's brief discussion on systems theory because we hope to use it in the organization of the subject matter concerned with the governance of teacher education.

"Systems theory," like all good basic theory, is a very simple notion with great utility. It is being used by modern physical and social scientists, by businessmen, by architects and builders, by the military, and by the space conquest missions among others. Indeed, it is claimed that *everything that exists can be at least partly described in systems terms.* . . .

The idea of systems is not new; it is part of the common lexicon of our culture. We speak of all kinds of systems and we use the term with considerable accuracy. For example, from childhood on we talk of:

Solar or galactic systems;

Transportation systems;

Ignition or fuel systems in cars;

Heating or cooling systems in homes;

Circulatory or respiratory systems;

Social systems among groups of humans.

In each case there is a complex of parts, one affected by the other, working together for a common purpose or task. One has no trouble recognizing many different kinds of systems.

Another characteristic of systems is that they have *outside limits or boundaries.* Systems are identified by drawing an imaginary boundary around the parts which are seen as related. For example, it is useful to describe a school system and to draw a boundary between it and its community even though no such neat line really exists.

Every system except the very smallest is composed of subsystems. For example, a school system has schools which in turn have classes and groups and individuals within the classes. A human system is composed of a number of subsystems such as the nervous and circulatory systems.

Similarly, all systems except the very largest have suprasystems of which they are a part. For the classroom system the school is a suprasystem. For the individual school the school district is a suprasystem.

The term "system" is applied to the level under consideration at the moment. At other times that level may be a sub- or supra-system.

All systems have similar properties and behave according to the same rules. Some of these properties include:

1. Open systems *exchange energy and information with their environments.* These are called *inputs and outputs.*
2. Systems tend to maintain themselves in a *steady state* or in a state of *dynamic equilibrium.* Essentially this means maintaining a balance between and among its parts. The word "dynamic" indicates an ability to change relationships but the word "equilibrium" indicates a stable tendency. Thus, it is normal for systems to resist change.
3. Systems have a tendency to *entropy*, which means that they have a tendency to disorder and inertia. That is, they tend to degenerate over time.

A central concept in systems theory is that of *feedback.* This is the process of returning output to the system as inputs by means of feedback loops. In effect this is the control mechanism which permits knowledge of results and subsequent adaptation so that purposes are achieved and balance is maintained.

Not only is internal feedback needed, however. Feedback from the environment also is important, particularly in social systems. The teacher education program that fails to monitor the opinions of those who hire its teachers is likely to be in trouble, particularly if employing systems have much choice of candidates.

Effective use of feedback tends to counter the tendency to entropy and thus keep the system dynamic and effective.

Systems are changed by inputs either to the system itself or to its subsystems. When done by a change agent, the inputs are termed *interventions.* Multiple interventions are much more likely to bring about change than are single efforts. This is because the old equilibrium is likely to be destroyed, thus forcing a new structure or patterns of behavior.

Systems analysts and systems engineers use their knowledge of systems in analyzing existing systems, in changing systems, and in engineering systems. Regardless of the complexity of the problem—whether engineering systems to place men on the moon or setting up a micro-teaching situation—the same basic principles and approaches are used. The objectives are identified and very clearly specified. The system and its needed elements are identified. For each subsystem the inputs, processes, and assessment of outputs are determined. The output is monitored and the results fed back so that the system may correct its own deficiencies. Coordination of the subsystems is provided by the system. (Howsam, 1971, pp. 15-18)

The application of systems theory to an analysis of the governance of teacher education may prove useful in understanding "what is," and perhaps eventually "what ought to be" in the process and structures for the control of teacher education. The systematic approach that is suggested here is to chart the course of the teacher education student from the time he enters a teacher education program until he is certificated and begins to teach, and to ask ourselves, "What are the agencies whose policies have influenced his total preparation?" and "What have these policies been?" As a rule, the student's program began with general education, progressed to subject matter specialization, and was permeated with professional education theory and practice. Focusing on the student should result in identifying all the influences on his program, whatever their source. These sources are of two kinds: (a) influences from within the institution of higher learning, and (b) influences from outside the institution. If the literature in the field can be classified into a system as shown in Figure 1, it might shed some light on the internal structure of the teacher education unit, which is a subsystem of the university as a suprasystem. The briefest form of such a systems model appears in Figure 1.

The basis of this report will be a historical review of those controls that have had some noticeable influence on the process of preparing educational personnel. Briefly stated, our purpose will be to fill in the blank circles in Figure 1; and it is hoped that from the accurate picture thus presented will emerge some guidelines for all professionals engaged in improving America's schools by preparing better teachers for them. Perhaps if present structure and procedures can be clarified, a few tentative evaluations can be made that may throw some light on how and by what agencies policy for teacher education ought to be made. Obviously, this will not be the final word. My analysis will have served its purpose if it presents what is now known from limited research and expert opinion in a logical and systematic manner and if it motivates others to fill in the many gaps in our knowledge as to how the major universities and colleges fulfill one of their most important obligations to the society that nurtures them—the preparation of professionals for the nation's schools.

Figure 1.
Influences on the Student in Teacher Education—A Systems Model

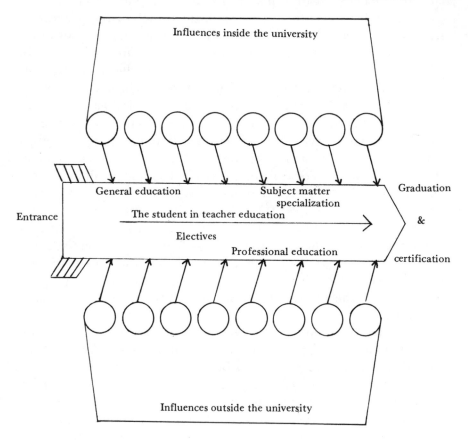

Summary

In a democracy the ultimate responsibility for education rests upon all the people, who feel free therefore to criticize their schools and the preparation of teachers for them. In recent years citizen unhappiness with education has probably increased because of the number and magnitude of social, economic, and political changes in American life. Professional educators have tried to respond to these developments but feel that their responses have been inadequate because they have not had the appropriate structures for providing better teacher preparation nor the finances and personnel necessary to achieve the desired innovations. If a systematic analysis of the many agencies having an influence upon the teacher education process can be made, then some perspectives on the governance process should ensue.

II

Development of Controls of
Teacher Education

There are three functions normally accorded to a college or university: the preservation of knowledge, the transmission of that knowledge to the next generation of students, and the application of that knowledge to the solution of the problems of society. During the Middle Ages, the major function of universities was the preservation of the knowledge of the ancients. A secondary purpose was the transmission of knowledge to students, but little thought was given in most instances to the application of that knowledge to the solution of the problems of the common people. The universities of the Middle Ages were primarily liberal arts colleges and universities.

Graduates of these liberal arts colleges eventually became teachers in those colleges, so that one of the functions of the colleges, perhaps the oldest, was teacher education. Graduation from a medieval university was the certificate of admission to the guild of professional teachers, and the traditional arts and literature curriculum was thought to constitute the ideal curriculum for the preparation of teachers. Whatever one's view is concerning education and teacher education—strictly liberal arts with emphasis on subject matter, strictly professional with emphasis on the child and learning theory, or some amalgamation of both—such views have a bearing on institutional governance, then and now.

In this chapter, we are primarily concerned with the nineteenth-century development of education and teacher education, and the governance of the latter. We can understand the early developments of teacher education in colleges and universities only if we recognize that traditional liberal education was thought to include the essential intellectual components of an ideal teacher education program. This is not to say that from medieval times up to the nineteenth century the importance of practical experience in supplementing the knowledge to be taught and the importance of theoretical insights in the teaching of it was not generally recognized; it was. We shall not go back to the origin of this tradition as set forth in Plato's *Republic*, but it is interesting to observe that it was recognized even in later medieval times that some kind of preparation was necessary if a student were to become an effective teacher.

The Infancy of Teacher Education

This recognition is well documented in the life and times of Richard Mulcaster. Mulcaster was born in England toward the end of the reign of Henry VIII. He graduated from the Eton preparatory school and later from Oxford. He taught for many years in the Merchant-Taylors School in London and lived to the age of eighty. He wrote several treatises, but their worth was generally not recognized for more than three hundred and fifty years. In more recent times, he has been considered the outstanding early writer of English educational theory and practice.

One of Mulcaster's revolutionary but eminently practical ideas was a demand for the systematic preparation of teachers. He wanted to make teaching a profession on a par with medicine, theology, and the law. (These were the three recognized professions in colonial times in North America, a recognition that continued until at least the middle of the nineteenth century.) In several of his writings, Mulcaster described the work and preparation of his contemporaries in education. In other places he set forth his recommendations for university courses in teacher training.

Mulcaster did not confine his recommendations to the preparation of teachers for higher education and secondary schools, but commented on the elementary schools as well, where he felt the worst teachers were to be found. Mulcaster believed that the preparation of teachers was a worthy undertaking for colleges and universities, but he was not unaware of the difficulties involved in persuading the faculties of these institutions to engage in this task. This point is well illustrated in the following observation:

> There will be some difficulty in winning a college for those who will afterwards pass to teach in the schools. There is no specializing for any profession till the student leaves the College of Philosophy, from which he will go to Medicine, Law, or Divinity. This is the time also when the intending schoolmaster should begin his special training. In him there.is as much learning necessary as, with all deference to their subjects, is required by any of the other three professions, especially if it be considered how much the teacher hath to do in preparing scholars for all other careers. Why should not these men have this competence in learning? . . . Why should not teachers be well provided for, so that they can continue their whole life in the school, as divines, lawyers, and physicians do in their several professions? If this were the case, judgment, knowledge, and discretion would grow in them as they get older, whereas now the school, being used but for a shift, from which they will afterwards pass to some other profession, though it may send out competent men to other careers, remains itself far too bare of talent, considering the importance of the work. I consider therefore that in our universities there should be a special college for the training of teachers, inasmuch as they are the instruments to make or mar the growing generation of the country, and because the material of their studies is comparable to that of the greatest professions wherein the forming of the mind and the exercising of the body require the most careful consideration, to say nothing of the dignity of character which should be expected from them. (Cole, 1950, p. 274)

For nearly three and one-half centuries, however, the recommendations of Mulcaster went unheeded. During the seventeenth and eighteenth centuries, teachers were not formally trained, as other professionals were. However, there were some early indications in western Europe in the seventeenth century, increasing in force during the eighteenth century, that teaching was developing as a recognizable profession. In western Europe the eighteenth century was characterized by the rise of nations and by the recognition that youngsters in the schools could be trained to be satisfied and obedient subjects of monarchial systems if they were given the "appropriate schooling." In general, teachers for these youngsters were trained in liberal arts and for the ministry.

This also characterized education in the colonial period in America: teachers for the elementary schools went directly from graduation from those schools to teaching in them; teachers in the secondary schools in the early academies went directly into them from the academies, although they occasionally completed the first years of the liberal arts programs of colleges or universities. The rise of Jacksonian democracy, however, saw the beginnings of specifically designated institutions for the preparation of teachers, particularly for the elementary schools. They were modeled after those in Europe, where normal schools designed for teachers in elementary schools were first developed. The word "normal" came from the French *norme* meaning model or rule, and it was an appropriate designation because the object of these institutions was to give teachers "rules for teaching."

Normal Schools

The first normal schools in America were private institutions, such as those established by Samuel R. Hall at Concord, Vermont, in 1823 and by James G. Carter at Lancaster, Massachusetts, in 1827. Thus, some of the groundwork had been laid for the work of Horace Mann when he persuaded the Massachusetts legislature to establish the first state-supported normal school in 1839 at Lexington, Massachusetts. By 1860 there were eleven state normal schools in eight states, and by 1898 there were 167 public normal schools in the United States, including county normal schools in the rural areas of many states and municipal normal schools in Boston, Philadelphia, Baltimore, and other cities (Butts, 1955, pp. 467, 547).

Further details on the development and growth of the normal schools are contained in Edward Krug's review of the movement. We have pointed out that in 1823 Samuel R. Hall, a minister, had opened an academy at Concord, Vermont. Hall added a course in the art of teaching and provision for some practice in the art somewhat later. He offered a teacher training course in 1830 at Phillips Andover Academy, which had been founded in 1778, built upon his book entitled *Lectures in School Keeping*. The idea of teacher training courses spread to New York, and by 1835 there were five academies in that state offering a course called "Principles of Teaching." What was significant about Horace Mann's venture at Lexington was the fact that it was a state-supported public institution. By 1856 there were four public normal schools in Massachusetts, with a total of 332 students, 290 of whom were girls. By 1860 there were thirteen public normal schools in the country, including one maintained by a city, St. Louis.

After the Civil War the movement developed more rapidly. The *Report of the United States Commissioner of Education, 1889-1890,* listed 135 public normal schools, state and city, with 26,543 students in the teacher training departments (Krug, 1964, p. 70). Normal schools did not have a monopoly on the training of elementary school teachers because high schools also undertook teacher training courses, starting with Chicago high schools in 1856. It was not until 1895, when Massachusetts led the way, that there was a change in the image of the normal schools: high school graduation became a prerequisite for entrance, a governance policy that was determined by a state board. By 1920 the major state universities were beginning to accept transfer credits from the normal schools and to apply the credit toward their bachelor's degrees. When the normal schools became teachers colleges, they began to grant their own degrees.

Teachers Colleges

During the last half of the nineteenth century, normal schools became two-year institutions and began requiring high school graduation for entrance; after about 1900 their number multiplied rapidly. Many became known as "teachers colleges" in the 1920s and 1930s, but they gradually dropped the word "teachers" from their titles. Increasing numbers of teachers colleges began to prepare high school teachers, which required greater breadth and depth in the academic subjects; these departments were added to the teachers colleges in the period from 1920 to 1940. Such vocational education areas as industrial arts, business, and home economics were also added. Later many teachers colleges added non-teaching curricula to their programs, although the majority of their students still became teachers. Early in the twentieth century many of these institutions, particularly those teaching high school curricula and training high school teachers, lengthened their courses to four years and began granting bachelor of arts and bachelor of science degrees in education. It was during this period that they changed their names: in the decade from 1920 to 1930, sixty-nine of the state normal schools became teachers colleges and by 1950 practically all of them had done so.*

---

*One example of these name changes characterized this writer's undergraduate institution. Founded in 1904 as a normal school, the Western State Normal School at Kalamazoo, Michigan, became Western Michigan State Teachers College in 1927, Western Michigan College of Education in 1941, Western Michigan College in 1955, and Western Michigan University in 1957.

Although speaking somewhat disparagingly of this movement, Paul Woodring has summarized "the short, happy life of the teachers college" and concludes as follows:

The three stages in the history of teacher education now seem clear. The normal school of the nineteenth century provided professional teacher training for students with an elementary school background. The teachers college of the first half of the present century offered high school graduates a program of teacher education combined with a modest amount of liberal education and some subject matter specialization. Teachers of the future will not be admitted to professional training until they have completed a considerable amount of liberal education at the college level and for many this will mean a liberal arts degree before the first professional degree. Teacher education will be no longer a thing apart but will be an integral part of higher education. (Woodring, 1963, p. 258)

The dynamic growth of the teachers colleges has resulted in critical problems regarding their institutional identity and the functions and purposes of their administration. Their organization into the American Association of State Colleges and Universities (AASCU) is an attempt to deal with these problems. In 1968/69 Fred Harcleroad and others made a study of the historical background and the current status and future plans of the developing state colleges and universities. Their findings were published in October of 1969. Data were summarized from questionnaires sent to over 200 state colleges and universities throughout the United States, and the report drew on site visits and other documentation. The investigators noted that the academic status of the state colleges and universities was rising and that these institutions were competing, with varying degrees of success, with the more established universities for the services of the new research-oriented Ph.D.'s being produced by graduate schools in state universities. At the time of the study there were approximately 2,400 non-profit institutions of higher education in the United States. Of this number, 284 were the group known as the "developing state colleges and universities." Harcleroad found that they were the fastest-growing baccalaureate degree granting segments of higher education in the country.

His review, therefore, of the historical development of these institutions is worth quoting *in extenso*, particularly because of his emphasis on the structures facilitating their governance:

In the 1920's and 30's, as the teachers colleges expanded their programs and grew in numbers of students, a need for completely different types of organization developed quite rapidly. Most of the colleges added registrars, first on a part-time basis and soon on a full-time basis. Sometimes the registrar was also the Dean of the Faculty or the Dean of Instruction. However, very soon it became necessary to have a person assigned the responsibility for instruction, another person responsible for business affairs, and Deans of Men and Women for Student Affairs.

The normal schools and teachers colleges, being single-purpose professional institutions, had a specialized administrative organization due to the presence of the training school or model school. The laboratory school was usually taught by a principal-teacher or a principal and one or two teachers. They were members of the small normal school faculty but were often considered a separate unit. As the institutions grew larger a department of education was often established with or without the laboratory school as a part of its responsibility. The American Association of Teachers Colleges reported an extensive study of organizational patterns in 1922 which included some specific data on this subject. Of 70 institutions responding to a questionnaire, 23 indicated that the head of the department of education was also principal of the training school. In 39 of the institutions the training school was separately administered. In eight institutions there was no head for the department of education and in one case, no training school. Cooperation between the training school and academic as well as education departments was a problem. Many of the teachers of academic subjects actually supervised the teaching of these subjects in the laboratory schools or training school. Thus, there was a critical problem of organization which called for very careful cooperative systems to be established.

As the institutions grew in size and in complexity another form of administrative organization gradually developed. Divisions were established in a number of colleges in the 1930's and during the 1940's and 50's. Divisional organization brought together in various ways groups of departments which had some type of cohesiveness. A divisional organization was usually based on the grouping of departments in the social sciences, humanities (sometimes including the arts), natural sciences (sometimes separated into biological sciences and physical sciences), and various professional divisions. Education divisions sometimes combined strange bedfellows, including such specialized subjects as home economics, physical education, business education, art education and often psychology. Some of these unusual combinations were the aftermath of the days when the institutions were solely single-purpose teacher-training institutions.

With the tremendous increases in institutional size in the last 10 to 15 years a number of the SCU's have moved into a university-type organization and in over 60 cases have been re-named as universities. In many SCU's unusual administrative organizations now exist. Divisions are side by side with separate schools of art and sciences, business, fine and applied arts, education and specialized professional schools. Where specialities have grown up (such as agriculture, social work, architecture, applied health professions or forest or marine sciences) separate schools are often established.

Since many SCU's have between 5,000-10,000 students, and a number will be much larger, a recent study of organizational patterns in institutions of this size has considerable pertinence (Oliver and Miller, 1966, p. 52). In the latter study the organizational charts were assembled for 54 institutions with between 5,000 and 10,000 students. Twenty-five of the 54 were AASCU-type institutions. The remainder were a wide variety of institutions ranging from large junior colleges to private universities and land grant universities. Although certain differences were quite apparent, the major one was the varying need for a vice president or high level official charged with development and fund raising. This position was found in many private universities but not in many of the public institutions. The organizational prototype suggested at the conclusion of the study recommended three vice presidents, one for academic affairs, one for student affairs, and one for business and finance. In addition, it was suggested that the president should have an assistant and that the assistant should work directly with the director of public affairs. Each of these officials was assigned long lists of major functions. The vice president for academic affairs was assigned the responsibility for teacher education in all of the facets as one of many academic functions of the colleges or universities of this size.

As the SCU's have grown in size and diversified their curricula the administrative organization has changed materially in order to provide for the new functions. Although the preparation of teachers was the primary, and in many cases the sole, function from 1839 until, in some cases, the 1950's this is no longer true. Almost all of the members of the American Association of State Colleges and Universities and a few comparable institutions which are not in its membership have become multi-purpose institutions and the organization and administration have expanded at the same time. (Harcleroad, 1969, pp. 74-76)

It is quite possible that too much attention has been given to the name change in these institutions and not enough to what they actually do. In the vast majority of them more graduates are still prepared for teaching than for any other professional career. As Samuel Wiggins has noted, "there is the continuing concern, of course, lest public and non-public colleges which have dropped the title may also drop their responsibilities in teacher education" (Wiggins, 1967, p. 232). Reports on their teacher productivity indicate that they have not.

Land Grant Colleges

Several attempts had been made to develop schools and colleges of agriculture in the 1850s—evidence of the growing trend toward vocationalism, which many of the state universities not only found impossible to resist, but even encouraged. Many small colleges introduced into their undergraduate programs such courses as chemistry, mechanical drawing, library science, and the history and philosophy of education. The coming of women into the colleges and universities strengthened this tendency toward vocationalism by helping to turn many colleges and universities into teacher training institutions. Indeed, by the end of the nineteenth century, American colleges and universities were producing more teachers than anything else (Rudolph, 1962, p. 339).

The attainment of college status for teacher education might be considered to have begun in 1862 with the land·grant college act, because in order to prepare vocational agriculture specialists it was necessary for these new "people's universities" to prepare teachers for agriculture and mechanical arts. The training of teachers for the land grant colleges was stimulated by the Smith-Hughes Act of 1917, but these colleges required more than half a century to achieve any respectable status in the hierarchy of American universities. Edgar B. Wesley has noted that

the land-grant colleges were so unblushingly utilitarian as to disqualify them as sharers of the heritage of liberal education. James McCosh of Princeton and Charles W. Eliot of Harvard cast aspersions upon them and clung tenaciously to the thoroughly erroneous notion that their function was to train farmers and artisans. The phrase "cow college" was used to imply the bucolic and backward atmosphere that alledgedly clung for many years to these land-grant colleges. (Wesley, 1957, pp. 93-94)

Thus, the land grant colleges rather early had the company of the teachers colleges in gaining a respectable status as teacher education institutions.

Further evidence on this point was summarized by John Hansen when he noted that teacher education in land grant institutions was at one time considered a sideline but is now recognized as a major function. He noted that, probably because of their somewhat unique concern with social and economic problems of the common people, they had made three types of contributions: the number and kinds of teachers prepared, the amount and quality of research they conducted on educational problems, and the services they rendered to public schools. The leaders in teacher education in these institutions listed eight issues and problems still unresolved, one of them being "tapping the creative and intellectual resources of the entire institution to strengthen teacher education, research, and consultative services to schools" (Hansen, 1966, p. 217). Hansen concluded his study of teacher education in the land-grant institutions by noting that "in over one hundred years, teacher education has steadily been earning full status in land-grant institutions. Its progress has often been made slow and difficult by legislative and institutional limitations on its programs and services. It has frequently been poorly supported, ill-housed, understaffed and unappreciated" (Hansen, 1966, p. 217).

The struggle for status by these institutions does not differ markedly from the struggle of the teachers colleges and the early state universities.

State Universities

The first hint that universities were to become interested in the preparation of teachers for the common schools occurred in 1831, when Ohio University announced its willingness to accept partial course, non-degree students in that year for the purpose of training teachers for the new common schools. Then in 1838 Lafayette College made known its intention of establishing a model or laboratory school to train teachers for the new public school system. These announcements, however, were simply tentative concessions to the growing numbers of young people who desired a higher education and probably reflected the educational impact of Jacksonian democracy.

The assumption of the responsibility for the preparation of teachers in colleges and universities did not come without considerable misgivings on the part of the faculty of those institutions, many of whom thought that the preparation of teachers was quite beneath the dignity of the university. (The remnants of this attitude colors the governance of teacher education in universities and large colleges to this day.) During the immediate post—Civil War period, however, the pressure was removed from the university by the unbroken development of the normal schools. Colleges and universities gradually began to accept their responsibilities because of pressures such as those Charles Kendall Adams described when he gave an address before the New England Association of Colleges and Preparatory Schools in 1888 entitled, "The Teaching of Pedagogy in Colleges and Universities" (Borrowman, 1965, pp. 86-92 and Borrowman, 1971, pp. 79-89).

Several institutions seem to take credit for beginning teacher education in state universities, but the most valid claim is made by the University of Iowa. Pangborn reported that in 1873 a permanent chair of didactics replaced an elementary normal course established in 1855 at the University of Iowa. The University of Michigan in 1879 and the University of Wisconsin in 1881 added professorships of pedagogy. Data from the reports of the United States Commissioner of Education showed that by 1891/92 there were chairs of pedagogy in thirty-one institutions and chairs of pedagogy combined with another subject, such as philosophy or mental science in forty-five others, while eight more universities had established lectureships in education (Pangborn, 1932, p. 21).

The second best claim must be accorded the University of Michigan which in 1879 maintained that it had established "the first chair in any institution of higher education for the science and art of teaching." The first person to fill this chair was William H. Payne, who

saw the purpose of his task to be the following: (1) to fit the University students for higher positions in the public school service, (2) to promote the study of educational science, (3) to teach the history of education and of educational systems and doctrines, (4) to secure to teaching the rights, prerogatives, and advantages of a profession, and (5) to give a more perfect unity to our state educational systems by bringing the secondary schools into closer relation with the university." (Cohen, 1971, p. 2)

The Regents of the University of Michigan established the present School of Education on May 27, 1921 (Cohen, 1971, p. 5).

For many years, the pleas of these early advocates of teacher education that education was a field worthy of professional designation went unheeded, despite their cogent arguments. This should not be surprising; even the basic sciences at one time were looked upon with considerable suspicion. Pangborn evaluated this attitude by noting an interesting inconsistency:

Departments of education were winning their way slowly; the professors in charge often felt that their colleagues considered them outside the pale of academic respectability. References were made in professional discussions to the "gentlemen who sneer at their own conceptions of what the study of pedagogy is good for," to the difficulty of seeing "how the university whose admitted function is education can pass by the science of education without discrediting its own work and virtually denying its own name," and to "the function of the university to furnish society with teachers."

In 1892, Professor Charles De Garmo of Swarthmore, in an address entitled, "Scope and Character of Pedagogical Work in Universities," urged that the pedagogical department be made effective through an organic connection with the rest of the university. He outlined a curriculum which would include psychology, educational administration, economic and political science, literature in English, history, and comparative education. Graduates of state normal schools were to be admitted in order that they might become specialists. (Pangborn, 1932, pp. 21-22)

The problem of acquiring professional status for the preparation of teachers in colleges and universities was a difficult one, and it was really not until the 20th century that teacher training reached significant proportions. Brubacher and Rudy point out, however, that

unaffiliated with academic institutions for the most part, it suffered the same inherent weakness that had earlier characterized schools of medicine and law. In spite of significant beginning of the theory of education, the academic mind refused to regard pedagogy seriously. This was even true until the end of the 19th century when departments of education emerged on college campuses as offshoots from departments of philosophy and psychology. But for that matter all the junior professions at first occupied a low rung on the ladder of academic prestige, as had the older professions in their earlier stage. No matter how much the practice of these occupations demanded more and more theory to meet the demands of a vastly more complicated America, people, and particularly academic people, ironically regarded them as utilitarian and therefore compared them unfavorably to liberal arts. (Brubacher, 1968, p. 213)

The remnants of this attitude still pervade the governance of teacher education on many campuses.

The presidents were the most important single influence in university governance prior to the Civil War, and for the older universities they remained so for some time afterward. However, as Schenkel has noted, "university governance of the contemporary American university is a complex system of checks and balances in which it is virtually impossible for a single person to dominate the government process" (Hodgkinson, 1971, p. 12).

The American university emerged in the decade following the Civil War as an institution that differed from the college of the pre-Civil War period: it enrolled more students in a wider range of subjects taught by a larger faculty. The distinctive features of the new universities later in the 19th century included graduate programs, professional schools, departmental structures, and research efforts. Governance changed from primarily sectarian control to a control that was primarily secular, whether private or public (Hodgkinson, 1971, pp. 1-2).

After 1890, when universities grew in size and complexity, the presidents developed a specialized core of administrators and university administration developed into a large-scale bureaucracy. During this period departments and schools within the university were established.

Other agencies and groups whose influence in university governance developed after 1890 would include the alumni, the faculty, the students (notably in the last ten years), state governments (through charters for private institutions and through appropriations for public ones), the federal government, and accrediting agencies. The result is that the modern university operates under many internal and external constraints. Hodgkinson quotes Schenkel's description of this situation:

Increasing number of constraints on the traditionally strong actors such as the president and governing boards, is reflected in this system of checks and balances which render it almost impossible for one person to make all major decisions alone. This fact is likely to prepare a base for either a university run in the truly representative manner or a new era of adversary factionalism in American university governance. (Hodgkinson, 1971, p. 23)

The foregoing historical review demonstrates that there have indeed been four periods in the history of teacher education. Because there are several excellent histories written by eminent authors, my purpose has been only to show that various philosophies of American education and of teacher education have led to several quite different institutional arrangements for its control, administration, and governance. These arrangements are clearly seen in the four periods of teacher education summarized by Cremin:

The history of teacher education in the United States, when seen against the development of American education in general, seems to divide itself into four chronological periods. The first of these is the Colonial period (1600 to 1789) during which there was little interest in popular education and virtually no interest in teacher education *per se.* A second period embraces those years between 1789 and 1860 when Americans laid the foundations of their state public school systems—particularly at the elementary level—and established the first normal schools to meet the growing need for professionally prepared teachers. A third period covers the years from 1860 to 1910, a period when the vast expansion of elementary and secondary education was reflected in the teachers college, the introduction of teacher education into liberal arts colleges and universities, and the development of educational programs for teachers in service. Finally, the fourth period covers the years since 1910 when rising enrollments, expanding curricula, and the growing efforts of state agencies and professional groups to raise educational standards have led to the upgrading of virtually every phase of teacher education. (Cremin, 1953, p. 163)

Evolution of Governance through Internal Structures

Some research has been conducted on the development of departments, schools, and colleges of education in the multipurpose state universities and land grant colleges. In 1957, Arthur Partridge made a study of the origin and development of the university school of education as a professional institution. Partridge felt that the faculties of these institutions could not perform effectively unless they understood the directional forces that have led to present practices and that have created present problems. He saw that the changing demands of the American people had been definitive in the training of teachers and had therefore had a profound effect upon the development of teacher training structures, including the university's school of education. He focused his attention on the relationship between the school of education and the social forces that have characterized the evolving American society and its relationship to the historical continuum of American higher education in general. After reviewing the general literature in the field, he traced the development of twelve university schools of education that had exerted a directional influence upon the entire school of education movement. His studies showed that the changing socioeconomic nature of American life and an increasingly industrialized society had placed on education at all levels, and especially on the public schools, demands that have altered the role of teachers and therefore required more thorough preparation for those teachers. This evolution created two conditions requisite to the establishment of schools within universities for the professional training of practitioners: a greater occupational specialization, and an accumulation of professionalized knowledge that practitioners must acquire.

In Partridge's view the histories of these twelve schools of education pointed to certain characteristics: (1) the schools originated with people outside universities rather than within them; (2) they shared the professional training functions with academic departments; (3) they defined professional training as consisting of the study of educational science and the development of scholarly and philosophical insights; (4) they generally prepared high school teachers, leaving to the normal schools the function of preparing elementary school teachers. Today, however, both types of institutions in a sense compete in the training of educators for all levels, because the normal school has evolved into a teachers college and then into an intermediate university.

Partridge identified four basic issues that confronted the university's school of education—issues he considered to affect all American higher education. These included the nature of general education, the relationship of general and special education, the content of specialized training, and the relationship of research to education. His analysis of the historical continuum of the university school of education suggested the following generalizations concerning the immediate future:

(1) The structural separation of the functions of providing general education and of providing specialized education seems unlikely at the present time. (2) Schools of education must continue to share the professional training function with other university departments. (3) Schools of education must resolve the apparent conflict between the educational and the research functions in their programs for the advanced training of educational specialists. (4) The schools of education must re-examine their purposes. The effective structuring of the functions which now engage in competition requires a clear conception of basic purpose. (Partridge, 1957)

Throughout any review of the history of teacher education and the structures in higher education to facilitate such education, there appears again and again the theme that the preparation of teachers, and of school personnel generally, even including educational leaders, is somewhat beneath the dignity of a university whose primary purpose is research, especially research in the academic disciplines. Collins approached this situation systematically when he raised such questions as, "What is included in the special domain of the faculty of education? What are the limits and what is the rationale of its jurisdiction? What is the substance of the content of professional education?" These questions raise others concerning the nature and definition of the discipline of education. The question was manifest as early as 1892 when Columbia University first rejected the petition from its teachers college for affiliation, and it has been raised many times since. The issue was confronted by Koerner, when he stated that education lacked significant knowledge as a basis either for dependable practice or for research and intellectual advancement of the field (Koerner, 1963). It went unanswered when, in 1958, Yale University dissolved its department of education. It was thought by the Yale faculty that teacher training appeared incapable of developing theoretical dimensions. Evan Collins, on the other hand, thought the field had substance but that its followers had not yet clarified the way to treat it, partly due to the confusion reflecting a lack of clarity concerning the real purpose of the educational system itself. Apparently, the autonomy of the teacher education unit in multi-purpose state universities has not been helped by the designation of education as an "applied discipline." Faculty discussions have raised the question of whether the orientation of teacher education units ought to be utilitarian, i.e., developing the profession of education, or whether these units ought to be reoriented toward the study of educational problems. To Collins, the important point is to keep the discussion going (Collins, 1969, pp. 77-89). The purpose of this review has been to note that these struggles for status among institutions of higher education has had a most significant counterpart in the internal governance of these institutions as they developed mechanisms to facilitate teacher education.

Several historians of the development of teacher education often refer to the relationship between the internal structure of a university and its governance. It is frequently remarked that there is no one ideal structure of governance equally applicable to all institutions to achieve a specified purpose such as teacher education. Most authors believe that the more democratic the governmental structure, the better for the institution, particularly for its faculty. However, Hodgkinson quoted data from the AAHE Campus Governance Project which indicated that the situation is much more complex than is generally recognized. He stated,

If people wish to, they can be dishonest and deceitful with each other regardless of the height of the governance hierarchy. Dewey is certainly at least partially right—democratic government is a *reciprocal* way for people to deal with each other. This fact transcends structure. There is no structure which will force people to trust each other, although some structures may facilitate communication and trust, at least for certain types of people (Hodgkinson, 1971, p. 144).

The latter assumption—which has been a foundation of my research on governance—has considerable credibility: some structures encourage appropriate individuals and groups to work together harmoniously to develop policies and programs in the administration of teacher education in multipurpose state universities, and other structures discourage such harmony.

There is a body of literature giving a few clues to the organization of colleges of education in the state universities under the general heading of the role of the deans of education, or for that matter, deanships in general. John Gould's study, *The Academic Deanship,* does not include an analysis of the role of the deans of the professional schools. Gould ignores the purely technical colleges and the professional schools of institutions and does not touch on the administrative organization for the preparation of teachers. However, he does outline the origins of the academic deanships. Gould implies that presidents needed no deans to help them, at least not until late in the nineteenth century. He quotes Ward, who had stated that the median date of establishment of the deanship in 319 institutions he studied in 1934 was approximately forty years after the median date of the founding of the institution itself, and the median date of the establishment of the deanship during a sixty-three-year period was 1913. By 1885, only 15 deanships had been established, but by 1913 the office had been widely accepted (Gould, 1964, pp. 2-3).

Another historian who traced the development of teacher education in universities, Edgar Knight, was well aware that teachers needed special preparation for their jobs. After describing the normal school movement, which as late as 1900 provided only two years of work beyond the high school, Knight showed the difficulties teacher education faced in gaining acceptance in universities:

When courses in pedagogy or education finally found their way to the doors of the colleges and universities, they were generally reluctantly admitted, assigned subordinate places, and kept in humility as long as possible. Some of the conditions which made them unwelcome in the colleges and universities also helped to keep them subordinate. The pioneer professors of pedagogy in these institutions were doubtless often effective and were generally picturesque, but they were not always standardized and orthodox products of the colleges and universities. Many of them had not bowed the knee to the gods of the graduate school. They were innocent of the idolatry of doctoral dissertations and the methods of scientific research. Their methods were anecdotic and reminiscent of their experience in teaching and managing schools. Organized materials for pedagogical instruction were scarce until after 1900, and the practical experience of the early professors of pedagogy formed a large part of the materials of their courses. The standard of their work, which was limited to a few fields, were not always high—probably little if any higher than the normal school standards—and their claim to scientific character could not always be supported.

     These and other conditions caused courses in pedagogy or education early to fall under the heavy prejudice of other departments. They still suffer from this affliction. (Knight, 1951, p. 335)

Although James Earl Russell must be considered an administrator (he was dean of Teachers College, Columbia University, from 1897 to 1927) rather than a historian, he certainly contributed to the making of teacher education history. He was one of the first to recognize the problems faced by teacher education in gaining acceptance in a university setting, and considered his administrative task that of keeping peace between two groups of faculty adhering to two different views of the field. He explained this over-simplified dichotomy as follows:

     Consider then, the connotation of the terms "academic" and "professional." I mean by "academic" that type of work which leads the student to a constantly expanding knowledge of the subject. It is scientific, logical, all-inclusive. Such work well done gives breadth to life and universality of interests. The work of the world however, demands concentration of powers and of interests on a particular job. This centering or narrowing upon a particular task is the chief characteristic of professional training. It does not follow, however, that subjects as taught in a professional school or an academic institution are perforce respectively either "academic" or "professional." The distinction comes not from the subject taught, but from the teaching of it. The fundamental fact is that teachers are either academically or professionally minded. (Russell, 1924, p. 23)

Woodring expanded on this notion recently when he observed that there were two distinct traditions of teacher education. The older tradition provides the basis for the academic or liberal arts view of teacher education, while the second is that of the professional educator and is most evident in the teachers colleges. Woodring described these two points of view as follows:

> The two traditions represent totally different concepts of the nature of man, of the learning process, and of the proper role and limitations of free public schools. Although both traditions stress the importance of the human individual, the older one holds that *formal* education is properly centered in the world of knowledge and is concerned with the development of the mind. The newer traditions prefer to place the stress upon the "whole child." It places great emphasis upon the learning process and interprets this process in a way which extends it far beyond academic or intellectual learning. (Woodring, 1963, p. 425)

The major function of a college of education in a university is to coordinate governance forces that will seek the reconciliation of both of these viewpoints so as to achieve the best of both worlds.

Emergence of the Profession of Teacher Education

When the Russians launched Sputnik I in the fall of 1957, the American people began to criticize their schools for not producing scientists that would have enabled the United States to be first. The public schools, as is so often the case, became the scapegoats for the social and economic shortcomings of our society. Why the public schools were singled out because they did not prepare scientists is somewhat difficult to understand, since later events showed quite clearly that science had the capability of launching a satellite from the United States much sooner than was done, and in fact it could have been done prior to 1957. The failure was not in science and mathematics but in the political decision which did not see the international propaganda value of such an accomplishment before 1957.

This public criticism was primarily an attack on the content of the curriculum in elementary and secondary schools rather than on the curriculum content of teacher education. It was not long, however, before university scholars in science and mathematics began to work with their colleagues in teacher education to revise the majors in those fields in order to update local school curricula by providing schools with better prepared teachers. The division between liberal arts scholars and teacher educators erupted into an all-out campaign of invective and vituperation during this period. Hodenfield pointed out that extremists on one side grabbed the floor (and the headlines) to proclaim that teachers were being taught *how* to teach but not *what* to teach, and that really if you knew your subject well enough you could teach it. Extremists on the other side reported that if you really knew how to teach, you could teach anything. Senior folk on both sides pointed out that a good teacher ought to know *what* to teach as well as *how* to teach, but their voices were lost in the din. (Hodenfield, 1961, p. 4)

Much of this controversy was overly dramatized by the news media. Most scholars on both sides of this so-called controversy would recognize that the word "teach" takes both a direct and an indirect object. One cannot teach something without teaching someone, and one cannot teach someone without teaching him something. It is as illogical to assert that what to teach and how to teach can be irreconcilably dichotomized as it is to assert that a coin may have only one side.

During the sixties, probably as a result of the accreditation requirements of the National Council for the Accreditation of Teacher Education (NCATE), and for many other reasons, mechanisms were developed in university teacher education programs for teacher educators and academicians to work together through what came to be known as all-university teacher education policy committees. This development will be further discussed in later chapters.

Perhaps the best review of developments during the period of the sixties is contained in Pomeroy's lecture, "Beyond the Upheaval," given before the annual meeting of the American Association of Colleges for Teacher Education in February, 1972. Pomeroy reviewed the development of teacher education after World War II and identified six major "crests." These included (1) identification of teacher education as an appropriate and important function for all types of higher education institutions; (2) the structuring of a national association of higher education institutions committed to improving teacher education as exemplified by AACTE; (3) the acceptance of the shared responsibility for teacher education by higher education, the practicing teachers in the school systems, and the public in general; (4) the development of a cadre of professional educators trained to meet the expanded demands of teacher preparation; (5) the joining together of academicians and teacher educators to meet the needs of prospective teachers; and finally (6) the expansion of governmental involvement in teacher education.

As Pomeroy looked to the future, he saw targets for professional action in such areas as education renewal sites and teacher centers using schools and communities as proper partners for the colleges and universities. Another approach to teacher education called for great involvement of colleges in the community, more feedback from the teachers in the field to their former colleges, the development of greater sensitivity to minority cultures, and greater emphasis upon performance-based teacher education, ideally one accommodating an improved accreditation procedure (Pomeroy, 1972, pp. 1-23).

What Pomeroy and others have left unanswered is the question of allocating authority and responsibility among the constituents in this partnership. When this allocation has been made, the profession of teacher education will have been finally established.

Let me conclude this chapter with a short review of another development in teacher education that has come to the fore in the last decade. This is the fact that, due to the enormous expansion of college and university enrollments in the past decade, higher education as a field of study has come to occupy a strategic place in the graduate programs of institutions of higher learning. For the American Association of Higher Education, James Rogers reviewed the programs in a number of institutions. Of the eighty-six programs in his study, including fifty-three that offered areas of major concentration at the doctoral level, eighty-four employed 468 faculty members and offered 889 courses. There were forty-nine major programs having an enrollment of 2,174 students. There were forty-four minor programs enrolling 842 students at the doctoral level. There were thirty-seven major programs that awarded 316 doctorates, and twenty-seven minor programs that had 354 doctoral recipients in 1967-68. He found that approximately 25 percent of the areas of concentration were found in student personnel work (Rogers, 1969).

Rogers found some evidence that programs in higher education were beginning to involve the faculty and other resources and agencies outside of professional education. "Without exception," he said,

the curriculum and faculty of every major program reported was based very largely on education. These faculties have been more responsive than others to the need in this area, and their competencies have had a more practical relevance for the organizational and management needs of institutions of higher education in the past. However, there is now an urgent need for concerted support of programs of higher education at the highest institutional levels, so that the richly varying contributions from many disciplines will be brought to bear on this increasingly complex field. (Rogers, 1969, p. 2)

Rogers cautioned that the eighty-six institutions offering course work in higher education referred to them as programs. He felt that this was quite misleading because many of them would not be considered bona fide professional programs of preparation for teaching in colleges and universities.

Summary

In retrospect, it is fairly clear that specialized programs for the preparation of teachers have had a long history, having had an advocate at the time of Henry VIII in England. In every century and probably in every decade advocates have struggled to make teaching a profession and to make the preparation of teachers an academically respectable component of higher education. The history of the normal school movement—from its beginning one hundred and fifty years ago, to the latest teachers college name change, to university status—illustrates this point. The founding and development of land grant colleges of agriculture and mechanical arts documents the same evolutionary battle. The establishment of "chairs of pedagogy," the expansion of such chairs to departments, and then their organization into schools and colleges of education in the multipurpose state and private universities is another example of the struggle for status of the professional preparation of all school personnel. Much of this history explains the frequently clumsy arrangements of the mechanisms for teacher education in too many institutions of higher education in this country today that make the development of wise policies for the governance of teacher education difficult. Teacher education in universities has a long history, and its academic respectability should be recognized.

III

Governance of Higher Education— General Considerations

We have defined governance in higher education as a sociological process: the interaction among human beings by which decisions leading to action are reached. Governance encompasses all the forces having an impact on the university—forces generated by the trustees or boards of education, the president, other administrative officers such as vice-presidents, deans and department chairmen, the faculty, the alumni, funding agencies, the state, and perhaps many others.

The governance processes of universities have been subjected to many strains in the last decade or two. The high visibility of student demands, the many socioeconomic maladjustments in modern society, and the demands of minority groups need no documentation. The American people are coming to believe that higher education should be used as a means of raising the quality of living for them—all of them—rather than to accept universities as traditional repositories of ivory-tower learning.

This general overview of the governance of higher education recognizes that the governance of teacher education is a part of the process and structure of governance affecting the university as a whole. Indeed, it is possible that more policies affecting teacher education may be made by non-teacher education agencies within the university than by the teacher education unit itself. It behooves teacher educators, therefore, to understand all-university governance. For an in-depth look at the all-university governance process, the reader is referred to a number of scholarly analyses of this subject, most of which have been developed within the last twenty years.

One of the earliest was John J. Corson's book, published in 1960, in which Corson reviewed the literature concerning the roles of trustees, presidents, deans, departmental chairmen, the faculty, and outside groups. Two other categories on which he obtained data were the administrative process and institutional studies. A good background on the theory of governance is provided by John D. Millett's book published in 1962. A more recent and very useful volume was produced by J. Victor Baldridge in 1971. A similar compilation of a number of essays on governance was done by Hodgkinson and Meeth in 1970. In recent years, probably because of the outside pressures already noted, the American Association for Higher Education has been quite sensitive to the newer developments in campus governance. The 1970 yearbook of the association, edited by G. Kerry Smith, has a section concerned with the disenfranchised on the campus, the campus ombudsman, and new configurations in governance. Collective bargaining and institutional autonomy are becoming critical problems. The 1971 yearbook of AAHE, also edited by G. Kerry Smith, has a section devoted to paradoxes in decision-making in the governance of higher education. These paradoxes are found in a redefinition of governing boards, home rule, mediation possibilities, campus power, and several other new developments.

The reader is referred to these and other studies if there is need for in-depth study of current analyses of the governance of higher education in the sixties and seventies. Our immediate concern is how the governance of teacher education is affected by these changing times as reflected in the governance of higher education in general.

Principles of Governance

Governance is a *process* participated in by people, and its *function* is to enable the institution to achieve its purposes. The *structure* of governance consists of the mechanism, the sociological groups, within which the university community as a group of individuals works to arrive at decisions for action. The *administration* of higher education is the implementing processes for translating decisions into action. Structures for governance and structures for administration may be the same or they may be quite different.

One of the basic principles of local public school administration is that those individuals and groups who are affected by policy decisions should participate in the process of reaching those decisions. Robert Isenberg elaborated on this notion when he commented that such an educational function "should be allocated to that unit closest to the people where it can be carried out with completeness, equity, and efficiency" (Isenberg, 1954, p. 182). One can accept no less a principle for the governance of higher education. Dehner recognized this when he noted that procedural systems developed in recent years for student-faculty home rule

emphasize the validity of the assertion that those persons who are most directly concerned and who know most about particular decisions should make those decisions. This is a principle of democratic community control of universities, but does not imply the one-man one-vote idea that administrators and faculty members rightfully find abhorrent. The principle also does not stand for participatory democracy in the sense that anyone making sufficient noise should be pacified with a decision-making role. It simply means that those who are directly affected or who have positive contributions to make should have the primary responsibilities for making decisions. Precisely how control should be allocated among students, faculty, administration, alumni, and staff is important, but a matter of secondary importance. This sense of democracy means that the influence of various groups will be relative to the decision being made. (Dehner, 1971, pp. 158-159)

There have been numerous suggestions for improving the effectiveness of campus governance in recent years, though many of these suggested reforms are full of paradoxes. O'Neil has noted the paradox of minimal change, among others, which is exemplified by the fact that "despite enormous pressures for reform, fundamental restructuring of university governance is remarkably rare." He also observes the paradox of disappearing power and the paradox of unselectivity; that is, no attempt is made to develop governance models peculiarly suited to academic conditions. The fourth paradox O'Neil discusses is that extension of participation has been undertaken largely without reference to its distribution among constituents. Fifth, there is the paradox of formalism, exemplified by the many recent studies that have focused on structures while neglecting process. Pressures for replacing internal decision-making processes have come from various sources, such as state legislatures, the courts, centralization of statewide systems which leave little to local option, accreditation, financial austerity, and the growth of collective bargaining. Improvement of local campus governance must recognize the power of these external forces. O'Neil has several suggestions for reform of university governance within these constraints. First, the institution must recognize that there is probably no one ideal model for all institutions; each must make its own. O'Neil goes on to say that a study of the functional aspects of governance may be far preferable to the structural approach commonly employed. Further, the claims of each of the campus constituencies that participate in the decision-making process should be appraised, and the governance structure should be fitted to the task at hand, to maximize options. The interdependence of the various forces within the university must be recognized, and external forces must be kept in mind because intrusive legislation, litigation, and law-enforcement surveillance may be not so much a restraint as an opportunity for reform of internal decision-making and distribution of power (O'Neil, 1971, pp. 172-178).

A review of the history of the governance of higher education shows that until recent times, the governance of institutions was predicated on a hierarchical form of organizational structure. Power flowed from the founder, or from the public through a charter or constitutional or legislative sources, to a board of trustees, which theoretically exercised absolute authority. The board then delegated authority to the president, and he in turn delegated authority to other administrative officers, deans, and department chairmen. Corson has noted that this hierarchical structure no longer corresponds to reality, because power no longer flows from a single source. "In a college or university," he states, "all power—that is the capacity to make decisions—does not reside in a single source at the top. It resides simultaneously and in varying proportions in three or sometimes four groups that make up the institution: the trustees and administrators; the faculty; the students; and sometimes the alumni" (Corson, 1971, pp. 180-181).

Improving Governance

Corson makes five proposals for modification of the structure of college and university governance: (1) Mechanisms should be established within the college or university to make possible community-wide participation in governance. Those now being established at many institutions include councils, senates, or assemblies, which recognize the institution as a political community made up of several factions whose voices are to be heard if decisions are to stick when made. (2) The redistribution of power should be made explicit as between and among trustees, faculties, students, and others, with the goal being to place authority where the required competence in knowledge and concern is based. (3) Leadership must be strengthened, particularly as it resides in the president, since he is held accountable by students as well as by faculty and trustees. All leaders must recognize that the university is run in the public interest and with reasonable economy and efficiency. (4) Every extension of authority must be accompanied by a means to enforce accountability. (5) The traditional structures of high schools, junior colleges, four-year colleges, professional schools, and graduate schools should be modified. The purpose of such modification would be to facilitate such new developments as off-campus centers, regional television colleges, flexible systems for earning credits and degrees, increased enrollments, internships, and restored campus autonomy in a statewide system (Corson, 1971, pp. 181-185).

The need for an analysis of the internal structures of colleges and universities and of ways to improve them was recognized more than a dozen years ago when Ayers and Russell studied the line-and-staff charts of some 608 institutions. Their study was designed to meet the growing need for a starting point for the modification and modernization of existing administrative structures. The authors emphasized the well-known fact that the chief function of an internal administrative organization is to increase economy and efficiency of operations, enabling faculty, students, and supporting staff to achieve maximum effectiveness. It thus contributes to the realization of the purposes of the institution within the broad categories of teaching, research, and public service. The report centered largely on the line-and-staff structure for the office of the president and his staff and made virtually no references to professional schools and colleges within the institution (Ayers and Russell, 1962, pp. 1-16).

Most critical observers of the governance of teacher education in complex universities would probably recognize that colleges and schools of education have in recent years had much of their "freedom of movement" noticeably curtailed by forces outside the institution. This is probably only a specific manifestation of the fact that "freedom of movement" for the institution as a whole has undergone considerable erosion. Important decisions affecting universities are made by the federal government, the military establishment, state legislatures, state governing boards, left- and right-wing students, accrediting agencies, and public critics in general. These may be referred to as environmental pressures, and their nature is analyzed in the organizational theory of sociology.

One of the most important characteristics of a profession is its ability to acquire and maintain its professional autonomy, defined as "the right to make critical task decisions based solely on the good of the client and on the expertise of the professional" (Baldridge, 1971, pp. 507-508). After reviewing considerable literature by sociologists and others in this field, Baldridge has stated a basic theoretical proposition as follows: "The higher the social insulation of professional organizations, the higher the professional autonomy within them. Conversely, the greater the environmental pressure, the lower the professional autonmy" (Baldridge, 1971, p. 508).

Five propositions were offered about three major factors: professional autonomy (the dependent variable), environmental pressure, and coping strategies. Briefly, they are as follows:

1. The greater the external control of resources, the lower the professional autonomy.
2. The more concentrated external resources are in the hands of a few contributors, the lower the professional autonomy.
3. The lower the professional control over client characteristics, the lower the amount of professional autonomy.
4. The greater the consensus between the school and its significant surrounding environment, the greater the professional autonomy of the faculty, and vice versa.
5. Other things being equal, high concentration of value-pressure groups on one side of an issue leads to low professional autonomy; high fragmentation of value-pressure groups leads to intense conflict and lower professional autonomy. (Baldridge, 1971, pp. 514-522)

If these propositions apply to the university as a whole or to any professional organization, they apply with equal effectiveness to colleges and schools of education, for the latter are subject to the same external pressures as the institution itself and are also caught in the web of those pressures external to the college but internal to the university. This is one instance in which basic principles of university governance are just as applicable, and useful, to the governance of colleges of education.

Governing Structures

In recent years the concepts and procedures of systems analysis have been used in organizing knowledge about a problem and suggesting solutions for it. This scientific approach might also be useful in viewing the problems of university structures and the functions they are to perform. I have noted that the purpose of structure is to facilitate the performance of function and the achievement of the university's purposes. In one sense, structure is simply the organization of people into groups—groups being defined in the sociological sense. In order for a group to be effective, there must be internal communication within the university as a whole. What does the university look like if we apply the systems analysis model to an understanding of its structure and function? The model has three major components: input factors, throughput factors (the internal processes of operation), and output factors. In industry these components are raw materials, labor, management and capital (input); the technological manufacturing processes (throughput); and the finished goods (output).

In the application of systems analysis to a university, Millett has stated that "the inputs are knowledge as represented by a faculty, students, research ideas, and capital (including land, plant, and equipment). The technology is made up of an instructional process and a research process. The output comprises graduated students, other students, and advancements in knowledge" (Millett, 1962, p. 139). Admittedly, it is difficult to quantify these three components, but the most important difference between an industrial enterprise and a university is the important role of the entrepreneur in the former and the almost complete absence of any ability by management to control the educational technology in the latter. Even with those deficiencies, however, Millett's analysis sheds some useful light on the university enterprise.

For example, the internal structure of a university recognizes faculty specialization, and this specialization can be broadly classified into the academic disciplines and the professional fields. The academic disciplines can be further subdivided into the humanities, the social sciences, the biological sciences, and the physical and mathematical sciences. The professional fields can be further subdivided into art, architecture, agriculture, engineering, teacher education, business administration, music, law, medicine, pharmacy, optometry, social work, public administration, and many others. These units can then be subdivided into separate departments of each discipline such as history, economics, botany, and physics, and into separate professional specializations such as painting, internal medicine, criminal law, accountancy, school administration, and landscape architecture. In other words, Millett states, "regardless of the interdisciplinary nature of various professions, various projects, and various problems of study, it remains clear that the basic specialization of university activity for instruction and research is by disciplines and by professional fields" (Millett, 1962, p. 144).

There is a great need for a university to develop structural clarity and precision by establishing a standard nomenclature for internal use and then observing some consistency in its use in all units. Millett suggests that "the word 'institute' or 'laboratory' be restricted to use in identifying specialized research units in a university and the label 'center' be used to identify interdisciplinary instructional units, although the designation 'school' might be equally employed for this purpose, and 'service' be utilized to identify programs or activities involving re-education and consulting assistance" (Millett, 1962, p. 147). All these units are considered to be basic operating units.

But another part of university structure of coordination is that of management. The structure of coordination consists of colleges and faculties and their assigned educational affairs. Millett, in referring to these, states, "we should employ the term 'college' to indicate arrangements for supervising and coordinating the instructional programs of a university. For two-year programs we might well have a general college. For a baccalaureate program we need a college of arts and sciences, and colleges of business administration, education, engineering, agriculture, nursing, and similar units. At the graduate level we need a graduate college. At the graduate-professional level we need colleges of medicine, law, dentistry, and other appropriate units" (Millett, 1962, p. 159). These colleges are concerned with student admissions, degree requirements, curriculum offerings, student counseling, evaluation of student academic performance, and instructional procedures.

The second structure of coordination needed, according to Millett, is in the area of faculty affairs and the standards governing them. Such standards should probably be university-wide in their development and application, and we must understand the functional distinction between supervision and coordination of an instructional program and the management of the faculty personnel resources of the university. If all these structures are clearly defined, and if all administrative, teaching, research, and service personnel of the university clearly understand their functions, it is Millett's belief that communication will be enhanced and the university will be better able to achieve its purposes.

It seems fairly clear that unless self-governance mechanisms of colleges and universities are understood and improved, the traditional autonomy of these institutions will be seriously curtailed. Several writers have repeatedly called attention to the influence of such external forces as accrediting agencies, professional societies, churches (in earlier days), and the federal government as having a long history of influence over colleges and universities. Observers have noted with some alarm the increasing incursions of governmental intervention, judicial rulings, statewide coordination and planning requirements, and multi-campus systems into institutional autonomy (Mortimer, Ikenberry, and Anderson, 1971, pp. 1-30). What educators must recognize is that conflict within the university is normal; it is recurrent; and it is probably inherent in the nature of higher education. What is important is that mechanisms must be improved in order to accommodate conflict in an age where all forces, internal and external, have become greatly intensified. Conflict that is uncontrolled and intense can reduce an institution to impotence, but conflict that is kept within agreed-upon parameters can stimulate progress and innovation.

One explanation of the vulnerability of colleges and universities to attack both from within and without is that their governance mechanisms have become obsolete. Their nature as complex organizations is poorly understood both on and off the campus. Ikenberry has stated that some of the problems inherent in the institution of higher education as an organization are (1) the absence of a widely shared understanding about the meaning and purpose of the institution; (2) the weakening of the forces of tradition; and (3) the diffusion of goals and values of the participants. He concludes his analysis by posing the cruel paradox that colleges and universities are of unequaled importance to both the individual and to society, while many institutions that are unsure of purpose, and bewildered by conflict are ready to recall the freedom of the academy in favor of certainty and order. It appears that institutions of higher learning have outgrown their organizational structures. The simplistic faculty, student, and administrative organizational patterns of the past were designed for a simpler time, for a different social institution, in a very different context.

Ikenberry apparently believes that the nature of colleges and universities as complex organizations is not well understood, either within the confines of the campus or beyond. The special qualities of the organization demand an understanding of purpose and ideology by all concerned, regardless of position in the hierarchy. This is not the case on most campuses, and consequently, colleges and universities are vulnerable to attack from both internal and external forces. Ikenberry concludes:

> One crucial task is the reform of the substructures of the American campus in such a way as to promote greater influence and personal contact by a great variety of individuals and groups. Recasting and strengthening student-faculty-administrative organizations is essential.
>
> Jurisdictional definitions need not and should not be tightly drawn. Demands for complete autonomy of authority, whether issued by students, faculty or administrators, should be treated as lightly as they are made. Because of the nature of institutions of higher learning as complex organizations, first efforts at restructuring and strengthening the organizational structure might well begin at the departmental level rather than with senates and boards of trustees. The eventual aim should be to enable institutions of higher learning to be the centers of free inquiry and havens of divergent and unorthodox thought they have so long professed to be. (Ikenberry, 1970, p. 13)

That organizational structure has not kept pace with modern demands is partially demonstrated by the development, largely within the last two decades, of large numbers of semi-autonomous research institutes and centers (although many are also teaching institutes and centers). Ikenberry has made several studies of this development, and in 1970 he estimated that there were probably 5,000 such units in operation in major American universities; in some universities, institutes were almost as numerous as departments. Why have they developed? What problems have they solved or created? They have generated some controversy and some complaints, and their emergence cannot be attributed to the failure of departments and colleges to develop innovations. Ikenberry explains his interpretation as follows:

> But no simple rationale will explain the rapid growth of institutes and centers. Certainly, not all of the impetus came from an inability of the conventional structure, primarily the academic department, to adapt to new functional demands. The impetus has come from a wide range of forces such as the availability of new sources of financial support, new constituencies, different faculty aspirations and role expectations, growing needs of administrators to exert academic leadership, increased urging from external sponsors, rising individual and institutional needs for status and prestige as well as the sheer burden of bigness and an obvious need to improve lines of communication and professional relationships. (Ikenberry, 1970, p. 2)

If institutions of higher learning are to develop new systems of university governance, it will be necessary not only to create new structures but to redistribute the power and authority traditionally found in the hands of the trustees and the president and his staff. But who will decide how this power, authority, and responsibility should be reallocated? Hodgkinson made a study to determine "who decides who decides?" Under his direction, the Center for Research and Development in Higher Education at the University of California, Berkeley, sent out over three thousand questionnaires and conducted nine hundred intensive interviews at nineteen institutions, in order to determine which individuals were considered knowledgeable and influential in problems of governance. The data showed that governance today is more complex and is subject to more internal and external factions than ever before. The ability of university presidents to control events on campus has declined, although they are still held accountable. Individual and group self-interest rather than concern for the institution as a whole and slow changes by accretion have made patterns difficult to change. The budget was a major source of friction because the faculty knew so little about it, but there was also resentment against state education departments, presidents, and deans of students. Organization of, or improved representation in, a campus-wide governing body was the most widely adopted suggestion for improving governance (Hodgkinson, 1968).

T. R. McConnell, who has investigated changes in governance, changing personal and social values, and the internal redistribution of power because of the influence of faculty unionism, student roles, changing roles of academic senates, and other considerations, reports that the Center for Research and Development at Berkeley has also developed several other documents on the subject (McConnell, 1971).

In 1971, a group of fifteen specialists in university organization and governance met at Airlie House in Warrenton, Virginia, to review the many issues concerned with restructuring the organization and governance of institutions of higher learning. Stanley Ikenberry, one of the participants, saw six major themes recurring at this conference. First, the participants noted a continuing decline in administrative, faculty, student, and institutional autonomy. Second, they saw increased procedural standardization—campus-wide councils, unions, and units for faculty and student appeal of grievances—all moving the institution from *ad hoc* approaches to more stable and well-defined mechanisms for university governance. Third, they recognized that conflict in governance is a fairly permanent characteristic and that mechanisms must be developed and used to improve the capacity of higher education to manage and resolve conflict. Fourth, they supported the notion that tension should be reduced through organizational insulation and decentralization, while recognizing that obstacles such as the emphasis on accountability for administrative officials sometimes mitigates against assigning too much independence to departments, component colleges, faculty, or students. Fifth, they acknowledged the need for a redefinition of the professional rights and responsibilities of faculty members with its attendant implications for tenure, academic freedom, and the need to accommodate to a different type of student. Sixth, the participants observed that "the higher education mystique, sustained by the largely uncritical affection of society and by its general lack of understanding and disinterest in the intricacies of higher education, has given way to a new level of interest, more careful surveillance, increased

sophistication, and not infrequent indignation and displeasure"
(Ikenberry, 1971, p. 428).

An observation repeated in the several reports of the Airlie
House conference was one that Clark Kerr has often promulgated;
namely, that higher education should be regarded as a quasi-public
utility. Ultimately, the university is a public institution; it is supported by the people, and they will require it to change its ways and
conform if it strays too far from their expectations. Mayhew put it
concisely when he said:

> Institutions of higher education are social institutions created to serve the
> public need. That need changes from time to time and those who work in
> colleges and universities are expected to change with it. A variety of forms of
> public scrutiny and demands for public accountability seem appropriate, and if
> faculties resist, public pressures rightly will increase. The present investigation
> of even such draconian measures as elimination of tenure and modification of
> academic freedom has come about because professors have been insensitive to
> public need and expectations. Only greater responsiveness on the part of faculties
> can reduce these threats. (Mayhew, 1971, p. 494)

The call for decentralization of the governance of higher education recurred in the several reports on the conference. Much of the
literature in this field, however, is unclear as to whether what is
required is a decentralization of the mechanisms of governance or a
decentralization of the processes of governance. The former would
suggest greater autonomy for such institutional structures as departments, schools and colleges, and university senates. The latter would
suggest a downward transfer of the authority, power, and responsibility from trustees to administration officials, to chairmen, to faculty,
and to students. As Marvin Peterson has indicated, there are apparently two dimensions of decentralization: the organizational
pattern of subunits and the pattern of decision-making for coordinating them. He states that "the pattern of these forms of decentralization is partially determined by factors in the external environment,
in the nature of the university organization and in the characteristics
of the faculty and student members or groups which make up the
university. In turn, judgments about appropriate patterns of decentralization may be evaluated against criteria related to the university's success in relating to its environment . . . , in achieving
organizational goals . . . and in relating to its members" (Peterson,
1971, pp. 522-523).

It is obvious that these trends have some significant implications for teacher education and the organization to provide it in multi-purpose universities. The "all-university function" as a concept in the governance of teacher education may have its significance reduced by any mechanisms designed to achieve decentralization of university governance. Yet the very obvious need to coordinate the resources of the university in the development and implementation of curricula and standards for teacher education may further argue for greater autonomy of the teacher education unit, as exemplified by colleges of education. The argument for greater autonomy may as well apply to other professional schools and colleges.

Emergence of Institutes

I noted above that one of the newer phenomena in the organization and governance of higher education in the last two decades has been the emergence of institutes, centers, bureaus, laboratories and other research, teaching, and public service mechanisms quite outside the established departmental, school, and college structures normally found in state universities. Ikenberry and Friedman have studied this development for several years and suggest in a recent publication the following reasons for the establishment of institutes:

1. There has been a combination of societal, professional, and institutional forces.

2. There is a growing dependence of society on scientific and technological innovation.

3. The last two decades have witnessed an influx of foundation, industrial, and government funds, especially R and D funds.

4. There are strong utilitarian, problem-solving motives.

5. The institutes make possible new ways of organizing and relating professional personnel into coordinated team efforts.

6. There has been increased emphasis on research and publication by faculties.

7. Institutes have provided career satisfaction for faculty members, plus funds for secretarial help, travel, and time for research.

8. Institutes were used to entice, recruit, and retain able faculty members, who were in short supply in the sixties.

9. There was a need to strengthen graduate programs.

10. Many administrators felt that institutes could be used to improve the university's modest academic reputation and prestige.

11. Need for departmental reform was noted by many administrators.

Not all of these forces were operative in any one institution, of course, and in some institutions the major impetus was generated by the faculty, while in others, the impetus came from administrative officials. Ikenberry and Friedman summarized by stating, "Yet nearly all successfully established and operating institutes met minimum criteria: they addressed a societal need; university administrative concurrence was given; and a core of faculty members was committed to bring the institute into being" (Ikenberry and Friedman, 1972, p. 118).

Institutes have varying relationships with departments in the university structure. Most institute staff members are appointed jointly with some academic department so that the institute member can have access to tenure, hold an appropriate professorial title, and participate in institutional governance. Ikenberry and Friedman noted that "if one were to distinguish between power (the ability to control rewards and sanctions) and its more informal counterpart, influence, one might suggest that institutes exercise considerable influence within the university authority structure but that power rests principally in the departments" (Ikenberry and Friedman, 1972, p. 122).

These authors also make six recommendations for improving the role of institutes and minimizing their negative aspects in the university: (1) make sure that the character of the institutes is congruent with the goals of the university, and devote more time to their supervision; (2) make university policy relating to personnel matters uniform irrespective of where a person is employed; (3) retain the special structural and functional characteristics of the institutes; (4) provide for effective and systematic review of institute programs and proposals; (5) give increased attention to the integration of institutes with the university in terms of organization, communication, physical facilities, and governance; (6) make increased use of institutes as organizational alternatives to academic departments in areas of instruction as well as in research and in public service (Ikenberry and Friedman, 1972, pp. 124-133).

With items one, two, four, and five I have no quarrel, but a caution should be raised regarding recommendations three and six. The real function of an institute, the reason for bringing it into existence in the first place, is to enable the university to do something it currently has no structure with which to perform the proposed function. Once an institute performs a new function effectively, the university should then determine the academic, professional, or service area most closely related to it and combine them, probably modifying both. Indeed, there seems to be a contradiction in giving credence to both numbers three and five. How can the institution simultaneously retain the special structural and functional characteristics of the institute and integrate it with the university in terms of organization and governance? One looks for some all-encompassing criterion to resolve this dilemma and can only suggest that the logical organization of subject matter, and the research, teaching, and public service within it, could be the unifying factor. In institutes of teacher education, the unifying criterion could well be the product of the university, the graduating teacher. Whatever unit governs the teacher education process should encompass an institute or should be modified to do so. Indeed, if one of the purposes of admitting an institute to the campus is to provide a vehicle for innovation, then the program of that institute should be incorporated into the most closely related academic or professional department in order to provide that department with a stimulus for innovation. Many departments could well be reoriented to encompass both a discipline-centered and a task-centered system of purposes and goals.

After sponsoring nearly four dozen publications, the prestigious Carnegie Commission on Higher Education finally analyzed the many-faceted problem of the governance of higher education. It defined governance as "the structures and the processes of decision-making," thus distinguishing it from administration or management (Carnegie Commission on Higher Education, 1973b, p. vii). The commission's report was primarily concerned with six issues of particular urgency: (1) adequate provision for institutional independence, (2) the role of the board of trustees and of the president, (3) collective bargaining by faculty members, (4) rules and practices governing tenure, (5) student influence on the campus, and (6) the handling of emergencies.

The commission noted nine major themes that permeated its background studies and reports, and made twenty-six recommendations, which observers hoped would form the basis for a new consensus about governance. It was most concerned that assurance would be forthcoming "that all who have a substantial interest in a decision may have their views heard about it, and that all who have competence to make the decision, and who must take the responsibility for it, have a chance, directly or through their representatives, to participate in making the decision. Both the products and the processes of decision-making are subject to evaluation" (Carnegie Commission on Higher Education, 1973b, p. 79).

One would hope that in the years ahead this principle would apply with special force to the governance of professional schools and colleges on the campus and especially to the governance of teacher education, because of the latter's complex relationships with all the resources in the institution.

Concept of the All-University Function

During the fifties and sixties teacher educators in multipurpose colleges and universities devoted considerable thought to the concept of "teacher education as an all-university function." This was doubtless encouraged by the new accreditation movement represented by the National Council for the Accreditation of Teacher Education (NCATE) and was supported by many scholars in the academic disciplines as they noted poorer scholarship achievement in the public schools. On many campuses, the result was the assumption of much decision-making in teacher education by university senates, deans' councils, and presidents with their administrative and advisory staffs. Additionally, at most institutions an "All-University Council on Teacher Education" was formed. These responses were attributable in large part to a failure to recognize the difference between *function* and *responsibility*. The whole university can and should contribute to the preparation of teachers. Its resources should be tapped wherever they are—in the liberal arts college, the vocational departments, the fine arts schools, and other professional schools such as nursing, law, or business. But whose is the *responsibility* for teacher education? Who is held accountable? Local school boards, parents, and local school faculties generally hold the professional education unit, its administrators, and faculty accountable. The governance of teacher education has been faulty precisely because the teacher education unit has not had the power to control its preparation program.

Teacher education is an all-university function, but not an all-university responsibility; university senates, presidential staffs, and teacher education councils are not the agencies to determine policy. These agencies can be helpful in an advisory and participatory capacity, but final decisions on programs and standards are the responsibility of the college of education. There is no more justification for all-university mechanisms to determine teacher education policies than for such agencies to determine policies for engineering, medicine, or law. These other professional schools and colleges also depend on resources outside their units and within the university for providing knowledges and skills for their students. Law needs much social science, medicine needs much chemistry, and engineering needs much physics, but the professional school determines how much of each its students need. In the same way, the teacher education unit knows what the curricula are in the public schools and hence what skills its students must acquire from the academic, vocational, and fine arts fields.

Summary

From the foregoing discussion a few principles seem to emerge:

1. Individuals and groups who are affected by policy decisions should participate in the process of reaching those decisions.

2. Decision-making should be assigned to that unit closest to the people affected so that the decision reached will be most complete, wise, and equitable.

3. Institutional governance structures must secure a balance between adaptability and innovation on the one hand and retention of proven values and stability on the other hand.

4. To raise the professional autonomy of colleges of education, it is necessary to grant them a higher degree of control over the internal and external forces that impinge upon them.

5. When currently available structures are unable to provide for their own governance and administration, they are replaced by new mechanisms. However, before such replacement is made, the current structure should be given every opportunity to make the necessary adaptation.

6. Teacher education may be an all-university function, but it is not an all-university responsibility. Responsibility lies with the unit designated for that purpose.

Should a university be organized according to the subject matter of specialization or the professional careers for which the student is being prepared? Conflict arises when it tries to do both simultaneously. This review of the research and professional writing on the problems and trends in the governance of colleges and universities in recent years shows that both structures and processes are now in a fluid state. This could be "the best of times" or "the worst of times" to make higher education serve the people of the nation. The outcome will depend upon our understanding òf the complex nature of the various systems of university governance and the willingness of leaders in higher education to solve these problems through the procedures of the academic tradition rather than through political expediency.

IV

Early Recognition of Faulty Structure

The purpose of organization and administration in education is to facilitate the performance of a specific educational function. The relationship between the organization and administration of elementary and secondary schools and the effectiveness of the education produced is generally well known. For example, it is recognized that small school districts produce poor-quality education. It is also recognized that a division of the responsibility for the administration of education among teachers, principals, superintendents, and school boards has a definite bearing on the effectiveness of the educational program in local school districts. Given certain inadequacies in the assignment of functions to personnel, certain inadequacies in the quality of education result.

The principle also holds true for programs for the preparation of elementary and secondary school teachers. If the teacher education program is not centrally administered, planned, and organized, it can be assumed that teachers are not as well prepared as in a program where the opposite conditions prevail. In a complex multipurpose institution, if the teacher education program is provided by several different schools, colleges, or departments, and if many individuals are responsible for the program, then such division might result in less effective preparation of teachers than would otherwise be possible. It is also recognized that the internal organization and administration of higher education is frequently characterized by tradition, by a certain amount of haphazard growth, and by a lack of fixed responsibility.

Surveys of Institutional Organization

Most of the material in this chapter has been revised from my review of research and writing on the subject of faulty governance made for the National Commission on Teacher Education and Professional Standards in 1958 and published by the National Education Association. Also included is a list of what were purported to be a "common set of underlying principles for the organization and administration of teacher education institutions or programs" developed by McLure some ten years earlier (McLure, 1948).

The purpose of these papers was to indicate the nature of the then current organization and administration in institutions of higher learning for the preparation of teachers, and to pose some of the problems and issues involved. Considerable opinion was expressed as to how teacher education should be organized and administered, but the research on the relationships between patterns of organization and effectiveness of programs was meager indeed. What is significant, however, is that so much attention was accorded to faulty governance structures to facilitate teacher education in many institutions so long ago. The research then produced had not been adequately disseminated, however, so the profession was not aware of the nature or the significance of the problem. In many institutions, nearly open conflict prevailed in the division of responsibility for the preparation of teachers, and there was considerable interest in this problem throughout the country.

The American Association of Colleges for Teacher Education (AACTE) analyzed this problem at its meeting in Chicago in 1955: G. Tyler Miller (1955) outlined the organization for teacher education at Madison College, Harrisonburg, Virginia, and J. R. Rackley (1955) did the same for the University of Oklahoma at Norman. In each of these institutions, teacher education organization had been divided among several different agencies, and the individuals concerned had been effective in bringing together, for discussion and planning purposes, the various administrators in the institution to develop a unified single teacher education program. The resulting organization was complex, but at least the assignment of functions to those units of the institution responsible for general education, professional education, and specialization was reasonably well defined.

In March, 1955, E. K. Feaster sent a questionnaire to the administrators of the teacher education programs in forty-seven state universities in as many states, requesting certain information about the scope, functions, organization, and administration of their graduate and undergraduate programs for preparing public school personnel. Feaster concluded by stating:

> I believe that my sampling of universities is reasonably representative for in perusing my analysis charts I feel that I have seen about everything. Organizationally the range is from simple departments of education in the liberal arts colleges through separate but close communion colleges of liberal arts and education to far-flung multi-campus and multi-purpose institutions. Administratively, they range from simple, direct, transmission to planetary gear systems which are doubtless appropriate, effective, and intelligible to the designers but which to the uninitiated appear wellnigh bewildering. The advertising slogan of a chain hardware system is, "If it's hardware, we have it." If it's educational diversity, American universities have it. (Feaster, 1956)

Similar inquiries and studies had been made by the universities of Wyoming and Nevada, the National Association of State Universities and Land Grant Colleges, and the North Central Association of Colleges and Secondary Schools. Interest in the proper organization and administration of teacher education was widespread in most institutions throughout the country.

Because the institutions differed, their organization for teacher education differed as well. Their sizes, resources, and purposes other than teacher education resulted in varying, but still effective, organization for teacher education. For example, the problems faced by a liberal arts college with perhaps a one- or two-man department in professional education were not those of the well-organized, single-purpose teachers college in which everyone at the institution recognized his responsibility for the preparation of school personnel. The situation would be still different in the typical land grant college, in which the primary purpose of the institution is the preparation of specialists in agriculture and the mechanical arts. And the problems of all three would be still different from those found in the typical state university with many professional functions to perform other than the preparation of teachers.

The best investigation of the various issues involved was done by E. B. Robert at Louisiana State University. In the fall of 1957, Dean Robert sent an inquiry to the multipurpose institutions in the country to determine the nature of their organization for teacher education. Replies were received from thirty-eight of these institutions. Eleven reported that the college of education was completely autonomous in the area of teacher education, with one particular individual, usually the dean of the college, having administrative responsibility. In seventeen institutions there was a division of responsibility for such activities as the planning of programs or the advising of students, and it was possible for students to become certificated for teaching while enrolled in some unit of the institution other than the school or college of education. There were three institutions whose organization was difficult to discern. In four institutions (and probably in more, since not every one of the respondents replied to this point) the recommendation for certification was clearly required by the dean of the college of education or the head of the department of education. Six institutions provided for a university-wide teacher education committee, but again there may have been (and probably were) many more who did so. Of the individuals who made this point (and not all did), ten deans recommended autonomy in the college of education for selective admission, for the planning and modification of teacher education curricula, for the advising of students, for recommendation for certification, for placement in teaching positions, and for follow-up of graduates. They also recommended that all students certificated for teaching positions be graduated from the school or college of education. Only one of the administrators recommended a cooperative arrangement between the college or school of education and some other unit of the institution, which would have responsibility for subject-matter specialization (Robert, 1957).

Perhaps the issue may be sharpened by quoting from one of the letters in Robert's study:

The College of Education at this University attained the status of a true professional school in 1944 without the slightest argument or debate. This was done through mutual understanding and agreement between the Dean of the College of Education and the Dean of the College of Arts and Sciences. Their joint agreement was approved by the President of this University. That agreement held without a murmur for nearly ten years through the administrations of two regular presidents and one acting president. During the last year or two of that period, some little agitation started in favor of permitting students in the College of Arts and Sciences again to take enough work to "obtain certificates to teach." The written testimony in my possession from the regular president who approved this much needed change and the acting president who succeeded showed that not one single protest, objection, or question had ever been raised by any student or parent to the system which was so happily worked out in 1944. The next regular president steadfastly refused to change the system in spite of the fact that during the last year or two of his administration the agitation referred to above got under way.

With the coming of a new president in 1953 who apparently, among other things, did not look upon public school teaching as being a true professional enterprise and who apparently felt that a school of education in a state university need not therefore be a true professional school for teachers, issued an "edict" which made it possible for students in the College of Arts and Sciences again to "get certificates" by completing the minimum requirements for such in the college of education. That president resigned effective last January. Since that time his institution, in my judgment, has been doing exceedingly well under an interim president. Under the circumstances I of course felt that I should await the coming of the next regular president to ask that the right status for our College of Education be restored. (Robert, 1957, p. 10)

Relationships between Structure and Effectiveness

Perhaps one of the best studies attempting to resolve the various issues in teacher education, particularly in multipurpose institutions, was undertaken by George H. Charlesworth at Washington University. Charlesworth obtained his information by visiting nearly fifty institutions and asking appropriate persons some forty-six questions. Of these questions, eighteen could be associated with the degree of centralization of control over teacher education and twenty-five dealt with possible effects of such control, due perhaps partially to its degree. Charlesworth had a panel of experts scale the degree responses on a one-to-ten scale in order to develop correlations between the degree of centralization and the "effects."

Charlesworth collected certain objective data largely from those institutions in the category of "publicly supported multipurpose institutions having a college or school of education." The data indicated that these colleges or schools of education enrolled all or most of the students who were being prepared for secondary school teaching. Students frequently enrolled in the junior year, following general education in the basic college or colleges of arts and sciences. Patterns of enrollment for secondary school teachers, where there was a school or college of education, seemed to be about as follows:

1. Joint enrollment for all, with dual professors and joint degrees.

2. Joint enrollment for a few top students who were willing to work harder and longer to meet standards and requirements for both the college of education and that of the major department.

3. Enrollment in only the school of education for all prospective teachers after their transfer from the basic college.

4. A very few, perhaps 5 percent or less, of the universities that had schools or colleges of education allowed some students to take courses toward certification without either single or dual enrollment in the school or college of education.

In response to the inquiry as to who advised and approved programs of study, including variations from catalog requirements, for students preparing to teach academic subjects, Charlesworth tentatively concluded that, with very few exceptions, the college or school of education did so. In most instances, "guidance" was related to the enrollment of students. The prospective student was usually required to have his course card signed by an adviser in the school of education before being allowed to take any courses beyond the general education level. In some instances, the adviser was a member of the academic department who had been approved by the school of education to teach a methods course and, therefore, was a half-time member of the faculty of the school of education. In decentralized teacher education programs this was not the case, and the students were advised by their major departments.

In studying the percentage of students enrolled in the school or department of education and in the academic departments of the liberal arts schools in multipurpose institutions, Charlesworth found a significant relationship between a high degree of centralization and (1) the percentage of students drawn into the teacher education program, (2) the ratio of education staff members to the number of students in education, and (3) the actual "holding of teachers" who became certified to teach because of a better program, better guidance, and higher motivation.

It was Charlesworth's belief that teacher education programs organized under schools or colleges of education were moving toward (1) enrollment of all who wished to take advanced education courses in the school of education; (2) allowing students with the inclination and the ability to enroll in a college or department of major interest as well, although these students had to be willing to spend perhaps a little more time in this dual preparation; and (3) centralization of control over the training of prospective secondary school teachers while moving "out" to include representatives of all academic departments in an "all-university committee on teacher education" chaired by the dean of the school of education.

After securing data through personal interviews at thirty-four multipurpose institutions, using an evaluative panel of twenty experts, and ranking thirty-four institutions according to the degree of centralization of their teacher education programs, Charlesworth concluded that "as the degree of centralization increased, the programs were likely to be improved" (Charlesworth, 1958).

In 1957, President Milo Bail of Omaha University sent a questionnaire to eighty-four multipurpose institutions in the north central United States and received replies from fifty-one of them. His purpose was "to collect examples of the organization for, the administration of, and current (promising, good, better, best, unique, usual as well as unusual) practices in teacher education in multi-purpose institutions." Although it is difficult to summarize Bail's voluminous report, a few outstanding characteristics of the organization and administration of teacher education in those institutions may be stated as follows:

1. Most of the institutions had a school, college, or department of education.

2. More often than not, the college of education had autonomy in teacher education.

3. Frequently, there were jointly appointed staff members with responsibility both to subject-matter departments and professional education departments.

4. Fifteen of the fifty-one responding institutions had a university council or committee on teacher education, and thirty-three did not have such a council or committee. The committee was largely advisory and policy-making in nature rather than administrative.

5. Thirty-six of the institutions recognized teacher education

as a function of the whole institution. By a margin of seventeen to eight it was regarded as primarily a function of the department or college of education, and by a margin of fourteen to two it was thought not to be a function of the subject-matter departments. Secondary teacher preparation was more frequently regarded as a function of both the subject-matter departments and the education department, while elementary education was more frequently regarded as the function of the education department.

6. Students preparing for elementary teaching were registered in the school or college of education in thirty-four institutions and in arts and science colleges in only five. Students preparing for secondary teaching were registered in the school or college of education in twenty institutions, in arts and sciences in eight, and in both in seven institutions. There were many variations in the place of registration for such fields as music, speech, home economics, and business education.

7. Counselors were drawn about equally from both education and the department of the student's major.

As early as 1958, Woodring appears to have recognized that the conflict in teacher education was one facet of a general conflict in public education. To oversimplify somewhat the conflict was between those who believed that teacher education should be controlled by the subject-matter specialists under the assumption that if you know, you can teach, and those who believed that there was a body of professional subject matter, that education, specifically teaching, involved certain skills, abilities, understanding, knowledge, and techniques that must be acquired in addition to the subject matter to be taught.

Concept of Centralization

In general, one might summarize the findings of the 1950s by stating that selective admission, teacher preparation curricula (including modifications of such curricula), advising students, determination of the school granting the degree, recommendation for certification, placement in teaching positions, and evaluative follow-up should be controlled by a single administrative unit representing the interests of, and concerns for, teacher education.

This concept had its official manifestation in the first guide and set of standards put out by the National Council for Accreditation of Teacher Education (NCATE). In Standard II, "Organizations and Administration of Teacher Education," the council stated:

> An organization will be regarded as acceptable for the development of policies when a single agency is made responsible for coordinating (1) the planning of teacher education curricula, (2) the development of policies that govern the admission of students to teacher education curricula, (3) the development of a system of registration and enrollment which makes it easy to identify all students preparing to teach and can be understood by students and faculty, and (4) the development of policies and standards for the satisfactory completion of all teacher education curricula. Such agency or unit should be representative of groups or divisions within the institution in proportion to their proper concerns, for teacher education.
>
> An organization that is effective in the continuous development and improvement of the total teacher education program will be typified by (1) a clear definition of objectives and criteria for effectiveness of important aspects of the program, (2) a continuous evaluation of the effectiveness of curricula and procedures, and (3) a consistent policy of development and testing of new and promising procedures.
>
> Responsibility for the total program will be regarded as clearly assigned when some one person is held responsible for the administration of the total program and when that person is in a position to speak authoritatively for the total program. This same person will normally be the one responsible for recommending students for teacher certification. (NCATE, 1954, pp. 5-6)

The National Commission on Teacher Education and Professional Standards (NCTEPS) of the National Education Association devoted its 1958 regional conferences to problems in teacher education, with special emphasis on the organization and administration of the teacher education program. The general conclusion of these meetings was that any institution preparing teachers must accept its responsibility in full; must assign administrative and leadership responsibility definitively; must encourage institution-wide cooperation of both practitioners and laymen; must adhere to the generally accepted standards of evaluation and accreditation; and must assume responsibility for identification, registration, and recommendation of students, including their selection and guidance.

The profession of education in 1958 was in the position of having accepted a certain number of fairly well stated principles and procedures and administrative organization for teacher education. Many of these had been enunciated ten years earlier by John McLure, who had suggested what he entitled a "Charter for the Organization and Administration of Teacher Education." In this charter McLure stated:

> The primary importance of free, universal, democratic education and, collaterally, the crucial significance of the role of professionally competent teachers for all children and youth, impose a major obligation upon all institutions engaged in teacher education. That obligation is to unify and center the responsibility for the organization and administration of teacher education exclusively in one properly qualified, major division of the institution. This principle should be applied in all institutions engaged in teacher education regardless of their source of authority, ownership and control, general plan of organization, method of administration, educational aims and objectives, or size. This is considered a fundamental principle in the organization and administration of teacher education. (McLure, 1948, p. 33)

Recommendations on Structure and Functions

McLure made only a few distinctions among three basic types of higher education institutions. In his view, the college of education in those institutions with a complex internal organization should be made the responsible agent of the institution for those functions appropriate for teacher education, including:

1. Developing a pattern of internal organization which facilitates the best and most intelligent utilization of the abilities and interests of faculty, students, members of the teaching profession, and all appropriate educational institutions and agencies in the formulation of broad policies and programs for teacher education.

2. Administering admission requirements, and selecting students for teacher education.

3. Administering the educational guidance and counseling program for students who are preparing to teach.

4. Recommending for appropriate degrees the students who have successfully completed programs in teacher education.

5. Making recommendations to the appropriate state authority of students who are eligible for teaching certificates.

6. Classifying students and graduates in terms of the requirements of various teaching positions and recommending them to school officials for positions for which they appear to be qualified.

7. Recommending persons of high character, scholarship, and professional competence for appointment to positions on the teacher education staff.

8. Developing and submitting to proper authorities the annual budget estimate for current expenses in the teacher education division.

9. Carrying on continuous study for the development of long-range plans and adequate plant facilities for teacher education, including plans for laboratory schools, whether owned and controlled by cooperating public school authorities or by the institution.

10. Developing, organizing, and administering all curriculums provided by the institution for the education of teachers, including graduate instruction and research as well as undergraduate programs and embracing in-service, as well as pre-service education. (McLure, 1948, p. 35)

The functions of a school or college of education in a complex university are necessarily broad in scope. They include, in addition to the regular undergraduate and graduate instructional programs: conducting educational research and publishing research findings; holding conferences for teachers, school officials, and others interested in the advancement of public education; providing consultative services to local school officials and teachers in the field; and conducting field studies and school surveys.

In a liberal arts college or in a college offering general education and pre-professional programs for other college students, as well as for students who are preparing to teach, the official designation of the division for teacher education should be similar to those of the other major divisions of the college. Usually the division for teacher education in these colleges is designated as a department of education. A person of recognized ability and professional competence should serve as head or director of the department.

The general structure and plan of organization being markedly different in the two types of institutions, the functions of and relationships in a department of education in a college cannot be identical with those of a school or college of education in a complex university. The fundamental governing principles relating to the organization and administration of teacher education are essentially the same, however. The department of education, in accordance with the basic policies and procedures of the college, should be made responsible under all circumstances for the following functions:

1. Providing educational guidance and counseling of all students who are preparing to teach.

2. Recommending for appropriate degrees the students who have successfully completed programs in teacher education.

3. Recommending to state certification authorities all eligible students who are applying for teaching certificates.

4. Classifying graduates and recommending them to school officials for positions for which they appear to be qualified. (McLure, 1948, p. 36)

In the single-purpose teachers colleges, of which there were many in 1948, the host of perplexing problems and obstacles that confronted teacher education in the multipurpose universities did not exist. Here both subject-matter specialists and professors of education knew they were preparing teachers, and both were fully supported by the institution's administrators. Today virtually all of these single-purpose institutions provide programs in many other areas, although they still prepare a very large share of the nation's teachers. Indeed, many are so large and complex that they hardly differ from the state universities, and they are now faced with the same problems of internal organization and control.

Teacher education should not—and probably cannot—be separated from state authority. Elementary and secondary education are state functions, and so too is teacher education. McLure noted this and also foresaw the necessity for a more rigorous system of accreditation of teacher preparation institutions and programs. He was well ahead of his time in recommending representation of the teaching profession on a state commission on teacher education and professional standards. He recommended that:

1. The certification of teachers should be administered exclusively by the state board of education or similar central state authority.

2. All state policies and plans regarding teacher education, including the approval of teacher education institutions, and rules and regulations for the certification of teachers, should be developed, adopted, and published with the full and continuous cooperation of representatives of the various types of participating institutions; together with representatives of the teaching profession as, for example, a state commission on teacher education and professional standards.

3. An institution desiring to engage in teacher education should be required to submit to the state education authority a statement setting forth the type of program proposed, together with full information about the institution as a whole, including history and traditions, predominant interests and purposes, attitude of board and faculty regarding teacher education, scholarship and competence of the faculty, libraries, and laboratories. To all of these should be added a full description of the proposed plan and facilities for teacher education, including the professional library, laboratory schools, curriculums and other facilities. Included also should be information as to scholarship, experience, and professional competence of all full-time and part-time members of the professional education faculty.

4. State policy should specify that, when certificates for teaching are issued on the recommendation of approved institutions of higher education, the state authority for teacher certification be required to issue such certificates only on the basis of the completion of approved teacher education programs, and only on the recommendations of the teacher education divisions. (McClure, 1948, p. 38)

Summary

More than a quarter of a century ago, educators expressed concern about the effectiveness of teacher education programs in many institutions. The relationship between structure and the performance of function in many colleges and universities was beginning to be recognized. A fair number of studies, largely of the survey type, were made to ascertain the nature of this relationship. The one common denominator they found seemed to be that given faulty structures, the misassignment of authority and responsibility to these structures, or both, inadequacies of teacher education programs appeared to ensue. The cry in the wilderness seemed to be for more institutional commitment to teacher education, a commitment that would be demonstrated by the organization of a unit within any institution of higher learning that would have rather complete control over all aspects of its teacher education program.

V

The Governance of Teacher Education— General Considerations

It is generally accepted that there has been a great deal of ferment over the structure and processes of governance in the institutions of higher education throughout the nation, most noticeably within the last twenty years. It is also generally accepted that there has been a great deal of ferment over the structure and processes of governance of teacher education in the larger state colleges and universities. The controversy in teacher education, however, has a long history. The neglect of the subject by colleges in the early years of our history led to the founding of the normal schools and teachers colleges in the nineteenth and early twentieth centuries, and concern for teacher education was reluctantly recognized by the state universities only in the last two decades of the nineteenth century. In these institutions teacher education was first provided by a so-called chair of pedagogy, later by a department, and finally by a school or college. This concept of the professional preparation of school personnel is still struggling for acceptance in such institutions. An examination of several of the criticisms of teacher education may shed some light on the governance of the teacher education organization and process in complex universities. One must retain perspective, however, by noting that such controversy is a part of a still larger parlor game of criticizing education all across its spectrum by self-appointed critics of such diverse types as parents, columnists, submarine admirals, and a few academicians whose last contact with the public schools was at graduation from high school. The critics allege that if education is bad, then the teacher must be bad, and if the teacher is incompetent, then the college that provided the preparation must be suspect; hence, the program and its architects are the real culprits.

The Need for Improved Organization

Unless one knows where the weaknesses of teacher education reside, he can do little to improve the process. To try something new only because innovation is the educational fashion of the seventies or only because some federal or foundation funds are available, and to use them will enhance the prestige of an institution and its administrators, is to miss the opportunity to give some useful personal help to each of next year's graduates of an effective teacher education program.

Horton Southworth has stated that what is needed is a revolution in teacher education. The implication for governance is contained in his request for a new political power base:

Some revolutionary shifts in attitudes about teacher education are basic to change. Rather than defend the present state of teacher education, teacher educators must provide (1) a new political power base capable of securing adequate finances for quality teacher education; (2) a recruiting system which properly selects and screens talent for teaching; (3) a new system of incentives based on performance and ability rather than years of service and credits earned; (4) a partnership which includes teachers, universities, school districts, communities, and related agencies; (5) data to support or refute the nature of teacher education; (6) a means to study, evaluate, and reformulate teacher education objectives which will be more responsive to societal changes; (7) adequate procedures and supervision of licensing that will contribute to professional standards; and (8) retraining for teachers through graduate in-service opportunities with the total support of the profession. Teachers must work in classrooms that are laboratories for learning and maintain professional dialogue. Additionally, if teacher behavior is changed, parents, whose maximum support is essential, must be made aware of the reasons for this change. (Southworth, 1968)

Some of the alleged weaknesses in the preparation of teachers can be laid at the doorstep of the liberal arts professors, not just the "educationists." If teachers of English or mathematics do not know their subjects, then those who prepared them in such subjects must assume the responsibility. Departments and schools of education should receive some praise for fulfilling, however imperfectly, a responsibility that the liberal arts faculties, beginning in the 1880's, not only refused to accept but even disparaged. New emphasis is needed on the means of communication and the conduct and strategy of intellectual inquiry as a way to reconcile the traditions of liberal education and specialization in the disciplines.

Silberman expects too much from the public schools when he implies that their major purpose is "to create a just and humane society," because he overlooks the 50 percent of a child's education acquired from the family, the television set, and the community. (Of course, a just and humane society has always been one of the goals of public education, and good teachers have long sought to achieve it, nebulous though it may be.) Silberman also overly dramatizes the debate between liberal and professional education and magnifies the differences and poor cooperation between the faculties of education and the faculties of arts and sciences (Silberman, 1970). Many internal cooperative structures, such as joint appointments and all-university teacher education policy committees have been developed in most institutions in the last twenty years.

The relationship between structure and the performance of function was noted twenty-five years ago by John McLure, who stated that one of the greatest handicaps to teacher education in many institutions was the lack of a properly integrated organization of the total institutional resources available for the education of teachers. McLure believed that the responsibility for the organization and administration of teacher education should be vested in one, and only one, of the major divisions of the teacher education institution, usually designated as the school or college of education (McLure, 1948).

McLure's analysis could well have been written in 1975. Why has it taken so long—a quarter of a century—for the teaching profession, the teacher educators, and particularly university administrators, to recognize what seems so obvious? It must be noted, however, that in a majority of the larger, more prestigious teacher education institutions, internal government is not the issue it once was. The emphasis has changed, and for them the real governance issues center around the role of the local school systems and the organized teaching profession. But effective internal organization is still a problem for the small and medium-sized institutions.

In this review of the reports available in 1958 it was apparent that the research which was needed to validate these principles of teacher education organization for governance of the process was all too meager. However, recommendations were plentiful that any institution preparing teachers should accept its responsibility in full, should clearly assign administrative and leadership responsibility, should encourage institution-wide cooperation, including cooperation between practitioners and laymen, and should assume the responsibility for identification, registration, and recommendation of candidates, including their selection and guidance (Cushman, 1958).

Attempts to Improve Organization

A recognition that faulty structure for policy formation and for policy implementation has been responsible for poor teacher education is now discernible. Such recognition has paved the way for several suggestions to improve teacher education organization. One such plea for improved organization to facilitate teacher education, this one through financial controls, has been made by Paul Orr, who suggested that some of the various planning, programming, and budgeting systems (PPBS) might be useful. The key to their use in improving structures for teacher education is the underlying assumption that a PPBS assists the university community to do whatever it decides to do more effectively; that is, to relate resources to goals within a priority system. Orr indicated that program budgeting was one of the vital components of any substantial change process simply because it provided a structure through which resources could be related directly to programs. He suggested that it might even be necessary to abolish traditional academic departments and replace them with an organization having much greater emphasis on programs and that a modified program budgeting system might encourage this step. Because teacher education utilizes the resources of the university in nearly all of its departments and colleges, it is already task-oriented in nature. Initially, however, it is suggested that faculty develop programs in their present departments, encourage interdisciplinary cooperation, and relate resources to curriculum development. Orr does not make a distinction between academic departments and professional departments (Orr, 1972).

Several attempts have been made in recent years to apply systems analysis techniques to the development of teacher preparation programs. Donald Haefele (1971) developed a project to help teacher educators and other professionals study the comprehensive Elementary Teacher Education Models proposed by nine universities and one regional education laboratory in cooperation with the U.S. Office of Education. Seven papers were presented that provided information and were designed to promote future planning through examination of systematic planning techniques. These papers reflected stages of thought and action proposals that teacher educators could use in responding to demands for better programs, sharper professional skills, and deeper knowledge. These comprehensive elementary teacher education models were developed by large universities, within and by their professional education units. The supporting academic disciplines were noticeably uninvolved in the studies of teacher education for elementary school teachers.

The need for more realistic teacher education programs with more input from the profession in the schools, and the need for programs designed for minority and culturally different groups, gave rise to considerable experimentation through the "Training of Teacher Trainers" (TTT) program, which was promoted with substantial federal funding by the U.S. Office of Education. The TTT programs were intended to help transform systems of educational training in the broadest sense by creating new organizational structures to provide effective roles for members of all groups that influence teacher education: professors of liberal arts, professors of education, school teachers and administrators, prospective teachers, concerned members of the community, and students.

Disciplines vs. Professions

It has been noted above that there has long been a conflict between those of the faculty who are members of a discipline and those who are members of a profession. The disciplines usually include such broad areas of academic subject matter as mathematics and English, such social sciences as history, economics, political science, and sociology, such sciences as biology, geology, chemistry, and physics, and such representatives of the humanities and fine arts as philosophy and music. The professions consist of those areas of study where the objective is to instruct students in the technique and skill of applying knowledge to the solution of practical problems in everyday life. The professions include such areas of endeavor as architecture, agriculture, nursing, medicine, engineering, teaching, and business administration. The professions rely on the basic academic disciplines for the justification of their practice, but frequently they develop new knowledge both in the discipline and in the practical application of it. In most professions, those who are responsible for the preparation of new practitioners are free to select that knowledge from the discipline which is most useful to their respective profession.

In recent years there has been an increasingly high degree of collaboration between the disciplines and the professions. Examples could be cited in engineering, in medicine, and in business administration. Teacher education is also a part of this growing collaboration, in which the faculty of a school of education might find itself engaged in research in social psychology, economics, public finance, or mathematical statistics as these subjects are applied to the solution of such school problems as public relations, school budgets, or sophisticated educational research. This trend is no doubt enhanced by the fact that more and more members of the professional faculties have advanced their competence as scholars in their respective supporting disciplines and also as more and more of the academic scholars have been drawn into the faculties of professional schools. It must be recognized, however, that the development of genuine collaboration will always be a continuing problem because of the nature of the two. The disciplines concentrate upon knowledge for its own sake and the extension of it through research, whereas the professions concentrate upon advancing the competence of their practitioners to solve the problems of society by utilizing all available and applicable fields of knowledge. John D. Millett has stated that "the disciplines and the professions are both essential to our concept of higher education in American society, and some means for their fruitful collaboration must be found in each university" (Millett, 1962, p. 101).

The academic subjects are usually organized under the administration of a college of arts and sciences and each subject is governed by its faculty, department chairmen, and its dean. Programs for the training of professionals are usually organized in the form of a professional school, which is governed by its faculty, department chairmen, and its dean. Nevertheless, as John J. Corson has noted, the administration of the professional school is different in many respects from that of the school or college offering the academic disciplines. The dean of a professional school usually deals with a smaller faculty, and the school has a greater unity of purpose than does one offering a broad general education at the undergraduate level and possessing high degrees of specialization at the graduate level, although this distinction is probably not as significant as it once was because so many professional schools—law, medicine, business, education, and engineering, for example—have extensive graduate programs and considerable specialization. Professional school faculties are often more closely knit than their academic counterparts, which enables the dean to exercise a greater leadership in educational planning, budgeting, and selection of faculty. Moreover, the nature of the profession requires its faculty to be more closely tied to their colleagues in the field, whether in lawyers' offices, medical clinics, banks, or public schools. Furthermore, the growth in size and complexity of the university, larger enrollments of students with definite vocational aims, larger faculties with a greater range of speciality areas, and other forces have brought a reassignment of responsibilities and attendant authority from the president to the dean, the department chairmen, and the faculty, as Corson noted in the fifties (Corson, 1960, ch. 4).

The decentralization of power and decision-making noted earlier is probably inevitable, given the expansion of higher education and the nature of the professional school. Morris Keeton has commented on the desirability of decentralization as follows: "The research of Likert and others on management of business and other organizations suggests the hypothesis . . . that colleges and universities would do well to explore patterns of decentralization which grant authority and rest accountability in subcolleges or subunits of government and management. . . . campuses should consider using subunits which, though small, have the authority to grant the degree or to manage a whole program. To implement this idea requires the collaboration of other subunits since a small unit cannot supply all of its own needed services. But if such a unit is free to enter into contracts with other parts of the institution for services which it cannot supply itself, many of the barriers to internal cooperation can be dealt with effectively" (Keeton, 1970a, p. 119). This sounds like a plea from most professional schools and especially from a college of education.

The growth in the size and complexity of higher education institutions in the last two decades is well recognized. What do such changes mean for higher education and for teacher education? Evan Collins has noted, for example, that the preparation of teachers and school personnel has failed to maintain the balance between practical experience and academic prestige. He believes that cooperating teachers in the public schools have not been treated as equals in the decision-making processes at a time when the organized teaching profession is claiming the right to decide who shall be candidates for the profession and by what standards teachers shall be prepared. Collins suggests that the solution lies in a definition of the purposes of the university and a power realignment of the agencies having a stake in the preparation of teachers (Collins, 1971).

One of the problems in campus governance as it affects teacher education is the failure on the part of so many in the university, professors and administrators alike, to recognize teaching as a profession. Professors are people who *profess*, and teachers in elementary and secondary schools *profess* no less than those who teach in institutions of higher education. It is difficult to fathom the rationale followed by university teachers who maintain that their work is highly respectable, yet deny such esteem to similar teachers in the public schools. But, be that as it may, what is a profession? What are its unique characteristics?

A recent summary of the nature of a profession has been made by Edgar Schein after he reviewed analyses made by eleven sociologists between 1957 and 1970 (Schein, 1972, p. 8). He defined a professional as having the following characteristics (somewhat abbreviated):

1. He is engaged in a full-time occupation.
2. He has a strong motivation or calling.
3. He has a specialized body of knowledge and skills acquired during a prolonged period of education and training.
4. He makes his decisions on behalf of a client in terms of general principles, theories, or propositions.
5. He is assumed to have a service orientation using his expertise on behalf of the particular needs of his client.

6. His service to the client is assumed to be based on the objective needs of the client irrespective of the professional's personal feelings and in a climate of mutual trust.

7. He is assumed to know better what is good for the client than the client himself, thus demanding autonomy of judgement of his own performance.

8. He forms professional associations which define criteria of admission, educational standards, licensing or other formal entry examinations, career lines within the profession, and areas of jurisdiction for the profession.

9. He has great power and status in the area of his expertise but his knowledge is assumed to be specific to his work and he has no license to be a "wise man" outside the area defined by his training.

10. He makes his service generally available but ordinarily is not allowed to advertise or to seek out clients.

Schein indicated that "these various criteria fit best the traditional, ancient, or 'learned' professions of medicine, law, and divinity. They fit in varying degrees professions like architecture, social work, engineering, teaching and management. . . . The ultimate criterion of professionalization according to most sociologists is the achievement of 'autonomy' which implies (1) knowing better what is good for the client than anybody else because of extended technical education or training, (2) subjecting one's decisions only to the review of colleagues, and (3) setting all one's standards pertaining to jurisdiction of the profession and entry into it through peer-group associations" (Schein, 1972, p. 10).

Some fields, like medicine, fit every criterion, whereas a field like management fits very few. Schein rates teaching somewhere in between, because it does involve a body of expert knowledge and skills learned over a period of time, has a body of professional ethics, and attempts to maintain professional autonomy. The identity of the client is somewhat unclear, because the teacher works for a publicly financed and controlled school system yet devotes the major portion of his talent to helping an individual realize his potential through his management of the learning process. His autonomy, therefore, is not as strong as that of the "ideal" professional, and colleague authority may be derived from the system. At the same time, Schein accords greater professional status to the college teacher; apparently that calling meets more of the ten criteria, but except for the greater preparation required, this granting of higher professional status is rather difficult to accept.

The extent to which education and teacher education can be considered a profession has been examined by a number of scholars in the field of teacher education and in higher education generally. When James B. Conant analyzed the question of who should be responsible for teacher education, he noted that the only group capable of maintaining control of events in university classrooms was the faculty itself, that the only agency able legally to certify a person to teach was the state; and that the "payoff" in any teacher education program was in the classrooms of local school districts. He proposed, therefore, a *restricted state-approved program approach* to teacher education. Conant not only suggested that the state focus its attention on practice teaching, but also urged all departments of the university to use a practice teaching arrangement as the basis for assessing the effectiveness of their teacher education programs. Here was the situation in which the "all-university" approach to teacher education could be made meaningful. The key to the success of this arrangement was the "clinical professor," one who had both knowledge of what to teach and skill and experience in teaching it. He would not be alone in assuring the state, the university, and the local school of the adequacy of the teachers prepared; he would be supported by his academic colleagues. The restricted program approach "would support the clinical professor when he urges the relevant university departments to eliminate persistent weaknesses of teachers being prepared, but the precise nature of the reforms will lie totally in the hands of the departments and of the university or college, or in its teacher education committees" (Conant, 1969, p. 137).

The development of control mechanisms by schools and colleges of education has been a problem of long standing in two very significant areas—one external, the other internal. Internally, much progress has been made over the past twenty years in combining more effectively the strengths of the academic disciplines and the departments and schools of education. Externally, the picture is not so bright, for as Felix Robb has noted, "the relationship between institutions that prepare teachers and the school systems in their vicinity leaves much to be desired. Despite notable exceptions, the chronic complaint persists that too many professors—especially in the academic disciplines, but also in professional education—spend little or no time in elementary and secondary schools and are really out of touch with education's mainstream" (Robb, 1969, pp. 262-263).

If there is one common thread that runs throughout the volumes of literature that (1) describe the current deficiencies in the preparation of teachers and (2) attempt to locate the general governance structure for its implementation, it is the notion that teaching and teacher education in colleges and universities are still struggling, along with some other professions, to establish themselves as professions. When one views the elements of teacher education—the general education, the academic and vocational components of the *what* of teaching, and the professional education component with its sociological, historical, philosophical, and psychological foundations—it is obvious that the profession's greatest need is coordination. When one understands the roles of the public school in the practicum and skill-building programs, and the role of the state as it attempts to assure the public, the schools, and the pupils of a prospective teacher's competence, it becomes even more clear that the basic problem is the need for coordination of the total process and the development of some structure to implement and administer the total process. To accomplish this coordinating function it is necessary to have some structure with authority and responsibility assigned to it in a complex university setting. The university cannot discharge its responsibility to those students preparing for careers in the profession of public education without internally organizing itself so as to facilitate that function.

In Howsam's rather philosophical analyses, we find a further rationale for the concept that education, and teacher preparation as a part of it, is a profession. Howsam has developed three theses: (1) education generally and teacher education in particular are disadvantaged by faulty governance systems and structures; (2) many of the problems of education stem directly or indirectly from these faulty structures; and (3) there is urgent need for a whole new set of assumptions about the governance of education and teacher education (Howsam, 1972, p. 1).

Using a systems analysis approach, Howsam examines the relationships that exist among the several systems and subsystems that constitute the educational system. The following systems are involved:

1. Teacher education as it exists on college and university campuses
2. The colleges and universities
3. The operating units (schools) which employ the graduates of teacher education programs
4. The organized teaching profession
5. Governmental units which have direct relationships with teacher education
6. Extralegal organizations such as accrediting associations
7. The broader society. (Howsam, 1972, p. 1)

In order to determine the role of these agencies, Howsam first analyzed the differences between the disciplines and the professions, concluding that:

1. The disciplines seek basic knowledge within a delimited area of specialization (history, physics, psychology, music, and mathematics);
2. The professional schools, borrowing from the relevant disciplines and conducting their own application research, seek to expand the capacity of the profession to serve human needs (engineering, law, and business); and
3. The professions purvey the services to clients within the society. (Howsam, 1972, p. 3)

From the Middle Ages until relatively recent times, universities were regarded largely as the repositories of knowledge. Their basic purpose was its storage, its expansion through research, and its transmission through teaching. They were generally quite unconcerned with the problems of society. Today, however, probably because its support comes from society rather than students, the university has a public purpose and a public responsibility. As a result, its structure has three components:

1. The disciplines. Customarily these are the departments of the college of arts and sciences, such as biology, English, political science, art.
2. Professional schools. Usually these are separate colleges or schools, each developing its profession and preparing personnel for it. Examples are law, business, pharmacy.
3. A variety of units charged with providing services, doing specialized research, cutting across disciplinary lines, etc. Usually such units have no students of their own. Examples might include a bureau of research and services, an office of international affairs, or a center for urban studies and services. (Howsam, 1972, p. 4)

These three units are subsystems of the university, and they have different purposes. "The disciplines seek to understand, the professional schools to apply and use" (Howsam, 1972, p. 7).

Where does teacher education fit into this structure? Is it a discipline or a profession? Howsam answers this question as follows:

> For decades teacher education has been the victim of an inability to decisively answer this question. On some campuses it has been a department or division of arts and sciences. On some it has had a separate college status but has been classed with the disciplines within the organization and in the minds of people. On still others the whole institution has claimed to be committed to teacher education. Finally, on some campuses it has had both the status and stance of a professional school.
>
> Undoubtedly there have been myriad reasons for the confused situation. It is beyond the scope of this paper to explore the question. It can be said with confidence, however, that both teacher education and public school education have suffered from the confused situation.
>
> In the opinion of this writer, teaching inherently is a profession. It belongs in the company of the decision makers. It meets the criterion of an important social service, and its decisions are based upon the social and behavioral sciences. To protest that it but poorly meets the criteria for a profession begs the issue and delays the day when the criteria might be adequately met.
>
> To categorize teaching as a discipline is to subject it to the control and the norms of the scholarly disciplines. Under such circumstances it can only suffer by comparison and be condemned in perpetuity to reputations of mediocrity. Professors of education cannot expect to be both scholar to the level of those in the disciplines and professional to the level of the other professional schools; to attempt to do so is to invite low status in both.
>
> The fact that teachers must study a discipline in order to teach within a specialized area should never be permitted to obscure the issue. The difference between a scholar and a professional educator is pedagogy.
>
> Some areas of concern within universities require collaborative effort between academic departments and professional schools. Traditionally teacher education is seen in this way. It is popular to speak of teacher education as "an all-university function." Both the American Association of Colleges for Teacher Education and the National Council for Accreditation of Teacher Education work from this assumption. Some programs within the U.S. Office of Education speak of "parity," and this has been interpreted by some as involving equal concern and responsibility.
>
> The reality is that teacher education is a high priority concern of the professional school of education and a low order priority for the disciplines. Under such circumstances, "marriages" are bound to fail. Such collaborative relationships as can be arranged will tend to be expedient and transient. The professor from the disciplines who chooses to involve himself in teacher education will, in most all cases, find himself receiving a slim share of the rewards and recognitions of his department. He simply is not doing what is valued. No amount of effort is likely to change this on an enduring basis.

The consequence is that, parity notwithstanding, the burden of producing and maintaining collaborative relationships falls on teacher education. Much of its energies often are expended in the effort. (Howsam, 1972, pp. 8-9)

If teacher education is a subsystem of the college or university that establishes it and supports it, what is its relationship to the organized, practicing profession? Howsam demonstrates that teacher education is a subsystem of the profession, but that it should not be subject to the direct control of either the state or local education units. From his model he observed that:

Teacher education is responsible to the teaching profession of which it is the training system and to the university or college of which it is an operating subsystem. Schools are responsible and accountable to the communities which they serve and to the state by which they are established. Since the employer of teachers is vitally interested in the quality of teachers and since the schools are needed as teacher training sites, a common interest exists. Each system needs to be responsive to the other. Hence a collaborative relationship is indicated; control is not. (Howsam, 1972, p. 14)

Implications of Teacher Education as a Profession

Again we are faced with the reality that there are many agencies having a stake in teacher education. Teachers can be prepared adequately only if all such agencies will contribute to the process in proportion to their abilities; but one agency, and only one, can and must act as a referee, must contribute an adjudication service, and must coordinate all forces. That agency must be the teacher education unit of the institution. Howsam's summary says it best:

1. Education should be viewed as the training function of the teaching profession.
2. On the college or university campus, education should be viewed as a professional school, sharing this with other professional schools such as engineering, law, and medicine. It should not ever be subordinate to another academic unit.
3. There should be considerably less emphasis on teacher education as an all-university function.
   a) The teacher education subsystem is the one with primary responsibility for the professional preparation of teachers.
   b) Other university subsystems with a role in teacher education (the disciplines) are no more critical to teacher education than they are to the other professional schools. They provide instructional service to the professional schools.

    c) Effectively, requiring education to jointly provide for the education of teachers with other units which have less interest and conflicting purposes makes education dependent and makes it responsible for behaviors over which it has no control.

4. The organized teaching profession should be actively encouraged to accept its role as the major suprasystem of teacher education.
   a) It should be strongly represented on the governing bodies of teacher education and viewed as full partners with the faculty of teacher education.
   b) It should, in the inevitable early contests with school units and the state, be strongly supported by the universities.

5. Accountability and responsiveness should be sharply defined and applied on the basis of suprasystems and related systems.
   a) Accountability is to the suprasystem.
   b) The profession should become the dominant system both for teacher education and for teachers. The university and the employers should accept this as a desirable reality.
   c) Teacher education and the profession should be responsive to the needs and preferences of states and communities. They should, however, be guided by the validated knowledge of the profession in making such accommodations.

6. As the organizational systems for teacher education—both preservice and continuing—are redesigned, every effort should be made to strengthen the profession and to reduce local and state governmental responsibility. (Howsam, 1972, pp. 17-18)

There are several other implications that follow from the foregoing analysis. In practical terms it means that

1. The university governance structure and procedures should grant the same self-governance and freedom to the college of education as to other professional schools. Teacher education should not be singled out as a special responsibility of the university senate.

2. The concept that education is an all-university responsibility is a false notion. It may be an all-university *function*, but it is the *responsibility* of the college of education.

3. College of education responsibility and autonomy means that anyone, undergraduate or graduate, in preparation for a position in the public schools, should be registered in, advised by, and graduate from the college of education.

4. The major role of the college of education is a coordinating one. It must have final responsibility, and commensurate authority, for seeking out and using all resources for teacher education programs, on the campus wherever they may be found—in other colleges,

schools, and departments—and off the campus from such sources as the state, the local schools, accrediting agencies, federal agencies, foundations, the organized profession, the public, and the profession of teacher educators.

5. Whenever experimentation, research, or development in teacher education is undertaken, particularly with outside funding, the program should be under the direction of the college of education and its components.

6. All-university teacher education policy committees should be advisory, rather than decision-making, bodies.

The problem has been that too many people have had too small a vision of what a college of education should be. It does instruct, but a mere department can do that. A college is needed because of the necessity for administrative leadership in a broadened role for American education and for teacher education to prepare its professionals.

Summary

This brief introduction to the complexities of the governance of teacher education in institutions of higher learning has shown that teacher education is a profession, a subsystem of the overall profession of teaching as practiced by educators in the schools of the nation. Some clarification has been made in the differences between a discipline and a profession, a clarification much needed in the multi-purpose universities—state, public, private, and municipal.

It becomes increasingly clear that teacher education is an endeavor worthy of commanding the appropriate resources of the university, but the responsibility for marshaling those resources rests with the faculty devoting all, or nearly all, of its professional time and energies to the preparation of school personnel. Although such a faculty should have authority commensurate with its responsibilities, it can be effective only when it also taps the resources of the practicing profession whose arm it must necessarily be. But educators devoting their lives to the preparation of all teachers and school service personnel also constitute a profession, and as such, they must be accorded the autonomy and responsibility granted to all other professionals.

The mechanisms for implementing these concepts vary enormously, and probably inexcusably, from one campus to another.

The evidence shows, however, that as many organizational patterns for facilitating teacher education are tried, certain structures will eventually be shown to be more effective than others. Some uniformity may be maintained without completely sacrificing diversity or insisting upon identical structures. This may be considered a hypothesis to guide investigation of many other ramifications inherent in the governance of teacher education.

VI

Governance of Teacher Education within the University

If systems analysis is a reasonably useful approach to the examination of university governance, then it might also be useful in viewing the university's commitment to the preparation of school personnel. Basically, systems analysis consists of three major components: (1) inputs, (2) processes, and (3) outputs. These components can be applied to the analysis of teacher education in the university in the following way: *Inputs* consist of the financing of teacher preparation, the students who wish to become teachers, the faculty who assist them in this process and who also receive research proposals, and the public, which is the "client" whom the teacher education effort of the university is presumed to serve. The *processes* consist of the admission of students, the appointment of faculty, the external and internal financing of projects and proposals, the determination of the public service activities to be undertaken, the utilization of the finance funds available for both capital structures and student aid, the provision of instruction by the departments, and the development of research through some such mechanism as a Bureau of Educational Research. *Output* would include the graduation of the teacher who is presumably prepared to begin to teach and who is placed with an employing school district. Other outputs are the retirement and resignation of staff, the reputation of the institution, the public services rendered, and the body of knowledge developed by research.

University Governance Structures

The purpose of university governance structure is to facilitate the achievement of university goals in teaching, research, and public service through its faculty specialization in the academic disciplines and in the professional fields. Two trends have been generally observable in the governance of higher education in recent years. One is the trend toward the democratization of the whole decision-making process. Power has flowed downward—from the trustees to the president and his staff, to the schools and colleges, to the departments, and to the students. Each of these groups has in succession assumed greater responsibility for the determination of policies that affect it both as a specialized unit and as a part of the whole university. This shift in the locus of power has been necessitated in the last two decades by the egalitarian spirit of the times and by the stupendous growth in student enrollment, in faculty, and in cost and complexity of programs.

Many observers see a second trend, a movement in the other direction. The size of institutions, the demand for efficient financial management, the requirement for greater teaching efficiency with larger classes, more impersonal relationships, the utilization of computers in accounting of students, finances, and programs have all resulted in the acquisition of powers by the higher levels of the university governance structure.

It is quite probable that these trends have also characterized teacher education, its structure, and its governance. The vast number of students who have come into teacher education, been graduated, and taken their places in the teaching profession in the rapidly expanding national educational enterprise since World War II has resulted in a mass production of school personnel in all categories—elementary school teachers, secondary school teachers, and school service specialists. This expansion has placed upon schools, departments, and colleges of education greater responsibilities and increased authority to discharge those responsibilities than they had prior to World War II. At the same time, the necessity for involving almost all of the other departments, schools, colleges, and faculties in the preparation of teachers has resulted in some measure of decentralization of the teacher preparation efforts of the institution. Demands for efficiency in the spending of funds and in teaching itself (the latter involving larger classes and participation of more faculty members and students), and the pressures on the part of legislatures, governing boards, and the administrative units of the university have imposed a number of restraints upon colleges and schools of education that often leave them less free than they would like to be to discharge their responsibilities.

These trends in the sixties, and there were others in the governance of institutions in general and in the controls of teacher education in particular, have produced a state of fluidity in teacher education in the large, complex university. This fluidity has led to a re-evaluation of the structure and authority of governance among schools and colleges of education as their faculties, administrators, deans, and department chairmen have sought new ways of making their efforts more productive at a time when the demands placed upon them have been enormous.

Walter Beggs has depicted the organizational pattern of higher education as a "Rube Goldberg" contraption that somehow works. But he agreed with critics who claimed that teachers produced by present patterns are inadequate for the challenge ahead.

> There is a sort of cultural universality about teaching which makes it just about everybody's province.
>
> The schools have been whipping boys for real and alleged problems, such as Russian space triumphs and race problems. Teacher educators have been blamed for the school's failures.
>
> While blamed for crises, school people and their collegiate trainers have been only partially in control of their destinies, and have been only a part of the whole training and controlling mechanism, which includes many agencies, organizations, and enterprises protected by bureaucratic walls.
>
> A major overhauling of the organizational structure for teacher education is needed. Internal organizations and structure tell the real story of a university's commitment to teacher education. (Beggs, 1970)

Beggs went on to criticize organizational fragmentation, divided responsibilities and authority, and unwieldy superstructure, such as committees and commissions that may be advisory and policy-making in function but that are "palliatives and not solutions."

Responding to these kinds of pressures, which were brought to bear not only by colleges of education but by other professional schools as well, many universities have revised their all-university governance structures in recent years. The typical (if there is such a thing) university governance structure consists of the faculty operating through highly decentralized local committees, departments, schools, and colleges, and quite centralized all-university faculties. Committees that include students are organized in a similar manner, and both faculty and students may be represented by the all-university senate. All structures include the departments that make up the various colleges, and in some cases they include the short-term institutes as well. Another structure is the council of deans, whose function is sometimes administrative, in other instances policy-forming, and in other instances merely advisory to the president and his staff.

A number of institutions have made studies of this structure, with emphasis upon department governance, such as the one completed in 1970 by Duke University (Departmental Governance, 1970). The report of this institution reviewed the policy-making processes within departments as well as the relationships between departments and central administration on the one hand and students on the other. The report examined and made recommendations regarding the office of the departmental chairman (i.e., his selection, term, and powers), the faculty mechanisms of departmental governance, the ways by which graduate and undergraduate students participated in university governance, and the composition of advisory committees under the direction of the dean of the faculty or a vice-president for academic affairs. Many institutions have undertaken similar self-analyses.

The Graduate School

One of the more difficult aspects of the governance of teacher education in multipurpose state universities is the governance of the graduate programs and the preparation of school personnel for advanced teaching, administrative, school service, personnel jobs.

In the summer of 1965, William McKenzie visited ten midwestern institutions of higher education and collected data from an analysis of their graduate bulletins, catalogs, and other printed information. He learned that many graduate deans were apparently only part-time, and were often assigned to additional offices such as vice-president for academic affairs or coordinator of funded research. As a result, they had little time to fulfill their responsibilities adequately.

Noting the necessity for an associate or assistant dean, McKenzie suggested that the graduate deans be given faculty and a budget of their own. He emphasized the need for the graduate faculty to have regular procedures by which to select a graduate council to form a policy-making body. He recommended that the graduate school deal consistently with all departments and colleges. McKenzie felt that the objectives of the graduate office should be stated as nearly as possible in terms of its function, placing service first, followed by stewardship and leadership. He recommended that the research function of the university be separated from the graduate office and be assembled into a separate unit of administration that would be provided with its own staff, equipment, and other resources. He believed that the primary function of the graduate office was improved leadership.

In view of the fact that graduate schools of education represented a considerable portion of the whole graduate school effort in these universities, McKenzie made a special analysis of the relationships of the graduate office to education. (The number of graduate students in education varied from 14 percent to 66 percent of all graduate students enrolled.) He reached the following conclusions:

> Graduate work in education should be recognized as an important part of the total graduate program, and accordingly should be given as much attention as it warrants. Graduate offices should not be allowed to think of such programs as something that is taking place over there in Education, in which real scholars would not be very interested nor a great deal concerned. If scholarship in Education is as poor as some graduate offices seem to think it is they should no longer be allowed to ignore the condition but be specifically charged with working toward its improvement. There should be no stepchildren in graduate studies.
>
> As mentioned above, the graduate office should deal with consistent units. If these units are to be departments, the departments in Education should be recognized on a basis of equality with all other departments. If they are not worthy of such recognition they should either be combined, realigned, or abolished.
>
> Graduate programs preparing scholars in any field should use the full resources of the university. Because of its eclectic nature, this is especially true in Education.

Advisement in Education should be distributed among the active scholars in the field. It should be considered an important part of the regular process of instruction and should be recognized as such.

Lastly, graduate offices must become better informed about graduate programs in Education, take a more vital role in their development, and help them to attain an indisputable status of equality with the graduate programs of other disciplines. To do less would be to fail a clear responsibility. (McKenzie, 1965, pp. 21-22)

McKenzie's assertion that "it is questionable whether education is a profession requiring professional degrees" leads him to the conclusion that practitioners in the teaching profession should be awarded academic degrees; he fails to differentiate between a discipline and a profession. However, his major motivation for suggesting this change seems to be that he feels professional degrees carry less prestige than the corresponding academic degrees (B.A., M.A. and Ph.D.). If this were true, though, awarding the academic degrees to graduates in other professions would raise their prestige, but other professionals have not demonstrated any desire for this.

The President and His Staff

The role of the president in the governance of teacher education in multipurpose state universities is probably no different, nor should it be, from his role in other professional colleges. He is, of course, the chief executive officer of the institution, and his effectiveness is measured largely by his capacity for leadership therein. He represents the institution and its faculty before the governing board in determining the institution's goals, administrative procedures, and operating mechanisms. The recent statement on the governance of colleges and universities by the American Association of University Professors sums up the responsibilities of the president in a general way:

It is the duty of the president to see to it that the standards and procedures in operational use within the college or university conform to the policy established by the governing board and to the standards of sound academic practice. It is also incumbent on the president to insure that faculty views, including dissenting views, are presented to the board in those areas and on those issues where responsibilities are shared. Similarly the faculty should be informed of the views of the board and the administration on like issues. (A.A.U.P., 1966, p. 11)

In recent years the role of the president as an educational leader has been eclipsed somewhat. The desire of the faculty to have more power in the academic community, the expansion and increasing specialization of knowledge, and the growing importance of research have all meant that the president can no longer be acquainted with many details and developments in professional fields. He is, however, still held responsible by the board, by the faculty, and certainly by the public for what transpires on the campus (Millett, 1968, pp. 186-191).

The National Council for the Accreditation of Teacher Education (NCATE) recognizes the importance of the president's role in teacher education with its requirement that he initiate the institutional self-survey and the NCATE evaluation that must precede accreditation of the institution's teacher education program. The president, not the dean of the college of education, is usually informed of the NCATE's decision to accredit or not to accredit. This is simply a recognition, of course, of the fact that it is the president who is ultimately accountable to the accrediting agency for the quality of the institution's teacher education programs. This is not to say, of course, that the dean of the college of education and its faculty are not involved; they are. Indeed, they are so much involved that the correspondence with the president is usually regarded as a courteous formality.

The Council of Deans

The staff that advises and assists the president usually consists of several vice-presidents: one for academic affairs, one for finance, one for student personnel, and one for institutional development, although these vary from one institution to another. He also works with a council of deans and administrative officers, and this group makes many decisions concerned with the number, scope, and extent of degree programs, the general enactment of student conduct regulations, the voting of degrees, the determination of recipients of honorary degrees, the general policies on promotion and tenure, the approval of curricula, the administration of student aid and admissions, and similar academic matters. These responsibilities also rest with an all-university academic senate in most institutions.

The governance of teacher education by this hierarchy is not thoroughly established in many institutions, where teacher education may or may not be subject to the same academic controls as are the other professional schools in the colleges of arts and sciences or the colleges of fine arts. To the extent that the council of deans does in fact represent the faculty, or is aware of their point of view, the governance of teacher education may be satisfactory. Most of the decisions of such a council concern all-university policies which colleges of education as well as other institutional units must abide by. Until recently, however, a group of this kind was likely to be insufficiently informed about the unique problems of teacher education. Consequently, the council of deans could make decisions based on lack of interest or inadequate information that could adversely affect the whole of the teacher education process. The same criticism may often be leveled at university senates, which frequently make decisions affecting a college of education that do not apply to other colleges and departments on the campus.

The school of teacher education, perhaps more than any other professional school on the campus, needs some clear-cut regulations governing the responsibilities of the day-to-day activity and authority of the president, the council of deans, and the university senate. The general principle that should determine such regulation is the one mentioned earlier: the allocation of governance responsibilities should be placed on that unit lowest in the hierarchical level that can best discharge it. This is another way of saying that university senates, councils of deans, and all other university-wide governance mechanisms should control teacher education only to the extent that they control all other professional and academic schools and colleges. In other words, the rules they formulate should be university-wide in their application. Rules, regulations, procedures, and assignments of responsibilities, both academic and financial, that involve only teacher education should be assigned to the faculty that is concerned with teacher education on a full-time basis, just as similar kinds of concerns are left to the faculty in the school of nursing or to the faculty in the college of engineering. The teacher education unit calls upon the resources of the whole university to build a strong program, suggesting that teacher education is an all-university function, but that should not be interpreted to mean that it is in the domain of all-university governance mechanisms. The unit that is primarily responsible for teacher education should have authority commensurate with that responsibility. Stating that teacher education is an all-university function is not the same as stating that it is therefore an all-university responsibility. Teacher education is the responsibility of that unit and faculty designated for the purpose of teacher education—i.e., a school, college, or department of education. Since teaching (and teacher education) is a profession, teacher education should be accorded that same authority and responsibility that is accorded professional education in law, nursing, business, architecture, medicine, or engineering. The council of deans should be concerned only with those policies that are university-wide in their application, not with the internal governance of the professional schools and colleges, including education.

The College of Arts and Sciences

The proper role of a college of arts and sciences in a large multipurpose university has been a subject of study and controversy for many years. Any review of the teacher education program will reveal that approximately 40 percent of the four-year preparation program for teachers at the undergraduate level consists of the academic disciplines taught in the colleges of arts and sciences. In addition, these disciplines provide the subject matter specialization in considerable depth for the secondary school teachers and in considerable breadth for the elementary school teachers. But controversy has developed over what agency or group may appropriately determine the relative amounts of these components of general education, subject matter specialization, and professional education.

The history of these controversies has been long and often bitter. From the founding of the first normal school in 1839, there has been a continuing debate as to the best means of educating teachers. Teachers colleges have always had their own academic specialists who knew they were training teachers and who provided the kind of subject matter content that the teacher expected to teach and that was appropriate for the pupils in elementary and secondary schools. From 1839 to 1900, most separately organized normal schools were preparing elementary teachers only, although some began training secondary school teachers after about 1880 and all were doing so by 1920. Colleges and universities had prepared secondary school teachers long before 1920. During the first half of the current century, the major universities began training elementary school teachers as well, and the old controversy—the liberal arts colleges *vs.* the teachers colleges and the academic faculties *vs.* the education faculties—grew more pronounced.

After World War II, particularly in the later 1950s when the technological revolution began to seep into the consciousness of the American people, the schools, and the universities where teachers were trained for them, became the targets for resentment for the alleged failures of education. The controversy between academicians and educationists grew acrimonious and was greatly magnified by newspapers, magazines, and television commentators, all of whom joined the academicians in placing the blame for local school failures on elementary and secondary school teachers and on the institutions that prepared them. While these critics did charge that teachers did not know enough subject matter because they were trained almost entirely in "methods" courses, the controversy between the liberal arts faculties and the education faculties has been exaggerated.

During the 1950s and 1960s there were many institutions that accepted the notion that teacher education was and should be a concern of the total institution. A survey made by the Council on Cooperation in Teacher Education during the summer of 1960 showed that there were a total of 1,074 senior colleges and universities approved for teacher education. When these institutions were asked the question, "Does your institution have a committee or council on teacher education?" almost half (360) of the seven hundred sixty-eight responding institutions indicated that they had established such a cooperative body. When those who responded "No, but" were taken into account, the survey revealed that perhaps as many as two-thirds of the responding institutions had set up some kind of all-institution committees on teacher education. Another significant aspect of the CCTE survey was that 87 percent of these committees had been established after 1950, and 40 percent in about 1960. It seems, therefore, that while controversy continued over the relative contributions of liberal arts and professional education to teacher training, at least there was a forum for reconciling those differences in most multi-purpose state universities (Hodenfield and Stinnett, 1961, p. 141).

In order to bring the so-called warring factions together on an active basis, a number of learned societies and the Teacher Education and Professional Standards Committee of the National Education Association held regional and national conferences at Bowling Green, Ky., in 1958, in Kansas in 1959, and in San Diego, Ca., in 1960. More than 4,500 individuals attended these conferences, representing the liberal arts, professional education, college faculty, public school teachers, school administrators, state departments of education, state education associations, the general public, and student NEA members. Summaries of the separate meetings that attempted to heal the "schism" in education showed that the quality and effectiveness of teacher education depended in large measure upon the extent to which it became a prime concern of the whole institution. In addition, they demonstrated the need for prestige institutions to become involved in teacher education and the need for sympathetic concern by their total staffs. The conclusion reached in these meetings was that a professional unit for teacher education in colleges and universities would continue, and the same kind of autonomy would obtain for it as obtained for other professional units (Hodenfield and Stinnett, 1961, pp. 139-144).

This academic/educator controversy was deliberately heated up again in the mid-1960s as the United States Office of Education gave grants for the education of the educators themselves in several programs. One of these was the TTT Program, the Training of Teacher Trainers. In the spring of 1970, the so-called year of the liberal arts, a conference was called at Phoenix, Arizona, which coincided with the Cambodian invasion, an event which colored the conference quite noticeably. In introducing the addresses delivered at the conference and the summaries of the discussions that were included, Donald Bigelow has implied that the development of specialized teacher education institutions can be partly explained historically by the trend toward the democratization of higher education in general. His analysis is as follows:

> The old democratic institution in whose hands lay the creation of whatever partial democracy we have had in the past was surely the state normal school. We have often felt that analogous schools for our time could come into existence. If the liberal arts colleges became good teaching centers, everyone would know about teaching and learning—but the liberal arts colleges have not so become. The last decade of NSF and Office of Education Activity, the Curriculum Reform Movement, the Title XI Institutes, the Regional Labs, and now the TTT, has been directed toward stopping the war between colleges of education and

colleges of arts and sciences. Yet the war goes on and children suffer, particularly children in locked-out communities.

Once in our history the democratic normal school provided all the training in teaching and in the liberal arts such as it was. Their functions were taken over by the teachers colleges and included liberal arts training in their curriculum. . . .

But the liberal arts colleges, with the dawning of the fourth revolution, must find a new democratic purpose; and it is hard to see how that purpose will be all that different from that of the old normal schools, though teaching styles, and curricula, and the level of profundity will assuredly be different.

Colleges of education and liberal arts colleges surely must be merged as centers of liberal knowledge. It does not matter which dies—the old arts college or the college of education; both are dead so far as American education is concerned. What matters is that the war cease and democratic education begin. (Bigelow, 1971, pp. xlv and xlvi)

As much fault is found with liberal arts colleges as with colleges of education, because they have been unable and unwilling to make a significant contribution to the preparation of teachers. It appeared that Bigelow's solution to the problem of governance of teacher education in state universities was simply to merge the liberal arts colleges and the colleges of education into some new unit. Clearly, the distinction between preparation for the professions and preparation in liberal arts, which has been made in the writings of Millett, Baldridge, and Corson, was not evident to Bigelow or to those who attended the TTT conference in Arizona in the spring of 1970. John Millett has stated this point clearly:

Regardless of the interdisciplinary nature of various professions, various projects and various problems of study, it remains clear that the basic specialization of university activity for instruction and research is by disciplines and by professional fields. This kind of specialization may be criticized as unduly narrow, as artificial and unrealistic, even chauvinistic on occasion, but the fact is still evident that this specialization of departments by disciplines and by professional subjects is the viable, enduring specialization within the university process. (Millett, 1968, p. 144)

During the decade following the conferences at which educators and academic specialists came together to find common ground for the preparation of teachers, there was some continuance of the notion that there was a battle royal taking place between these two groups. There are undoubtedly differences between individuals in either camp, but the implication that professors of education and professors of subject matter areas constitute distinct institutionalized entities is untenable. One must review the syntax of the words "to teach" in order to recognize this fact. The words "to teach" must have both a direct and an indirect object. One cannot teach something in a vacuum. One cannot teach someone without teaching him something. One cannot separate the *what* of teaching from the *how* of teaching because they are, in effect, two sides of the same coin. Consequently, in recent years there has been general acceptance of the notion that teacher education is a cooperative enterprise requiring a community of interest between teachers of the various disciplines and specialists in professional education. Cooperation among scholars in academic subject matter fields and in professional education on the same campus is not furthered by calling for a "confrontation," as Bigelow does in the very title of his book. Cooperation and community of interest are much more productive than opposition of forces.

Educational research might be one way to bridge the gap between faculties of education and faculties of the liberal arts. Some of the conditions that would lessen the gap and support both contact and exchange of intellectual resources between education and the liberal arts must include institutionalizing contacts between educational researchers and the liberal arts, and using joint education and liberal arts committees to direct the studies of advanced graduate students. Bringing liberal arts trained researchers into schools of education should be supplemented by encouraging educational researchers to affiliate directly with professional societies in the liberal arts (Brown, 1966).

Vocational Departments

In most universities, there are departments other than those in liberal arts colleges that are concerned with teacher education. On many campuses the vocational departments also contribute to teacher training. In the land grant colleges the subject matter preparation of vocational agriculture teachers is usually provided by the college of agriculture. The preparation in the *what* of teaching for home economics teachers is usually found in the college or department of home economics. The preparation of art or music teachers in their knowledge and skills comes from the art departments and music departments of colleges of fine arts, and in a similar manner the skills of business educators are learned in schools of business. Some institutions such as colleges of engineering, business, public administration, or agriculture, have separate departments for distributive education and trade and industrial education. It should be noted in passing that these vocational departments in multipurpose state universities and land grant colleges have had to struggle for status among academically oriented and discipline-centered institutions and faculties as hard and as long as did professional education itself.

Professional Schools

Other professional schools whose resources are often used in training both elementary and secondary school teachers include the law school, sometimes used to provide courses in school law, and the school of medicine, which may provide courses in hygiene, anatomy, and public health. Colleges of business often provide courses in public finance and public administration that are most valuable for prospective school administrators.

One of the newer developments in public schools is the utilization of differentiated staffing, which was prompted by the realization that a school does not function best with a single teacher for each classroom. This has long been recognized in secondary education, but the diminished utility of the self-contained classroom in elementary schools has become evident more recently. Specialized teacher resources and supplemental staff services are required if the flexible pattern of adjustment to this new development and its processes is to be made available. A teaching team is required for a master teacher to be used effectively, and various other technical personnel, such as those for guidance services, evaluation, field trips, materials processing, and others, must have places on a team to work imaginatively and constantly with student groups in the development of better education in elementary and secondary schools. These two patterns of staffing, individual teaching and team teaching, should be used in university teaching to serve as an example to teachers in training. Most university teaching is done by one teacher in a classroom of college students. If team teaching is to be demonstrated, then the college of education must call upon other professional schools, the college of arts and sciences, and vocational departments to supply members for the team as appropriate. If colleges of education are to improve local elementary and secondary school learning environments, they must set an example for their students while still in training.

The Professional Teacher Education Unit

The central component of the teacher preparation program in a multipurpose state university is the professional teacher education unit, whatever it may be called. One of the problems that colleges of education face is how to structure the internal organization of this relatively discrete unit. It can be organized in terms of elementary, secondary, and higher education areas of specialization—in other words, by levels—or by such specialized areas as educational foundations, curriculum, methods, and research. ("Educational foundations" usually includes the psychology of learning, sociological bases for schools and their operation, a philosophical orientation to education in a democracy, and as much educational history as is relevant for today's teachers.) There are nearly as many systems of internal organization and components of the professional teacher education unit in the university as there are institutions. One of the things that professional teacher educators need to do is to determine the essence of professional education and organize the students' experiences in some logical manner so as to assure the development of the skills and competencies required.

The competency of professional educators in academic or vocational subject matter is too often ignored. Most of them have taught these subjects in the public schools. They probably need greater depth in these fields, however, not to achieve greater respect from their academic colleagues but to know more about what is taught in local schools. We would recommend that all professional education faculty members should have an academic or vocational subject matter specialization equivalent to the competency required for teaching at least freshman and sophomore level courses in the university. (This question is treated at length in Chapter IX.)

Student Organizations

Finally, considerable attention has been given in recent years to the role of students in the governance of teacher education. This notion was developed by Donald Cottrell when he pointed out that the "silent generation" of students, if indeed there had really been one, has passed. It has been replaced by a generation of students who can and do have opinions and speak their minds publicly concerning their goals in life and their education for the realization of those future responsibilities. Cottrell developed this notion as follows:

> Today's students are ready to accept the long-term challenge of educators to take the responsibility for their own education. This is no less true of students whose career aspirations have been reasonably definitely identified than of those who are still in the stage of general orientation to the life situations with which they seem to be confronted. Prospective teachers are finding out on their own what good teaching is and what kinds of education they shall be needing to serve as teachers. Students must now be enlisted as partners in the task of shaping the appropriate teacher education programs. It must be a shared task in order that the curriculum process and product shall neither be too abstractly theoretical nor be improperly limited or dominated by immaturity or in-adequate understanding of the greatness of the human adventure—the deeper meanings of the good life and society. Neither the empirical reproductions of commonly observable institutional practices nor utopian fabrication of sup-posedly better ones will yield a defensible teacher education program. Com-mitted study of the real, the possible, and the desirable, by deeply purposeful teachers, will do so. Teacher education faculties must learn to treat their students as junior professional colleagues in such a quest. This will require many new approaches in universities, often shattering accepted organization and practice, and will require flexibility where the set for efficiently manipulated "production" of teachers is more often the rule than the exception. (Cottrell, 1970(a), pp. 14-15)

Students have participated in teacher education policy-making procedures in England nearly as long as they have in this country. M. D. Shipman has noted that a high level of social activity, universal participation, and close relationships between the principal, staff, and students were in evidence at Worcester College of Education in 1961. A social structure was produced by the interaction of a number of interrelated factors in the early history of the college. In 1967 there was a resurgence of students' interest in participating in policy determination at Worcester College of Education, although by that time the increased size of the institution resulted in more formal and limited social relations between staff and students not merely because of new facilities and a new sense of intimacy but because the motiva-tion to participate had not been as strong as formerly. It appears from

Shipman's review that it is difficult to sustain continued student interest in college governance (Shipman, 1969).

In this country, the National Education Association (NEA), through its subdivision, the Student National Education Association (SNEA), has promoted a similar kind of student involvement in decision-making for teacher education. The NEA has proposed some guidelines for developing greater student voice in teacher education through a student-faculty committee. Two alternatives have been suggested: (1) provide student representation on existing departmental committees or (2) create a new committee with student and faculty representation. In either case the committee would be charged with the responsibility for ensuring that students would actively participate in determining matters of importance to them. As far as possible, all students, not just those on a committee, would be involved.

The most important consideration involved in student participation is not whether students will be involved, but how much and in what areas. Thus, care must be taken in establishing a philosophical base for policy determination so that it lies within the context of the goals of the institution, and care must also be exercised in determining just how comprehensive student participation will be. As a guideline, the general statement by the NEA may be helpful:

> The development of greater student participation in the decision making process of teacher education must be based upon a consensus by all elements of the teacher education community that student involvement is important enough to be considered part of the total democratic and educational process of the institution, and that it is compatible with the purposes of the university community. If serious apprehensions exist about the degree to which the policy of involvement constitutes a threat to the primary academic functions of students and the faculty, the effort to secure involvement will falter at every turn. On the other hand, if it is commonly agreed that an opportunity for students to advise on and share in administrative policy decisions is valuable in building a strong institution, a strong faculty, and an understanding, loyal, and democratically oriented student body, then there is good chance for success. (National Education Association, 1968)

Student participation in determining policy for a college of education began in 1950 at the University of Illinois College of Education, when the idea of students participating in determining college policy seemed to arise simultaneously from the faculty and students. All parties recognized some valid reasons for tapping the reservoir of student ideas: students were vitally interested in their education, were mature enough to have their judgement trusted, and had ideas that would help materially in the formulation of sound policy. The faculty also recognized the value of producing teachers who were committed to democracy in school administration. The first plan of organization provided for representatives from each of the professional education classes to draw up a charter and establish a student forum, theoretically having 130 members, although only about half of those eligible actually attended. The major input of the students was through representatives of this large group who were members of the College Faculty Policy Committee. Graduate students also sat on this committee. Problems considered included curriculum, library hours, a five-year preparation proposal, professional standards, pay scales, and similar problems. Difficulties encountered were similar to those reported by Shipman—inadequacy of representation, need for sustaining interest, and lack of communication of participants with the colleagues they represented. Benefits derived from this arrangement included improved communication between students and faculty, improvement in the quality of teaching, and improvement in the relationships between instructors and learners. Some educators felt that this type of teacher-student planning would result in better teachers (Henderson and Brown, 1950).

Summary

The development of appropriate and effective governance mechanisms to determine policies for teacher education in complex, multi-purpose universities is a most difficult one. Historical accident, tradition, and the socioeconomic pressures that emanate from the demands of modern life explain in part the nature of current structures and what they do. But adherence to the academic tradition of searching for truth, for principles, and for objective evidence must surmount such accidents and pressures. What is needed is some defensible rationale for correcting current deficiencies in organizational patterns and constructing plans for the future. Teacher education on most campuses must respond to many forces: the general governance structure, the graduate school, the president and his staff, the council of deans, the colleges of arts and sciences, vocational schools or departments, other professional schools, and student organizations. The professional teacher education unit has usually been held responsible for its results by all these organizations, but it usually has had a minimum of control over their demands and contributions. More than anything else, teacher education in a multi-purpose university needs coordination and central direction. Differentiation must be made between contributions and controls. The professional teacher education faculty must be accorded the authority to make such a differentiation.

VII

Influences on Teacher Education
by Funding Agencies

In Chapter VI I discussed the governance structures of teacher education and the factors influencing it from within the university itself. Chapters VII, VIII, IX, and X will be devoted to an analysis of governance structures and the influence of agencies outside the university on such structures. The vast amount of literature in this field can be classified into about ten major categories, which in turn can be grouped under four useful headings: (1) influences on teacher education by funding sources, (2) the role of state agencies, (3) governance by the practitioners in the teaching profession, and (4) governance by the profession of teacher educators.

The major funding sources (other than state appropriations) referred to in the first heading include philanthropic foundations and the federal government. State agencies include the state government, the State Board of Education, or Board of Regents, and the state teacher certification agency. Practitioners in the teaching profession include the National Education Association (NEA), the American Federation of Teachers (AFT), many scores of subdivisions of these organizations, and the local education agencies (LEAs), i.e., school districts and schools. The profession of teacher educators includes such national organizations as the American Association of

Colleges for Teacher Education (AACTE), the Associated Organizations for Teacher Education (AOTE), the Association of Teacher Educators (ATE), the Society of Professors of Education (SPE), and the Deans of Education in the Association of Colleges and Schools of Education in State Universities and Land-Grant Colleges. Certain learned societies, many of whose members are extremely knowledgeable in teacher education are somewhat arbitrarily included. The heading also includes the National Council for the Accreditation of Teacher Education (NCATE).

In this chapter I shall analyze the influence of two funding agencies, the foundations and the federal government, on teacher education.

Philanthropic Foundations

Very few philanthropic foundations have had a greater influence upon teacher education than the Ford Foundation, and its predecessor, the Fund for the Advancement of Education. During the last two decades this foundation has achieved a national, even international, reputation for its philanthropy, and the improvement of education as an essential to democracy has always been one of its priorities. The Fund for the Advancement of Education was created in 1951 to encourage useful changes within education. It has confined itself largely to single purpose, short-term, pilot projects, and it made some five hundred grants, totaling approximately $50 million, during the 1950s (Ford Foundation, 1961). These grants were for such purposes as the training of liberal arts graduates for teaching by developing teacher scholarships, the promotion of the use of teacher aids, the development of patterns for team teaching, and the encouragement of use of new technology such as television, tape recorders, teaching machines, and other media.

In the late 1950s and early 1960s, the Fund for the Advancement of Education and the Ford Foundation were consolidated under the latter name. At this point, the foundation's emphasis shifted slightly, to development rather than research to bring about improvement in public schools.

The route they chose was better preparation of the nation's teachers. The foundation provided some seventy million dollars to investigate ways to make a breakthrough in the education of teachers.

In the early sixties, James C. Stone evaluated the impact of this campaign by visiting and reviewing the reports of forty-two colleges and universities that had operated forty-three of these "breakthrough" programs.

Stone found a number of major accomplishments. The new curricula had attracted a high quality of teacher education candidates, and more than 4,000 of these able young people completed the programs. There was a tendency for these graduates to stay in teaching several years after graduation in about the same percentage as regular graduates. The foundation-supported programs placed great emphasis upon subject matter, especially for elementary school teachers, and upon the teaching internship. The public schools were brought into a more vital role in the professional aspects of teacher preparation. Although all these programs had common objectives, institutions used a variety of approaches to achieve them. In many institutions, the new programs replaced conventional ones even after the foundation support was discontinued.

One of the most noticeable results of the new curricula was an emphasis on cooperation between education and academic faculties. Forty-one of the forty-two institutions Stone studied reported a high degree of such improved working relationships. Stone noticed a high degree of support for, interest in, and commitment to the experimental programs on the part of academic professors, particularly those in English, the social sciences, the life sciences, foreign languages, and mathematics. These good working relationships

appeared to be equally vital regardless of the institutional pattern of organization for teacher education. Whether it was a school or college of education within a university, a department of education in a liberal arts college, or no identifiable education unit . . . all forms of organization seemed to make for cooperative relationships because, within these new curricula and within the minds of those who were involved in designing and operating them, there was a new spirit of working together toward a common goal. (Stone, 1967, pp. 175-176)

Stone recognized that the Hawthorne effect hovered like an invisible cloak over the many identifiable accomplishments, and indeed, many institutions capitalized on it as a means of enhancing the program's impact.

The Ford Foundation's campaign to improve teacher education

gave rise to another program, which came to be known as the "Comprehensive School Improvement Program" (CSIP). One of its twelve purposes was to encourage "school and university partnerships for curriculum improvement, and pre- and in-service teacher preparation" (Nachtigal, 1972).

A comprehensive evaluation of the experience of the Ford Foundation in the 1960s has been made by Paul Nachtigal and several associates. We are here concerned not with Nachtigal's assessment of the efforts and the grants to local public schools, but only with the ways by which the foundation had an impact upon universities as they were involved in the comprehensive school improvement program and in the improvement of their teacher education programs.

Nachtigal has indicated that a partnership of schools, colleges, and universities was thought to be essential for improving education, and the collaboration was expected to be mutually rewarding. It was hoped that better education and better trained teachers would result if the expertise of higher education could be brought to bear on the problems of elementary and secondary education and, in turn, the study of actual problems within the schools would be available for teacher training. Nachtigal's report showed a total of twenty-six projects, with a total expenditure of $30 million, were funded by the Ford Foundation during the 1960s, but only six of these had project directors who were university based. About 29 percent of the funds involved went directly to public schools, and another 29 percent went to state education agencies, while universities served as fiscal agents for the remaining 42 percent. This does not mean, however, that 42 percent of the funds were spent on university campuses; much of it was spent in the local public schools even though the business offices of the universities had been appointed to account for the funds. During the whole twenty-year period between 1950 and 1970 the foundation had made three hundred grants, with 84 percent of the funds going to colleges and universities under the Fund for the Advancement of Education; but in more recent Ford Foundation grants the figure was only half that size. Evidently, the foundation began to realize that there were limits to the capacity of universities to provide innovative leadership for solving the major problems in the schools, so it started to finance projects directly within the local school systems.

Two of these undertakings to improve local school practices were nevertheless university oriented. One was the Alaska Rural School Project, sponsored by the Department of Education of the University of Alaska, and the other was a model for teacher retraining that originated in the center for coordinated education at the University of California at Santa Barbara. Most of these seemed to be reasonably successful.

A primary objective of the CSIP, at least from the foundation's perspective, was to bring the universities and the schools into a closer relationship. Some of the CSIP projects were designed specifically to develop university-school collaboration, and to a limited extent, these efforts were effective. For example, personnel from the universities and schools experimented with new types of instruction, some university staff members were exposed to basic problems within the public schools, and the notion that teachers had much to contribute to the design of college teacher education programs was emphasized. One by-product of this experimentation observed by Nachtigal was that in one way or another the experiences of these programs later contributed to the design of federally funded programs that either encouraged or required collaboration between schools and universities. Nachtigal, however, was rather pessimistic with regard to the usefulness of universities in the improvement of public school education. He felt that much of the cooperation was rather superficial; i.e., both universities and public schools portrayed their relationships as closer than they actually were. Nachtigal concluded that university schools of education had gained little from the experiences that would lead them to alter their teacher training programs.

The lesson drawn from the CSIP efforts was more specifically detailed in ten rather critical comments. With regard to the usefulness of the university in the improvement of either in-service or pre-service teacher education, Nachtigal made the following observation:

Seldom did the power of the university *as an institution* function as a force for improvements of educational quality in elementary and secondary schools. The university was not seen by any of the parties as an instrument of educational reform for the nation's schools. Hence, our university faculty members worked in schools and with teachers, they functioned as part-timers—individual professionals—who necessarily promoted new ideas, could not become involved in the nitty-gritty, and did not carry with them a university-expressed commitment. (Nachtigal, 1972, p. 43)

This summary of Nachtigal's analysis could not set forth his explanations as to why the universities were not more responsive, but the fact that they were not and the fact that the foundation appeared to be rather disappointed in their contributions occurs frequently in the report entitled, *A Foundation Goes to School.*

Another foundation that has had tremendous influence on teacher education is the Carnegie Corporation of New York. Chartered many years ago, the Carnegie Foundation for the Advancement of Teaching has usually followed the format of sponsoring publications and paying outstanding authors for writing either research reports or expert opinions, but has not generally provided grants to local educational agencies.

For example, the Carnegie Corporation financed the study published by James B. Conant under the title *The Education of American Teachers* (Conant, 1963), although the fund was administered by the Educational Testing Service of Princeton, New Jersey. In a like manner, the Carnegie Corporation sponsored John R. Mayor's monumental study, *Accreditation of Teacher Education: Its Influence on Higher Education,* done in 1965 under the auspices of the National Commission on Accrediting.

In more recent years, the Carnegie Corporation has sponsored the Carnegie Commission on Higher Education, under the able chairmanship of Dr. Clark Kerr. Several dozen publications have ensued from this effort, but few of them are concerned with teacher education, although the publication entitled *Professional Education: Some New Directions* by Edgar H. Schein (1972) has many implications for the preparation of school teachers.

For many years the W. K. Kellogg Foundation of Battle Creek, Michigan, has had a noticeable impact on education through its promotion of consolidated schools in the upper Midwest and, more recently, through the development of several programs for improvement of junior colleges and the preparation of administrative personnel for them. The Danforth Foundation's influence has been minimal, despite their praiseworthy efforts to provide for the upgrading of faculty members in higher education through financing of leaves of absence for faculty members, including teacher education personnel.

A fifth foundation having an influence upon education in general and upon teacher education in particular is the Charles F. Kettering Foundation, which has increasingly supported educational research and development. Its programs under the IDEA and IGE were well known. Its emphasis upon Individually Guided Education (IGE) has been an incentive to provide teacher education with programs to enable teachers to recognize the nature and magnitude of individual differences among pupils. A sixth foundation, the Brookings Institution, has made many grants to institutions of higher learning in the area of economic and political science. Other major foundations worthy of note, all of them in New York, would include the Rockefeller Foundation, the Andrew W. Mellon Foundation, the Alfred P. Sloan Foundation, and the Commonwealth Fund of New York.

The *Foundation Directory* lists more than 6,000 such organizations. It is impossible to mention from among this group all those that have a major interest in, and a long history of support for, improvement in the education of teachers. However, the foregoing discussion provides sufficient evidence to make a point: one of the great influences upon teacher education in colleges and universities has been that of foundation support for research and development in teacher education.

The Influence of Federal Agencies on Teacher Education

Throughout most of the nation's history, the federal government has had little more than a peripheral interest in the preparation of teachers. The Land Grant College Act of 1862 provided funds from the sale of public lands to promote "agriculture and the mechanic arts," and sixty-nine colleges and universities received funds under the act. The establishment of the United States Office of Education in 1867 gave no impetus to federal involvement in teacher education even in these vocational fields, although in 1890 the office (then called the bureau) did take on the responsibility of administering part of the second Morrill Act for land grant colleges. The Smith-Hughes Act of 1917 granted funds to the states with which they could develop state plans for vocational education. With subsequent federal approval these plans were then the basis for financial support for vocational education in agriculture and home economics in the local schools with some funds allocated to teacher education in the land grant colleges.

During the first half of this century, two massive studies were substantially funded by the federal government. One was the National Survey of the Education of Teachers, directed by Dr. Edward S. Evenden of Teachers College, Columbia University, between 1927 and 1933. Well documented with statistical data, this report was the first national overview of the institutions, the curricula, the faculty, and the students then engaged in teacher preparation. The second study was done by the Commission on Teacher Education of the American Council on Education and directed by Dr. Karl Bigelow, also of Teachers College, Columbia University, in 1946 (Borrowman, 1965, p. 224). In neither of these studies, however, did the federal government assume any responsibility for developing innovative changes in the preparation of teachers; the federal role was only that of a reporter.

The George-Barden Act of 1946 made the responsibility for teacher education more explicit. Vocational education and federal sponsorship of teachers for the field were both given great impetus by the Vocational Education Act of 1963. With the passage of the National Defense Education Act in 1958 and its amendments in 1964 and later years, the federal government made a major step forward in teacher education and stimulated improvement in specific subjects in elementary and secondary schools. One feature of the NDEA, as it came to be known, was the provision for undergraduate student loans and graduate fellowships and loans. The loans included important forgiveness features if students became teachers. Science teachers and those who planned to teach were given preference in applying for such loans. Here then was the beginning not only of federal involvement in teacher education but of an obvious attempt to assume some of its direction. The opening paragraph of the NDEA is significant in this regard: "The Congress hereby finds and declares that the security of the nation requires the fullest development of the mental resources and technical skills of its young men and women. The present emergency demands that additional and more adequate educational opportunities be made available. The defense of this nation depends upon a mastery of modern techniques developed from complex scientific principles" (U.S., Congress, 1958).

Although most of the act dealt with financial aid to the states and their subdivisions as sponsors of educational programs, particularly those strengthening science, mathematics, and foreign languages, through the purchase of equipment and materials and remodeling of space, there was considerable emphasis upon the preparation of new personnel to administer and teach these programs. Consequently, the act called for the establishment and maintenance of programs of testing in counseling and guidance training institutes, the establishment of centers and institutes in foreign languages, research in the use of audio-visual media, and the extension of vocational education to residents of areas inadequately served. There were several amendments in 1963 and 1964, and in the latter year the reference in the section on student loans to special consideration for those planning to teach and those with superior capacity in mathematics, science, engineering, or foreign languages was defeated. It was in these later amendments that a new feature was added: the development of institutes for those who were preparing to engage in teaching disadvantaged youth (U.S., Congress, 1964).

The major purpose of the NDEA was the provision of increased numbers of teachers in specified categories, not for better or different preparation. The design of the training program itself was still left to the institutions of higher education and to the public schools associated with them.

The relationship between level of education and economic welfare has long been recognized; as early as 1848, Horace Mann had stated that education prevented one from being poor. The federal government recognized this connection when on August 20, 1964, President Lyndon B. Johnson signed the Economic Opportunity Act and declared a "war on poverty." As the preamble to the act declared, "It is therefore the policy of the United States to eliminate the paradox of poverty in the midst of plenty in this nation by opening to everyone the opportunity for education and training, the opportunity to work, and the opportunity to live in decency and dignity" (U.S., Congress, 1964).

Surely the preamble to the Economic Opportunity Act, and the NDEA some years before, stated a national policy for the federal government's participation in education, and involved with this policy was the evident need to become involved in and direct the future development of the preparation of school personnel. The latter act provided for the preparation of teachers in many categories by granting to colleges and universities vast sums of money for regular programs, for innovative programs, for such new areas as counseling and guidance, and for preparation of teachers for the newly created job corps.

One of the earlier attempts to develop more meaningful programs for children of low-income families was the establishment of the Teacher Corps. Don Davies describes it as follows:

> The Teacher Corps was established by the Congress in 1965 to increase the educational opportunities for poor children by enabling colleges and universities to improve the ways in which teachers are trained, and to permit school districts to improve the ways in which teachers are used. The training and use of teacher-interns in teams led by an experienced teacher are the means by which new approaches are introduced and tested. This has proven to be a workable strategy for accelerating the adoption of educational change, and the Teacher Corps has also become a vehicle for the dissemination of promising ideas developed by the National Center for Educational Research and Development, the Office's regional laboratories and others.
>
> In fiscal years 1969 and 1970, as in previous years, the emphases which the Teacher Corps has attempted to establish in its programs are a catalogue of these developments: in the universities, inter-disciplinary involvement in educational research and training, relevant course-work, new instructional techniques, competency-based education; in the schools, team teaching and differentiated staffing, individual tutoring, the introduction of new curriculums, and community involvement which increases parents' interest in their children's education. These emphases are intended to change educational systems to increase awareness of the actual conditions under which poor children are expected to learn, and to encourage institutions to seek new ways to best prepare teachers to serve these children. . . . (Davies, 1970, pp. 69-70)

From the foregoing description it is quite clear that the U.S. Office of Education was encouraging the development of new approaches to teacher preparation and to their utilization in the public schools. It encouraged programs that developed flexible models of teacher education based on performance criteria. It urged involvement of other college and university departments outside the school of education. It suggested granting credit for the internship period and using local faculty and even community members in the teaching staff. In short, the primary purpose of the Teacher Corps program was not just to produce more teachers but to change the way teachers were prepared and the way they taught.

The U.S. Office of Education stated that since the Teacher Corps was intended to encourage and assist changes within the institutions which prepared teachers and educated children, those submitting proposals must identify in their proposals the changes that the Teacher Corps could help them to achieve within the ensuing three to six years.

The Education Professions Development Act (EPDA) of 1967 recognized the fact that the teacher, the administrator, and the other personnel who serve the schools are central to the effectiveness of the education of the nation's children. This act gave the Commissioner of Education considerable flexibility to meet a broad range of problems by removing certain categorical restrictions of previous legislation and enabling him to identify priorities and allocate resources for them. One of the major provisions of the act that had a bearing upon the preparation of teachers for the schools was the Career Opportunities Program:

> The Career Opportunities Program encourages low-income men and women to start their careers as education auxiliaries at whatever level their abilities and interest permit, then follow a career lattice to more responsible, more remunerative, and more challenging jobs in low-income area schools.
>
> Career Opportunities help school districts and universities create programs that are more relevant to the needs of the participants themselves. Training combines academic study toward high school equivalency, the associate of arts, and the baccalaureate degrees, with classroom work in low-income area schools supervised by experienced teachers, who serve as team leaders and cooperating teachers. A combination of courses approach, including practicum, will enable participants to earn 30 credits per calendar year.
>
> Each COP auxiliary begins his career in education at whatever level his abilities and interest permit, then pursues his own career development as far as he wishes from teacher aide to assistant teacher, intern teacher, and ultimately to teacher certification and a baccalaureate degree. Auxiliaries work in such school fields as teaching, counseling, and library and vocational studies. In addition, they supervise "youth tutoring youth" components, helping low-achieving youngsters improve their own self-image and learning by tutoring younger children. (Davies, 1970, p. 69)

Probably the most clear-cut examples of the effort of the U.S. Office of Education to influence the preparation of teachers and other school service personnel is found in the TTT program. In the other acts, the effort was directed toward improving the preparation of the personnel going into the public schools either in a pre-service program or in an in-service program. However, the target for the TTT program was the educators themselves. The deans of education, the professors of education, the supervisors of student teaching, anyone who had any part in the preparation of personnel for the schools could be affected by the program developed by the TTT section of the Education Professions Development Act. The gist of the program is contained in the following paragraph:

> The Trainers of Teacher Trainers Program (TTT) provides a process for engaging the full resources of universities, schools, and communities in creating effective new cooperative institutional arrangements for preparing educational personnel. To this end the program supports projects in institutions of higher education, and in local and state education agencies designed to strengthen the preparation of key agents of change; the individuals who teach or lead, or who aspire to teach or lead, as well as teacher trainers and those who train teacher trainers. During fiscal years 1969 and 1970 major emphasis of the TTT program and virtually all of the projects it supports has been to enable university teachers and high level supervisors and administrators to prepare trainers of teachers, and through them teachers, who can deal effectively with the educational problems of low-income youth. This concern is reflected in the instructional programs, in the practical or clinical experiences provided, and in the administrative structure of the projects themselves. To insure the relevance of these projects, community representatives, particularly from low-income areas, serve on planning and administrative committees and often assist in the instruction of the participants. Nearly all participants in TTT programs are specifically prepared to provide special training to their students—the future classroom teachers—to meet the problems of educating under-privileged children. (Davies, 1970, p. 72)

The report by the U.S. Office of Education the following year, 1970-71, elaborated on the details of the TTT program, particularly its governance mechanisms. The guidelines practically required that the controls be exercised jointly by the colleges of arts and sciences, the schools or colleges of education, and the local community. It was hoped that out of such settings new patterns of teacher preparation would evolve and that new organizational structures to facilitate the process would be established. This is quite evident in the following summary from the 1970-71 report:

> Participants must include university or school personnel responsible for the preparation or leadership of teacher trainers. Graduate students and school or college teachers, supervisors, and administrators preparing to be teacher trainers, are also eligible. Other school or college personnel who will serve on clinical teams or whose training provides practicum experience for teacher trainers or trainers of teacher trainers may also participate.
> The TTT is intended to help transform systems of educational training in the broadest sense by creating new organizational structures to provide effective roles for members of all groups which influence teacher education:

professors of liberal arts, professors of education, school teachers and administrators, prospective teachers, concerned members of the community, and students. (U.S. Office of Education, 1971, pp. 11-12)

The Elementary and Secondary Education Act (ESEA) of 1965 as amended included teacher training. Title IV of this act amended the Cooperative Research Act of 1954 to authorize the development of research and development laboratories that work with state and local authorities, colleges and universities to develop and demonstrate educational innovations and to train teachers in their use.

A separate bureau for the professional development of educational personnel was established in 1968. It brought together the Teacher Corps, the administration of the NDEA fellowships, and teacher training institutes and similar programs. These advanced study institutes served teachers in the public schools, while the graduate fellowships provided support for the development of qualified college teachers. The Vocational Education Act of 1963 and its amendments in 1968 authorized financial aid to students in teacher training programs.

Another well-known agency of the federal government designed to improve the preparation of teachers is the National Science Foundation. In a general way, its programs can be divided into two categories. The first category includes programs for the preparation of in-service teachers by providing remedial training, background training, updating of undergraduate programs, and graduate level preparation. These programs were developed by institutes that provided intensive instruction during the academic year, by summer institutes consisting of six to ten weeks of education, by in-service institutes for teachers in service in evenings and on Saturdays, and by the cooperative college-local school science programs. Generally, these were centered in colleges and universities despite the involvement of the local public schools.

The other category of National Science Foundation program was the undergraduate pre-service teacher preparation program, which was designed to assist colleges and universities in improving their preparation of prospective science and mathematics teachers. This was done to encourage greater mastery of subject matter and the art of planning courses, developing teaching materials, and modifying other teacher preparation instructional programs (Deighton, 1971, pp. 523-544).

One of the more recent developments in the federal government's involvement in teacher preparation may be derived from the newly established National Institute of Education (NIE). This bill, signed into law in 1972, established new programs of student and institutional aid, and extended and revised almost all existing higher education programs. A director has been appointed, and the institute became operational early in 1973. In March, 1973, the president appointed the fifteen-member council, whose role is to establish general policies for and to provide a review of the institute. The council also advises the assistant secretary and the director of the institute on programs to be supported by NIE.

Although the institute's policies are still under development and funding is regarded as less than adequate, program activities are planned in four major areas: (1) the collection, analysis, and dissemination of information on education, particularly higher education; (2) the research and development of resources; (3) the improvement of current practices in educational systems; and (4) the identification of major problems in education and the development of new forms in education (U.S., Congress, 1972).

This search for new structures is evident in another program sponsored by the U.S. Office of Education called the "Program for Improving the Undergraduate Preparation of Educational Personnel" (UPEP). This program had had its legal and funding basis in the Education Professions Development Act (EPDA), or PL 90-35, enacted in 1967, which amended Title V of the Higher Education Act of 1965. Part D of EPDA authorized grants and contracts for improving the "qualifications of persons who are serving or preparing to serve in institutional programs in elementary and secondary schools or secondary vocational schools or to supervise or train the persons so serving." Part D was amended by the Education Amendments Act of 1972. Section 11 of the Amendments Act authorized "programs or projects (including cooperative arrangements or consortia between institutions of higher education, junior and community colleges, or between such institutions and state or local educational agencies and nonprofit associations) for the improvement of undergraduate programs for preparing educational personnel, including design, development, and evaluation of exemplary undergraduate training programs, introduction of high quality and more effective curricula and curriculum materials, and the provision of increased opportunities for practical teaching experiences for prospective teachers in elementary and secondary schools."

In August of 1971, the division of the U.S. Office of Education known as the National Center for the Improvement of Educational Systems (NCIES), which provided for the implementation of the UPEP program, funded a three-year project under the title "Study Commission on Undergraduate Education and the Education of Teachers," directed by Dr. Paul A. Olson of the University of Nebraska. The "commission" consisted of some 40 to 50 members scattered throughout the country, representing public schools and institutions of higher learning, and its' work was overseen by the NCIES. The staff of the commission under Olson's direction was called the directorate.

The commission held a number of meetings, not always attended by all members of the commission and more often than not including people outside of the commission. Speeches were given, discussions were recorded, and the conference results were published. The commission published a newsletter summarizing its activities and proposing areas for future study. It also has published four booklets: *Education for 1984 and After* by Olson, Freeman, and Bowman (1971), *The University Can't Train Teachers* by Olson, Bowman, Freeman, and Pieper (1971), *Of Education and Human Community* by Bowman, Freeman, Olson, and Pieper (1972), and *Nothing But Priase* by Pino (1972).

The position of the commission has been stated by Olson in the five-page letter that is the introduction to the book, *The University Can't Train Teachers*. Olson recommends that any future Office of Education funding of higher education should be developed as follows:

1. The grant should be an "institutional reform" grant rather than a "temporary systems" or "purchase of services" grant.
2. Before the grant was given, commitments to follow up the changes created through it should be obtained up through the governing board of the institution and, in some cases, the state legislature.
3. Grants should require some form of program budgeting across arts and science colleges and education colleges; and common, fully integrated systems of curriculum formation, evaluation of college teachers as teachers of teachers, and related promotion and pay features should be required.
4. Preference in grants should be given to places which have abolished or

seriously modified departments and created some kind of common arts and sciences-education learning community as the basis for educating education personnel.

5. Each program should have a clear program for governing inter-systemic questions which relate the college and the schools to each other: e.g. such questions as the staffing of clinical schools, leading new teachers into the schools, protecting academic freedom in the school, need to be handled in a systematic way and across systems. The Study Commission and UPEP will have to create the tools to make higher education take note of the above recommendations. (Pp. v and vi)

Olson goes on to report the recommendation of the second meeting of a Study Commission committee with superintendents of schools and principals:

The professional aspect of the training of teachers needs to be centered in the schools and controlled by them as a "technical training" comparable in some ways to industrial training. The role of higher education in the education of teachers should be to provide a good general or liberal education in the first three years of college. School-based professional training should be offered in the fourth and possibly the fifth years. (P. vi)

Despite this recommendation, however, both the deans and the local school administrators agreed that if teacher education were centered in the local schools, it should not be controlled by them, because local schools lack the intellectual resources of the typical college of education and are overly conservative.

As a means of assuring compliance with locally based programs Olson suggested that

The AAUP and/or other organizations which "guarantee" academic freedom be encouraged to participate in the development of school-based undergraduate training for teachers and also be invited to participate in developing guarantees of freedom for student teachers where technical education is controlled by higher education.

That higher education either reshape, or give up in its claim to offering, technical education in education areas and assign it to the schools, industry, community agencies, etc., which have extensive educational programs and can possibly provide their own technical education. (P. viii)

Several comments need to be made by way of explanation and clarification of Olson's letter, only part of which has been quoted above. First, Olson's title originated from the following statement, reported on page 71 of the book, by Richard L. Foster, then superintendent of the Berkeley Unified School District in Berkeley, California: "I have come to the conclusion that the university can't train teachers. I am saying they can't be trained on the university campus; that fourth year or fifth year, whatever it is going to be, has got to be in the school." But perhaps a more accurate title would have been, *The University Can't Train Teachers Alone*. That fact has long been recognized, and universities have either had their own laboratory schools for observation and student teaching or they have used the public schools. However, the implication of the Olson title is that the university cannot train teachers at all.

I would also take exception to Olson's suggestion that Office of Education grants should be institutional reform grants rather than temporary systems or purchase of services grants. The commission recommends that before a grant is given, commitments to follow up the changes created through it should be obtained from the governing board of the institution and, in some cases, from the state legislature. If there is any more direct way for the federal government to control teacher education programs than through the granting of funds, it is difficult to envision. The idea that the recipient institution must commit itself in advance to put into practice whatever the federally funded experimental program develops, whether good or bad, seems unworkable. Taking this commitment to the state board of higher education or the board of regents of the institution and perhaps even to the state legislature implies direct federal control.

A third notion in this suggestion for future Office of Education funding is the requirement that there must be a combined college of education and college of arts and sciences faculty and programs, and that this combination must be crystallized through a single budgeting process. It calls for a fully integrated system of curriculum formation and evaluation and professional controls over faculty in the combined organization. This will be enforced by according a preference in the grant "to those places which have abolished or seriously modified their departments and/or schools of arts and sciences and education." There are probably no clearer procedures for abolishing colleges of education and abolishing or modifying colleges of arts and sciences than this kind of forced amalgamation through the granting of federal funds. The study commission provided no evidence indicating that such a modification and amalgamation is any more productive of better teachers than the many procedures now used by inter-departmental curriculum committees, all-university teacher education policies committees, or joint appointments between arts and sciences faculties and college of education faculties. However, the commission rather presumptuously assumed that this would create a better learning environment for prospective teachers. If this were true then a similar amalgamation should be sought with such other professional schools as engineering, business, law, and nursing.

Later in his introductory letter, Olson recalls the commission's concern with regard to the need for education statistics based upon the need for educational personnel. The educational profession is well aware that the teacher shortage has long since ended. But what the commission failed to realize was that such educational statistics are already quite well known, readily available, and are quite revealing of the needs for various kinds of educational personnel. A more recent publication of the commission reveals a clearer understanding of the complexities of the teacher manpower situation (Olson, 1973). (Not available, of course, to the Commission at the time of the publication of the 1972 document was the study produced in 1973 by the Carnegie Commission on Higher Education.)

At one point in the 1973 publication it is remarked that the professional aspect of the training of teachers needs to be centered in the local schools and controlled by them as a "technical training," comparable in some ways to industrial training. One might object to this questionable use of "technical training," because it is used in industry in the preparation of technicians, not school personnel. Denmark referred to this point in his address to the annual meeting of the American Association of Colleges for Teacher Education in Chicago in February, 1973, when he said, "Obviously, teachers want to be and should be significantly involved in designing and implementing training programs for their professions. But their involvement should be as partners in a cooperative enterprise, not as sole determiners" (Denmark, 1973, p. 2). The study commission's report of the position of the deans of education and of arts and sciences described in Olson's report states a somewhat similar position, namely that "the professional education of teachers needs to be centered in schools but not controlled by them because the schools in most districts lack the intellectual resources of a typical college of education and secondly, the schools have very conservative administrations and school boards and neither educational innovation nor academic freedom would be protected in school-based settings."

Olson's introductory letter makes several further references to the fact that federal financing should be "institutional reform" grant funding. The notion that there is greater wisdom residing in Washington than in the several hundred accredited colleges of education, their faculties and administrators, among the associated liberal arts faculty, and the supporting clinical experiences in the public schools seems rather an arrogant one. The teacher education community is moving in the direction of cooperative sharing of the governance of teacher education policies among such groups. Sagan and Smith, for example, have suggested several alternative models for the cooperative governance of teacher education programs and several procedures that universities, local schools, and state education agencies might develop to achieve such a partnership (Sagan and Smith, 1973).

There is another rather interesting item in Olson's introductory letter outlining the proposed work of the commission. "The group said that the teacher education program should be directed toward the reshuffling of certification so that a teacher's being allowed to teach would not be simply a matter of getting a degree or credentials but of the teacher's being certified as a person who is appropriate to teach in a specific school or specific context. The group said that there should be a program involving parents in the local community to 'certify' at the district level." One can only call attention to the fact that the procedure of local lay certification of teachers characterized American education from the colonial period until the first quarter of the last century. Having parents evaluate teachers and give advice to school administrators and the school board is one thing, but having them certify teachers is something quite different.

The February 1, 1973, study commission's newsletter reported that "one of the categorical programs which appeared to have been cancelled is the UPEP (Undergraduate Preparation of Education Personnel) program, which was to have had one million dollars in fiscal '73 and three million in fiscal '74 and more later." Olson implied that the reform movement by the National Center for the Improvement of Educational Systems, the Career Opportunities Program and the Urban-Rural Programs will have to go forward under private or local auspices.

However, this prospective USOE failure to provide further funding did not deter the commission from issuing guidelines for the UPEP program (Olson, February 1, 1973). These were concerned largely with recommendations to the federal agency which also had created the commission in the first place. The commission was about to publish in the *Federal Register* the proposed guidelines for granting funds to institutional and local educational agencies for the preparation of teachers. This is an interesting way to force compliance with the proposed guidelines, because publication in the *Federal Register*, after due comment by individuals affected, usually on short term notice, gives such guidelines the force of federal law. The proposed guidelines included such major components as the scope and purpose which involved the need for reform, the eligibility of institutions, the types of grants to local educational agencies, the involvement of state education agencies, the program objectives, and the program conditions. In a general way one can summarize the guidelines by pointing out that they attempted to implement the concepts and procedures set forth in Olson's introductory letter of June 15, 1972.

The March, 1973, newsletter of the study commission reported on the institutions having innovative developments in teacher education. These included team teaching in the learning center at Temple University, better preparation of teachers for inner-city schools at Duquesne University in Pittsburgh, a teacher internship program of the Wisconsin Improvement Program at Green Bay, and a renewed emphasis upon training of teachers for urban areas, particularly the black ghettos of the inner city, at Chicago State University. There were reports of other special programs for students who intend to teach in urban communities described at Livingston College, a unit within Rutgers State University, and the internship program for teachers and social workers by the College for Human Services in New York City. Also reported was the combined program of Malcolm X College and the University of Massachusetts, who together have formed an urban teacher education program that confers a bachelor of science degree in elementary education upon completion of 18 months of course work and 60 semester hours of credit (Olson, 1973).

In 1970 and 1971 several individuals in the United States Office of Education developed proposals for reforming American education by establishing "teacher centers" and funding "educational renewal sites." The proposals conspicuously ignored teacher preparation in higher education. Concern over this action prompted the American Association of Colleges for Teacher Education (AACTE) to appoint in January, 1972, a Higher Education Task Force on Improvement and Reform in American Education (HETFIRE). A HETFIRE panel was then identified and appointed jointly by AACTE and USOE with Denmark as its chairman and Joost Yff as the task force coordinator. These authors produced a document, later endorsed by the AACTE board of directors, that recommended the principle of collaborative effort—of a partnership in the task of improving education. The partners were listed as the teacher education institutions, the public schools, the federal government, the states, and the local communities (Denmark and Yff, 1974).

The influence of the federal government on education in the United States has changed remarkably since its original statistics-gathering assignment of 1867. Its current role goes beyond one of simple reporting, of merely disseminating a congressional appropriation, of compensating for poverty, and of remedying cultural disadvantages. Its purpose is clearly to influence local education in general by influencing the preparation of personnel for local schools. It is quite clear that the procedures for distributing federal funds have been used to secure the adoption of the notions of federal officials as to the kind of education they believe is good for the American people. The four-fold nature of federal purposes has been observed by Schmeider:

> The fundamental mission of the United States Office of Education and of other federal educational agencies is to administer programs authorized by Congressional legislation. These programs generally have four major purposes: (a) to provide information and statistics about the state of education in the United States; (b) to promote interstate cooperation and sharing of educational experience; (c) to respond to emergency situations related to the national welfare; (d) to support experimentation and demonstration programs that are in the best interest of improving American education but which cannot be afforded by local and state education agencies; and to provide developmental, nation-wide assistance in the installation of large-scale service programs growing out of (c) and/or (d) above. (Schmeider, 1973, pp. 57-58)

Most of the publications of the Directorate of the Study Commission on Undergraduate Education and the Education of Teachers carry the USOE disclaimer that "the opinions expressed herein do not necessarily reflect the position or policy of the U.S. Office of Education, and no official endorsement should be inferred." Nevertheless, USOE support of the study commission at the University of Nebraska surely is a long step forward in achieving the fourth purpose mentioned by Schmeider: "to support experimentation and demonstration programs . . . and to provide developmental, nation-wide assistance in the installation of large-scale service programs. . . ." The USOE may or may not support the notion that "the university can't train teachers," but support of the idea with federal funds surely gives it wide publicity. Much can and should be said for the opposite view—that the university *can* and *should* prepare teachers.

Teacher education is too often merely reactive to criticism and new developments such as the master of arts in teaching (MAT) programs, science education institutes, the teacher oversupply, PBTE proposals, and new certification designs. Teacher educators should begin to take the initiative, because the university is a center for intellectual reflection, for research and evaluation, for personal support and growth, and for learning new skills, knowledge, and values (Nash and Ducharme, 1974). The university is not only the best place but probably the only place where prospective teachers can acquire the knowledge and abilities they need in education's supporting disciplines: psychology, anthropology, sociology, philosophy, political science, and history. Research, experimentation, and development are more often stimulated in university settings than in public schools, where even in-service programs are usually minimal. The vast majority of university-based teacher preparation is capably staffed, academically solid, and professionally sound (Cushman and Steeves, 1976). It would be interesting to see the federal government through the U.S. Office of Education finance a program that suggested what is right about teacher education.

Some evidence suggests that federal policy in education may now change its course. Vast sums of money are not being committed as they once were, and the USOE, engulfed by the huge Department of Health, Education and Welfare, does not have the political clout to compete for funds with such commitments as social security, unemployment compensation, aid to dependent children, medical aid, and public welfare. Michael Kirst has noted that the higher levels of government can affect local schools in six ways: it can provide general aid, stimulate through differential funding, regulate, discover and make available knowledge, provide services, and exert moral suasion (Kirst, 1976, p. 155). Such avenues are also available for affecting teacher education through universities.

Several objections to the work of the study commission at the University of Nebraska were voiced by George Denemark, who withdrew his endorsement because "debate and reflection were ended in favor of advocating governmental solutions" to teacher education problems. This curtailment of debate is suggested by the fact that in his Acknowledgments, Olson had stated that "the group began to formulate its final recommendations shortly after it came into existence . . . in January, 1972" (*Teacher Education in the United States,* 1976, p. xix). Most "study commissions" gather their evidence first and then make recommendations on the basis of that evidence.

Summary

An exhaustive treatment of the many avenues through which the federal government and foundations have sought to influence the preparation of school personnel should be undertaken, and the measurement of the extent to which such efforts have been effective in modifying teacher education practices in colleges and universities awaits further research. The experience of the last decade suggests however, that higher education, and particularly its administrators, should be alert to the possibility that the determination of many significant decisions concerning how best to prepare the nation's teachers may pass from their hands. In general, professional educators welcome experimental opportunities to improve their work, and the funds they have received from foundations and federal sources have undoubtedly had considerable impact upon their programs of teacher education. That these teacher educators are receptive to, and actively seek, new ideas in teacher education is evidenced by the several hundred new practices reported by them in the Distinguished Achievement Awards program promoted by the American Association of Colleges for Teacher Education since 1965. Private and public funding to improve the quality of teacher education can and should be continued—but this does not imply the assumption of governance of teacher education by such funding agencies.

VIII

Role of State Agencies

One of the fundamental tenets of American education is that the states are responsible for education. By "state" I mean all the people of a state acting under the educational provisions of the state constitution and through the legislature, which is responsible for the creation of a state department of education and intermediate and local school districts. In most cases, either the constitution or the state legislature provides for a board of control for the management of the institutions of higher education in the state. These units of state government are the legal foundation of the agencies that discharge the states' functions in teacher education. In the final analysis, therefore, the governance of teacher education rests with each of the fifty states.

State Government

State constitutions may provide for certain kinds of control over teacher education. For example, the constitution of North Dakota established the university, as well as other institutions in the state, and in a general way allocated the responsibility for teacher education to these institutions. Under constitutional provisions, the

North Dakota legislature some years ago established various colleges on the campus of the University of North Dakota in Grand Forks. That law provided that "there shall be a College of Education at the University of North Dakota," and it listed such other colleges as Arts and Sciences, Business and Public Administration, Engineering, Law, Medicine, and Nursing as well (North Dakota, *Century Code* 15-11-04).

Although state government can legislate colleges into existence, its major influence on the governance of higher education lies in its power of appropriation. The amount and distribution of funds appropriated has a definite bearing on what the university as a whole can do and on what the college of education can do. Recommendations concerning that distribution are made by the institution, including the college of education, in its budget. The state governing board and the governor and his staff then make a total budget recommendation to the legislature, which determines the funding level.

Another state agency having a bearing on the governance of teacher education is the court system. As the courts interpret the laws and hand down decisions and injunctions concerning the administration of schools and the relationship of the teacher education institution to those schools, they determine the freedom of movement exercised by the college of education. For example, in recent years the courts have handed down several decisions concerning the liability of students in student teaching; colleges of education, therefore, have had to comply with these directives by acquiring insurance coverage to protect student teachers from liability during their student teaching experiences.

State legislatures also have enacted into law certain policies, such as requiring equality of educational opportunity, permitting local boards of education to establish programs of adult education, or allowing local schools to consider work experience as a part of vocational education. More recently, some states have passed "accountability" laws. Several states—Texas, for one—have required by law that performance based teacher education (PBTE) be established. In Oregon and California the Teacher Certification and Professional Practices commissions have tried to achieve the same purpose through the authority granted them by their legislatures.

Frequently, the state legislature may control teacher education by enacting specific laws imposing curriculum requirements on the institutions of the state, or it may authorize the state department of education to impose such requirements. Many states require all prospective teachers to take courses in physical education (since those states also require that subject to be taught in local schools), or courses in American history, state history, economics, political science, state geography, or conservation. The legislature also regulates licensing requirements for teachers, such as bachelor's or master's degrees, the minimum number of semester hours in professional education, and such specific provisions in vocational education as a definite number of credits in vocational agriculture or practicums in business education. Many states have similar requirements for such school service personnel as superintendents, principals, guidance counselors, and other specialists. Once enacted, these laws remain in the state school code long after they become obsolete, and they can impart a certain rigidity to the whole teacher education curriculum.

State Board of Higher Education

Although one might consider the control exercised by the state board of higher education or by a board of trustees to be a part of the internal control structure of a university, it seems clearer to regard these entities as external agencies representing the public, because appointments to them are usually made by the governor and confirmed by the state senate. In addition, they represent many external social and economic forces and agencies outside the university.

Governing boards usually make final decisions concerning matters of educational policy, the approval of the university curriculum, financial management, the appointment of personnel, the conditions under which personnel work, and the development and maintenance of physical facilities. Although the day-to-day management of these affairs may rest with such administrators as the president, his staff, deans, department chairmen, and faculty, the board makes or approves most general policies, and that is the essence of governance.

The American Association of University Professors (AAUP), the American Council on Education (ACE), and the Association of Governing Boards of Universities and Colleges (AGBUC) have made many attempts in recent years to develop some kind of under-standable relationships among the various governing mechanisms of the university. These groups issued a joint statement on the govern-ance of colleges and universities, asking the institutions of higher education to recognize the inevitability of interdependence among governing boards, administrators, faculty, students, and alumni, and called for joint planning among all groups in the academic community. The statement was an attempt to divide the total governance re-sponsibilities among these groups, with the board of higher educa-tion, or governing board, being the only group able to speak for the whole institution. The statement called for the broadest possible exchange of information and opinions in designing the future develop-ment of the institution, in determining the requirements and priorities for physical facilities, and in budgeting. The governing board was expected to help the institution relate to the community and to have final authority in matters of educational policy, operations, and management, although it was expected to be guided by the judgment of the administrative staff and faculty. The need to maintain public interest in higher education could be handled more effectively by the board than by the administrative staff or the faculty of the university (AAUP *Statement*, 1966). Additionally, the faculty is usually unaware of the costs involved in many budgetary conditions, and it is unaware of the difficulty of administering and implementing many academic programs. Although not exactly financially irrespon-sible, the faculty, because of its limitations, must recognize that the governing boards may necessarily feel compelled to overrule faculty decisions (Millett, 1968).

Obviously the assignment of these functions to the governing board has a significant bearing on the governance of teacher educa-tion by the state board of higher education, which is charged with representing and safeguarding the public interest in the preparation of school personnel. (There are other agencies designed to safeguard the public interest in teacher education, but the state board of control is the most significant.) Either the State Board of Higher Education or the governing board has the final responsibility for determining the structure of the university and therefore, the structure of the college of education. While the faculty, the deans, the presi-dent, or the university senate may make recommendations with regard to what the components of the college of education should be, the board of higher education has the ultimate authority for determining them. It also approves the budget, both in terms of requests from the legislature and in terms of final allocations for the college of education. But perhaps the most important effect the board of higher education has upon teacher education at the university is in determining the scope of its program and approving its internal organization. The board decides whether the college of education will prepare undergraduates only, or both undergraduates and graduates; whether it will have vocational departments within it such as industrial education, business education, and home economics, or whether it shall be strictly academic; whether it shall have a public service function in extension education and off-campus classes, or whether these shall be assigned to the extension division of the institution. It approves the various majors and minors available for specialization among secondary school teachers and decides whether the program will reach downward to include preparation of kindergarten and nursery school specialists or extend upward to include the preparation of junior college administrators, teachers, and professors of education in other institutions. It has the authority to approve or reject the preparation programs for superintendents of schools and other school service personnel, and decides what programs extend through the specialist degree and the doctor's degree. The extent to which authority is invested in the board varies, of course, from state to state.

State Education Agency

A casual view of teacher certification by departments of public instruction in the fifty states shows that their impact on teacher education has been very great. The obvious reason is that the department of public instruction is the legal agency for licensing all teachers and all school service personnel, under the authority granted to it by the legislature. The certification division of the state department of public instruction, sometimes called the department of education, also approves the programs and the institutions providing such programs in a manner not unlike the procedures used by accrediting agencies. A review of their guidelines indicates that these departments are much more concerned with the preparation of teachers, whether in academic or vocational fields, than are either the National Council for the Accreditation of Teacher Education or the regional accrediting associations.

Certification of teachers started in 1794 when the Society of Associated Teachers was organized in New York City. This society examined aspiring teachers and certified those they found worthy. Thus, certification at that date was by "the profession" (Cottrell, 1956). Later departments of public instruction were organized in each state as it entered the union. Very early in the history of the state education agencies, the assignment was given them by the legislature, although the responsibility was often assumed by strong state chief school officers, to oversee the initial certification of teachers and their in-service growth and development. Departments of public instruction in earlier years conducted many institutes at the city and county level for the improvement of teachers in service, because they had also assumed the responsibility for renewing teaching certificates. As education became more complex and a greater diversity of practitioners entered the profession, a number of different kinds of certificates designating expertise in a particular area such as administration or psychology were issued by the state education departments. Early in this century, the leaders of the certification agencies within departments of education in various states began to form their own national organization and to develop uniform standards that would enable them to evaluate their work. This National Association of State Directors of Teacher Education and Certification (NASDTEC) has been effective in giving assistance and direction to the states' legal licensing agencies.

Thus, the legal accreditation or approval of institutions and programs for the education of teachers became the responsibility of the states. The state education agencies acquired the authority, by constitutional or statutory provisions, to do two things: first, to accredit or approve both private and public institutions and programs for the education of teachers; second, to establish the regulations and machinery by which such authority might best be discharged and its purposes accomplished in the public interest. These two prerogatives were necessary in order for the department of education to regulate the licensing of individual practitioners. This authority, deriving from the people in each state, is most commonly vested in the department of education, its controlling board, and the chief state school officer (NASDTEC Proposed Minimum Standards, 1952-1966).

Between 1950 and 1952, NASDTEC, assisted by staff members of the National Commission on Teacher Education and Professional Standards of the National Education Association (NCTEPS) and of the United States Office of Education, developed its first proposed minimum standards for state approval of teacher training institutions. These standards were published by the Office of Education as circular 351 rather than by NASDTEC.

As a result of the 1954 transfer of the professional accreditation of teacher education institutions from the American Association of Colleges for Teacher Education to the newly created National Council for Accreditation of Teacher Education (NCATE), NASDTEC began to revise its standards and cooperate with NCATE in the new accreditation procedures. The result was the production of the 1966 and 1968 editions of the proposed standards for state approval of teacher education, which was, in turn, superseded by the fourth edition in 1971. A few revisions of the 1971 edition were adopted by the organization at its meeting on June 20, 1972. One of the most significant dealt with authority:

> Each state department of education is involved directly or indirectly in the accreditation or approval of teacher education programs within both public and private colleges and universities of the state. In some instances this function is specifically provided for by statute and is supplemented by rules and regulations of the state education agency. Where statutory authority is lacking, the State board of education or State department of education supplies the legal authorization necessary, usually as an application or extension of its authority in teacher education and certification. In the absence of specific statutes, a State should provide explicitly, through board of education regulations or administrative policies of the department, the legal authority for the approval of teacher education programs. (NASDTEC, 1972, p. 1)

Each state department of education retains enough autonomy to establish the procedures for the accreditation or approval of teacher education programs that will be most effective in meeting state requirements. The National Education Association (NEA) has promoted the development of advisory groups to these state departments of education. This is recognized in the 1971 edition of the NASDTEC guidelines: "It is appropriate and desirable for the state departments of education to seek the advice, counsel, and assistance of an advisory group or groups, representing as nearly as possible a cross-section of all segments of the education profession and others interested in the schools." The guidelines go on to say that its membership should include professional educators from elementary, secondary, and higher education and from the state education agency, and should include both citizens concerned with teacher education and minority groups (NASDTEC, 1972, p. 2).

The new guidelines also expected the state departments of education to take other accrediting agencies into account. There is a great potential for competition among the state directors of teacher education and certification, the National Council for the Accreditation of Teacher Education, and the professional educators in higher institutions. Therefore there is much need for considerable interchange of information and for cooperation between these three major components of all the forces governing teacher education. The state directors were cautioned to give due consideration to the National Council for Accreditation of Teacher Education and the six regional accrediting agencies. The National Council for the Accreditation of Teacher Education includes representatives of this group of state certification directors, and whenever a visiting team from NCATE arrives at the campus of an institution undergoing visitation and accreditation, a representative of the certification division of the state department of public instruction is a member of the team.

The state departments of public instruction have an influence upon the organizational structure for the preparation of teachers within state universities and teacher education institutions. Chapter II of the 1971 edition of the NASDTEC standards is devoted to the organization and administration of teacher education and covers the organizational, administrative, and operational provisions and support of the teacher education program. Its recommendations begin with the requirement that the institution provide a statement of purposes and objectives for teacher education. The statement must also include policies for admission and retention of students, descriptions of faculty resources, curriculums, facilities, and relationships with the nearby public schools. Provisions for evaluation of the teacher preparation programs must also be included. The NASDTEC standards review the curriculum requirements for basic, or undergraduate, programs and advanced, or graduate, programs, and describe the role of the organizational structure in an approved program:

2.2 *Organization.* Sound instructional programs can be operated effectively only when supported by competent administrators and a board of control committed to institutional purposes. Consequently, attention should be given to the manner in which the administration operates, its responsiveness to institutional needs, and its efforts to appraise its own effectiveness in terms of the following criteria.

2.2.1 *Board of Control.* Control should reside in a board of trustees or otherwise designated board. Terms of office should be arranged to provide desirable continuity within the board.

The function of the board should be that of assuring for the institution sound philosophies and policies, facilities, and leadership which will provide the best possible services to the students and faculty, and will insure for the college and the students a sound educational program. In the discharge of this function there should be clear evidence of the board's appreciation of its responsibilities in providing a program of teacher education.

2.2.2 *General Administration.* Under the direction of the president as the chief administrative officer, adequate provision should be made for the performance of all administrative functions affecting teacher education by personnel competent in their respective lines of activity. A chart showing the organization of the institution should be available. When evaluating the administration of teacher education in an institution, appraisal should be made of suitability of the organization, the competence of the personnel, and the way in which functions are performed. Consideration should be given to salary schedules and rank, retirement allowances, tenure, group insurance, sabbatical leave, sick leave, funds for in-service development of the faculty, and service by the faculty in professional development on a State, regional, or national basis.

Institutions which prepare teachers should provide information for administrative and faculty members outlining the applicable administrative policies. Such information should state and interpret the functions of the board of control, the faculty, and the staff of administrative officers with particular reference to teacher education.

Institutions which accept responsibility for education of teachers should establish and designate the appropriate division, school, college, or department within the institution charged with accountability and authorization to act, within the framework of general institutional policy on all matters relative to the teacher education program. [Italics mine] (NASDTEC, 1972, pp. 7-8)

These guidelines for the directors of certification in state education departments do not differentiate between governance structure for policy formation and the structure for the administration of teacher education programs. There is, of course, a close interrelationship between policy formation and policy administration in institutions of higher learning, and some of the mechanisms used for policy formation are identical to the mechanisms used for policy implementation. It is important to note, however, that the state education departments' guidelines for approving teacher education institutions call for a clearly established and clearly designated division, school, college, or department of education charged with accountability and with the commensurate authority to act. In this respect these guidelines are in agreement with the standards of the National Council for the Accreditation of Teacher Education (NCATE *Standards,* 1970).

The 1972 revisions of the NASDTEC standards did not recommend changes in an institution's governance structure, but suggestions were made to accommodate experimental or innovative programs of teacher education. The guidelines proposed that if an institution desired approval of such a program it would submit a proposal to the state education agency outlining the program's professional rationale, objectives, plan of operation, and the provisions for its evaluation. Presumably, governance of such a program would be provided by the same structure that governs the standard program (NASDTEC, 1972).

State certification of teachers and state approval of the programs that prepare them is an idea that is not without its detractors. An oft-repeated criticism is that accreditation, both state and national, evaluates the *process* rather than the *product,* and that the state certification system for teachers evaluates the teacher's pre-service education rather than his in-service ability to bring about the learning of children. Critics suggest that teachers' colleges, local schools, and state education offices must work together to revise certification procedures; the schools themselves must ultimately decide on the licensing standards (Lierheimer, 1969).

In recent years, state departments of education have exercised controls and contributed to policy formation by exercising leadership. Many state departments of education have conducted workshops and conferences as part of in-service programs, published curriculum guides (with which prospective teachers must be familiar) for local elementary and secondary schools, and conducted research on teacher education problems. In their more recent role of approving institutional programs for teacher education, state departments have become intimately involved in many curricular details of such programs, and their influence has been significant. They have exercised leadership in many new fields as the result of financial support by the U.S. Office of Education, as that federal agency has been influential in strengthening state education agencies under the provisions of Title XI of the Elementary and Secondary Education Act.

Summary

Since all education is a function of the state, the state has the ultimate authority and responsibility for preparing teachers and school service personnel for all children living in it. The people discharge this responsibility through their constitution, their legislature, and their court system. The state department of education and the state board of higher education are the most significant implementing agencies. Policies for teacher education are determined by legislative appropriations for institutions that train teachers, by state departments of education that provide legal licensing, by local schools that employ teachers, and by the internal management of the whole process by colleges of education in the states' higher education institutions. Some means of coordinating these agencies and some governance structure to reconcile their conflicting interests is an obvious necessity. Just as legislatures and controlling boards granted authority and assigned responsibility to the single-purpose teachers colleges between 1900 and 1940, they must now delegate similar authority and responsibility to colleges of education within universities.

IX

Governance by Practitioners
in the Teaching Profession

The teaching profession in the United States has approximately 3,470,000 members. The National Center for Educational Statistics (NCES) of H.E.W. analyzed that figure in its *1975 Digest of Educational Statistics* as follows:

Teachers in public elementary and secondary schools 2,184,000

Teachers in private elementary and secondary schools   231,000

Administrators, supervisors, consultants, researchers and other specialists in public and private elementary and secondary schools (estimated)   300,000

Professional personnel in higher education institutions   654,000

Professional staff members in professional organizations, in government offices of education, in accreditation offices and in private agencies with educational programs (estimated)   100,000

Total membership of the teaching profession   3,469,000

It is not presumptuous to designate these 3,470,000 people as a profession. Teaching does indeed have most of the characteristics of a profession, as noted by Edgar Schein (1972), although its very size and its great diversity prevent it from being accorded the same status as law, medicine, or engineering. As Schein notes, however, most professions control the entrance of new practitioners into their ranks. The question that presents itself, then, is: "What influence should elementary and secondary school teachers, administrators and other school service personnel exert on the training of prospective teachers?"

The Teaching Profession

In recent years, the organized teaching profession has demanded greater control over the preparation of new teachers. The National Education Association has been moving in the last ten to fifteen years toward greater control over teachers' working conditions and salaries. In addition, the NEA has tried to influence input into the profession by participating in the design of preparation programs, setting up standards for admission to such programs, and regulating the licensure of new teachers.

In 1965-66, the National Education Association held a series of regional conferences in eight cities, as the third phase of the major effort by the National Commission on Teacher Education and Professional Standards (NCTEPS) to improve continuing education and career development for teachers. The NEA sought new ways to solve old problems: the lack of time to plan and teach, the lock step in-service education requirements, the lack of direction for beginning teachers, the excessive non-instructional duties to which teachers were subjected, and the lack of cooperation between local public schools and the colleges that prepared teachers. The emphasis of the conferences was on career patterns and career teachers (Edelfelt, 1966). NEA involvement in teacher preparation has continued since the 1965-66 conferences, and in recent years the NEA has produced a number of publications concerned with self-governance for educators. (It should be noted that in much of the literature on this topic there is considerable confusion in differentiating the governance of the profession from the governance of education. Governance of the profession has to do with internal professional questions, such as preparation, entry into the profession, and standards for competent, ethical performance. Governance of education refers to the control mechanisms for school operation usually exercised by the public through boards of education and other agencies, depending upon the scope, level, and nature of the education being governed.)

The governance of education currently rests with state legislatures, local school districts, boards of education, and legally appointed administrative professionals. The governance of the profession sought by teachers is the governance of many conditions surrounding their work. The statement developed by the NEA illustrates this point:

> We want a teaching profession act in every state, created by law. That act should give to members of the profession the legal power to: establish requirements for teaching certificates and to issue certificates; to determine and establish the procedures to be used in deciding which institutions of higher education are qualified to prepare teachers (accreditation). (This could include standards for school district-initiated and sponsored programs of continuing education for teachers, based on teachers' needs); to define performance criteria for teachers for both beginning and later-career roles, the context of minimum working conditions under which teachers will provide services; to conduct a continuous study of teacher standards and practices and recommend needed changes; to revoke, suspend, and reinstate certificates when teachers, after a full and fair hearing, are found to be in violation of the state's Teaching Professions Act or the standards established under it; to adopt rules and regulations to implement the teaching profession act, including the power to employ staff and legal counsel, to subpoena witnesses and records, to place witnesses under oath, and to establish rules for and hold hearings, or cause them to be held, in appropriate places within the state.
>
> The Teaching Profession Act in each state should provide for the selection, by their peers in education, of a number of professionals who will serve on a standards board and/or a practices commission which will have legal power to carry out the above duties. These groups should be accountable to the entire profession for their decisions.
>
> A Teaching Professions Act at the state level will undergird what can be done at the local level, just as a state professional negotiation law does.
>
> We also want, in governance, expertise and know-how at the local level in including standards matters as a part of negotiation procedures, wherever appropriate. (NEA-NCTEPS, 1970, pp. 7-8)

In attempting to implement these goals, the Teacher Education and Professional Standards Commission collaborated with its National Commission on Professional Rights and Responsibilities and its general counsel. From this collaboration, from the aforementioned eight regional conferences, and from extensive discussion with over 2,000 professionals in all levels of education, a model teacher standards and licensure act was developed to represent the NEA position on such legislation. Among the seventeen issues that the commission raised regarding implementation of this model law were several concerned with the impact that such governance has on institutions of higher learning. One issue was the question of whether the same act can regulate teacher licensure and grant accreditation to teacher education programs. Another was whether the act should encourage reciprocal licensure to facilitate the movement of teachers without loss of teaching privileges among the states. The third issue concerned financing: should the commission be supported solely by licensing and other fees paid to it or be funded from a state treasury? Section VI of the proposed act makes it clear that the authority for issuance of licenses rests with the commission, whose membership is provided for in the act, but the role that colleges and universities are expected to play in the model teacher standards and licensure act needs much clarification.

Section IX of the proposal concerns accreditation and indicates that the commission shall "investigate, study, evaluate and accredit teacher preparation institutions. The commission by rule-making procedures shall promulgate and put into effect the procedures and standards governing accreditation. It may in its own discretion adopt as its own, with or without modification, the accreditation standards, procedures, or findings made by other accrediting agencies." It is conceivable, therefore, that such a state commission could accept the accreditation recommendations of the National Council for the Accreditation of Teacher Education. The commission in the model act is also authorized to enter into agreements with agencies of other states for reciprocal accreditation of teacher preparation institutions (NEA-NCTEPS, 1971, p. 14).

Much of the energy for the acquisition of more control over teacher education by the NEA arises from the so-called accountability movement. The NEA uses 'accountability' and 'responsibility' interchangeably in several of its publications and apparently believes that teacher educators are actively seeking more responsibility for professional matters because they feel that they are held accountable by the public and by local school boards for the performance of teachers. The association believes that the profession must assume the responsibility for deciding what constitutes adequate preparation for any teacher, in what institutions teachers should study, who should be licensed to teach upon the completion of those programs, and, finally, how the teacher, once on the job, can keep his or her skills up to date.

In December, 1971, the NEA did a brief analysis of the licensure and accreditation processes of some other professions compared to those of teaching. Comparisons were made with accounting, dentistry, medicine, law, nursing, engineering, and architecture. In practically all of these professions the initial licensure is made by an agency of the profession with some legal sanction. In addition, the accrediting agency in some way represented the profession as a whole. The NEA's analysis did not accord that status to the National Council for the Accreditation of Teacher Education, probably because its focus was the legal state agency. The study revealed that in some professions accreditation was required of an institution, while in others, including teaching, accreditation was voluntary. What the NEA appears to have overlooked is the fact that the teaching profession includes not only teachers in the public elementary and secondary schools, but also college professors, administrators, and professional personnel in state departments of education and in educational accrediting agencies. These individuals are within the profession; in effect, they represent the profession in the licensure of practitioners and in the accreditation of teacher education programs. It must be recognized, however, that the policies of licensure in education, although administered by professionals in state departments of education, are determined by one or both of two lay agencies: the state legislature or the state board of public school education. The gist of the NEA's position is that the responsibility for shaping such policies be transferred to an autonomous commission of professionals sanctioned by legislative act.

While national organizations like the NEA are sponsoring the formulation of improved models for the preparation of teachers, however, educators like Koontz and Flaherty claim that the country does not have enough institutions of higher learning able to adapt the best aspects of these models to their own needs. (They make this claim in spite of the fact that the nine well-known teacher education models for the preparation of elementary school teachers were in fact developed under federal sponsorship by some of the major universities in the country.) Koontz and Flaherty feel that colleges are unwilling to accept responsibility for results of teacher preparation programs and that the state departments of education cannot be held accountable for adequate teacher preparation. In addition, neither the public nor the accrediting agencies can be held accountable: the former, because of its disorganized nature; the latter, because they, like the interlocking directorate of the colleges, universities, and state departments of education, are simply incapable of self-governance (Koontz and Flaherty, 1970).

To generalize, it appears that the trend is for educators to feel that the governance of the profession should be undergirded by legislation and policies for the protection of rights and responsibilities as well as by machinery to deal with malpractice, unethical performance, and all other forms of professional or legal violation. If the profession is to achieve autonomy, a number of legal and policy provisions are essential. These laws and policies must include provisions for benefits, protection, and certification, and the processes and mechanisms for implementing them must be through accreditation and professional certification. Among the benefits and protection recommended are academic freedom, tenure, leaves, retirement, minimum salary, publicly financed liability insurance, tax sheltered annuities, and other personnel policies. The mechanisms for achieving these benefits and protections were, of course, the professional practices commissions and local negotiations committees.

As mentioned earlier, it is difficult to make a clear distinction in practice between the governance of the profession and the governance of education. It is one thing to have a profession govern the welfare of its members, but quite another to determine the procedures by which the professionals are prepared. Evidently the profession wants to control preparation and licensure and negotiate for the conditions surrounding their work once the teachers are employed. As other writers have commented, the profession is in need of further clarification of the distinction between governance for preparation and entrance and governance of professional welfare (Becker, 1972).

As a matter of fact, at the state level there are now two parallel agencies controlling entrance to the teaching profession: the state board of education, a legal agency, and the state professional practices commission, a professional advisory agency. The functions of the state board of education are clearly delineated, and they complement the work of the professional boards and commissions, whose membership is largely teachers and practitioners. They are created in many states to regulate the preparation and licensure of new teachers, to monitor practices in service, and to aid in the improvement of in-service or staff development programs. They provide due process for cases of unethical professional behavior. In some activities they are largely advisory; in a few they are determiners of policy.

One gets the impression that the National Education Association, or at least certain of its constituent organizations, is using the current popularity of accountability as an excuse for the acquisition of power. If individual teachers cannot be held accountable for what children learn in their classrooms, then who can? Why is any legislation necessary to make responsibility and accountability in teaching acceptable and accepted aspects of the classroom teachers' job? This is quite a different kind of accountability from accountability for the welfare of the teaching profession as a whole. Yet a recent president of the NEA claimed, "It is sure a myth that a classroom teacher can even be held accountable, with justice, under existing conditions. A classroom teacher has either too little control or no control over the factors that might render accountability either feasible or fair" (Bain, 1970, p. 413).

The one segment of the teaching profession that should be held accountable for the preparation of teachers includes professional teacher-educators in colleges and universities, deans, department chairmen, supervisors of student teaching, and others who are fully committed as professionals in the preparation of school personnel. The structure and governance mechanisms for the preparation of individuals who enter the teaching profession should be separated from the controls over the professional behavior of individuals once they become practitioners.

In 1972, the Representative Assembly of the NEA created a Task Force on Practicing Teacher Involvement in Teacher Education to work under the direction of the NEA Department of Instruction and Professional Development (IPD). The overall goal of IPD was to establish an ongoing and continuous study on practitioner involvement in all aspects of teacher education, including

initial preparation; advanced or graduate preparation; governance, including accreditation and certification; legislation—federal or state—affecting teacher education; any research and development in the area of teacher education; any and all activities—local, state or national—which directly affect the practitioner. (NEA, 1974, p. 87)

Much of the time after July, 1973, the NEA-IPD Council and staff were engaged in work-study sessions with the NCATE constituents, renewing the funding of part of NCATE's expenditures, appointing additional members both to NCATE and its coordinating board, and encouraging the teachers' own in-service training in their local school districts.

The NEA-IPD Council also reiterated "the necessity for NEA's and state associations' giving high priority to creating legal professional standards boards that would have responsibility for licensure of teachers and for accreditation in any state." The council went on to specify that "such standards boards should have at least a majority of K-12 practitioners serving on them. Both California and Oregon have such commissions with responsibility for certification and accreditation. Minnesota and Pennsylvania have just created boards with considerable power, although they are technically advisory to the state board of education" (NEA, 1974, p. 89).

NEA's position on the membership composition of the proposed state standards boards is not acceptable to the organized profession of teacher educators. At its 1975 spring meeting, the Associated Organizations for Teacher Education (AOTE) reacted to the NEA's long-held position that classroom teachers should hold most of the seats on state licensing boards. The AOTE Advisory Council, according to a report in the *AACTE Bulletin* for July, 1975, "encourages the establishment of teacher licensure boards in each state with membership primarily drawn from the community of professionals in education: the fulltime classroom teachers, teacher educators, and school and college administrators and supervisory personnel." The AOTE Council also endorsed the principle that "each state determine the specific allocation of positions to achieve balance among the constituent groups in the community of professionals in education and appropriate lay personnel." The council position was that no group of educators or laymen should be in a majority on state licensing boards, but that classroom teachers may be the largest single group.

Three avenues have been used in recent years by the NEA to influence teacher education: recommendations on accreditation, suggestions to state teachers' associations, and establishment of state commissions. Its 1976 representative assembly readopted the following resolution concerned with accreditation:

The National Education Association believes in the importance of national accreditation for all teacher preparation institutions and supports the concept that a single national non-governmental agency perform this function.

The national agency must be broadly representative of the teaching profession and the preprofession and must include students preparing to teach and equitable representation of K-12 teachers in all matters of policy and function (69, 72, 73, 76). (NEA, 1976b, p. 26)

To utilize the second avenue, the NEA urged its affiliates to exercise thirteen steps to implement the general resolution quoted above. One of its affiliates, the Student National Education Association (SNEA), was urged to take an active part in representing student interests in teacher preparation programs. The 1976 representative assembly adopted the following resolution concerned with teacher education:

The National Education Association believes that teachers and students preparing to teach must be directly involved in evaluating and improving the standards for teacher preparation and certification. The Association insists that teacher involvement is necessary in planning and implementing quality teacher education programs.

Teacher educators must be certificated and experienced in their instructional areas.

The Association also believes that preprofessional practicum experience is an essential phase of teacher preparation. The responsibility for the practicum experience must be shared by the public schools, the institutions that prepare teachers, and professional associations.

The Association urges its affiliates to—

a. Take immediate steps to evaluate and improve standards for entrance into the teaching profession.

b. Critically assess current college and university programs of teacher education and make specific recommendations for changes.

c. Support inclusion of training in the dynamics of intergroup communication and human relations courses in requirements for certification and the provision for in-service workshops in these areas for experienced teachers and administrators.

d. Support legislation providing legal status and liability protection for student teachers.

e. Develop guidelines for qualifications of cooperating teachers and college coordinators of student teachers.

f. Support inclusion of instruction in school law and in the values, ethics, responsibilities, and structure of professional teachers organizations.

g. Support the teaching of methods courses by teachers currently employed in elementary and secondary schools.

h. Support requirements in state certification standards for specific course work in reading instruction.

i. Formulate standards for school systems receiving student teachers. Supervising or cooperating teachers in a student teaching program should have reduced teaching loads and be given a minimum established compensation.

j. Recommend Student NEA membership before participation in pre-professional experiences and student teaching.

k. Take immediate steps to improve the selection of persons entering the profession through more effective screening of applicants for the pre-professional practicum.

l. Offer guidance to teacher preparation institutions to prepare teachers in numbers consistent with projected need for teacher positions.

m. Support inclusion in master contracts or school policies that acceptance of student teachers be on a voluntary basis. (NEA, 1976b, pp. 27-28)

It will be noted that although the NEA suggested that the "public schools, the institutions that prepare teachers, and professional associations" share in the responsibility for the practicum phase of teacher education, no similar insistence was made for other components of teacher education. The NEA also emphasized control of entrance into the profession by urging higher education institutions to be more selective in the admission of teacher education students and to make such selection in numbers consistent with demands for graduates.

The third avenue through which the NEA is attempting to influence the preparation of teachers is through the development in each state of a state commission on teacher standards and licensure. As we noted above, the NEA in 1971 developed "A Model Teacher Standards and Licensure Act," which, if adopted in each state, would set standards for entry and continuation in the profession as well as decide how and where teachers should be prepared. In its "Resolution F-1 on Professional Autonomy," the NEA passed in 1969 and reaffirmed in 1976 the following resolution:

The National Education Association believes the profession must govern itself. The Association also believes that each state should have a professional standards board, with a majority of K-12 public school classroom teachers. Professional standards boards should have the legal responsibility for determining policy and procedures for teacher certification, approval of teacher certification, approval of teacher preparation programs, recognition of national accreditation of preparation programs, and programs designed to improve teacher education. (NEA, 1976b, pp. 41-42)

In 1976 the NEA recognized that their model act was not appropriate for all states and issued "Guidelines for Standards and

Licensure Legislation." In these guidelines the association recommended, among other provisions, that the model act provide for "teacher licensure, accreditation of teacher education programs, and power to initiate needed related research." The members of the standards boards should be appointed by the governor with the advice and consent of the legislature after nomination by teacher organizations or petition of licensed individuals. The board should include "a majority of full-time teachers, grades K-12, full-time supervisors and/or administrators, full-time teacher educators, and other full-time educators," and it was to have full power for making decisions.

As we have noted, in only two states, California and Oregon, do the boards have full legal powers. Nine other states have boards that meet NEA criteria for Standards and Licensure or Standards and Practices commissions, or boards created by legislative act to be advisory to the state board of education. Twelve other states have a Practices Commission only, which were created by legislative act to be advisory to the state board of education. Another fifteen states have legislation either being planned or pending. In view of these developments, the IPD concluded: "It is still too early to determine the effect of increased teacher involvement in accreditation and state approval. It appears safe to say, however, that teachers are no longer content to let higher education 'own' teacher preparation, or to let lay persons (present state boards of education) continue to set standards for teacher preparation" (NEA, 1976a, p. 28). Clearly, the attempt by the NEA to control preparation, accreditation, and licensure through state law will, if successful, effectively bypass higher education as the primary and coordinating agency for teacher education. The only way for colleges and universities to assure themselves of their appropriate role in preparation and accreditation is to write such a role into that state legislation.

The teaching profession is more than the National Education Association. The organized profession must also include the American Federation of Teachers (AFT), representing several hundred thousand classroom teachers. A perusal of AFT publications reveals that the federation has no great concern for the governance of teacher education at a national level. The AFT is primarily concerned with the conditions under which classroom teachers take on the added responsibility for supervising student teachers, recognizing that student teaching is a most important phase of the professional preparation of the teacher. The AFT has been more concerned with the pre-service and in-service teacher education arrangements and opportunities than with such other aspects of governance as institutional curricula and licensure.

The public schools have tended to regard student teaching as a function of the colleges to which they could choose to contribute, with the result that the colleges and universities have remained the primary decision-makers on student teaching policies and practices. During the last twenty years, however, as universities have expanded their programs and required many more student teaching stations, the AFT has become increasingly concerned with protecting the rights of both the supervising classroom teacher and the student teacher. Typically, the process of arranging student teaching opportunities involved too little participation of the local teachers, who become frustrated with the ambiguity of their role and responsibilities and their limited involvement in the development of the policies and procedures that governed these programs. As a result, the AFT, like the NEA, has urged union locals to negotiate with boards of education the conditions under which classroom teachers would cooperate with local administrators and college personnel in student teaching programs. Negotiation centered around the issues of selection and assignment of supervising teachers, their rights, their compensation (usually paid by the college), and the use of student teachers as substitute teachers. In the AFT's *Negotiations Manual*, Kuchar has suggested that for pre-service teacher education these issues be clarified and solutions to problems be agreed upon through the usual contract negotiations process among the parties involved: the local AFT, the local school board, and the teacher education institution.

In-service teacher education is more directly under the control of the AFT, which has recognized that most in-service courses, both those provided by institutions of higher education and those developed in the schools by administrators, have had a negligible effect on teachers' classroom performance. The AFT believes that the teachers must be more actively involved in planning and implementing their own self-renewal programs. Since this costs money, the local district should pay these costs and the teacher should decide what the program should be. The AFT has urged that contract clauses on in-service education should increasingly utilize the local teachers' center concept, with resources chosen by them for their own self-improvement. Thus the resources of higher education would be used at the discretion of the local teacher. Nationally, the AFT has been much less concerned with overall policy for determining teacher education decisions than has the NEA.

Local School Districts

The object of the considerable pressure by the National Education Association for a greater voice in the preparation of the next generation of teachers is the local teachers' association. Teachers in the local school district are the extension of the National Education Association, and since the local school district provides most of the professional laboratory experiences, observation, and student teaching, it occupies a critical position as a governance mechanism. Directives from the NEA and AFT may sometimes be in conflict with the desire to cooperate on a partnership basis with the nearby college or university that is assigning student teachers to its classrooms.

The local district should be primarily concerned with the control structure that determines what the policies shall be, who will have responsibility for certain aspects of the professional laboratory experience, and who must ultimately assume the role of accountability in the total process. Most of the student teaching procedures have been studied for several decades by the Association for Student Teaching (AST), and their many publications are extremely valuable for college supervisors and for the local schools' cooperating teachers. This has been even more true in recent years with the association's change in name to the Association of Teacher Educators (ATE) and with its broadened membership base.

During the sixties, the question of developing better relationships between the local schools and the higher education institutions became a critical one because of new developments within the schools, such as team teaching, greater use of audio-visual aids, and updated, more relevant curricula, to name a few. Another impetus was the increased demand for new teachers on the part of the schools and the large numbers of teacher education students in the colleges. As a result, the American Association of Colleges for Teacher Education, along with the Association for Student Teaching, began to study the ways by which cooperation between local education agencies and the colleges might be improved. In 1964 the AACTE published and distributed to its members and other interested persons the first report of the subcommittee of its Studies Committee dealing with this problem. In 1965 a second report was issued, building upon the experience of the first and describing in more detail several partnership programs that were being developed. The reports noted three trends:

1. State-wide plans involving the cooperation of state departments, colleges and schools are being expanded. In some instances legal procedures for formalizing such arrangements are being made. Texas is moving in this direction with a proposed law which is quite comprehensive. Under the leadership of the National Commission on Teacher Education and Professional Standards a joint committee representing a number of professional organizations has been formed to make recommendations regarding state responsibility in student teaching. Proposals for state-wide cooperative structures with colleges and schools are being discussed. The Association for Student Teaching in its discussion of Federal and State aid proposals is reviewing state-wide plans for student teaching. Attention must be given by everyone concerned to the delineation of responsibilities and roles if state direction of student teaching programs becomes a reality. The universities and colleges must consider which controls they can relinquish safely to cooperative administrative bodies without jeopardizing their unique responsibilities for the professional education of their students. If they are to be responsible for the education of the teacher then they must have a strong voice in the school laboratory. State-wide programs could strengthen the hand of the college but they could weaken the university's position if means are not provided for the exercising of leadership by college representatives.

2. The cooperative ventures on which progress reports have been submitted show a marked advancement in formalizing administrative structures. Constitutions, by-laws, and standard operating procedures are emerging as working documents to several of the projects. They are being carefully devised to provide flexibility and means for permitting the injection of new ideas into the machinery of administration. Means for taking joint responsibility in planning, in decision-making, and in executing proposals are the hallmarks of these administrative structures. They all allow for the open interplay of powers and concerns from each of the cooperating institutions, while at the same time the arrangements seem to encourage decision and action. Local organizations such as these will need to run smoothly if the more grandiose cooperative schemes for regional, state-wide and inter-state projects are going to become possible.

3. The structural molds seem not to be solidifying present practices. Instead they seem to be providing a helpful means for fostering new ideas and experimental proposals. There was a feeling expressed at the Wayne Conference of project leaders last fall that the profession could now do some things for the improvement of teacher education that were not possible under the old regime of divided responsibility. College and school personnel when finally placed on an equal footing in the business of teacher education seem to prod each other toward new horizons. (Smith and Johnson, 1965, pp. 1-2)

As the subcommittee reviewed the descriptions of a number of administrative structures in Michigan, Minnesota, Utah, Ohio, Texas, and West Virginia, and saw cooperative ventures by universities in Oregon, New York, Missouri, Pennsylvania, Michigan, Maine, and Wisconsin, it noted a number of changes in professional laboratory experiences. For example, student teaching was increasingly being moved from college laboratory schools to the public schools because of the rapid increase in the number of students preparing for teaching careers and because of the need to develop more realistic settings for prospective teachers than the institution-based laboratory school generally afforded. This, of course, brought up problems of responsibility, control mechanisms, and financial support as well as the need to acquire more professional education faculty in the institutions and more cooperating teachers in the local schools. The subcommittee was able to identify a number of specific elements in the newly developing cooperative relationships. These included (a) joint curriculum decisions in laboratory experience programs, (b) joint selection of supervising teachers, (c) joint selection and provision of needed facilities, (d) joint placement of student teachers, (e) joint action on funding, and (f) joint evaluation of laboratory-experience programs (Smith and Johnson, 1965, p. 68).

After studying these various experiences and models developed among the various states, the subcommittee felt there was general agreement that a cooperative framework should evolve primarily on a local basis. This was because various school systems and colleges required different structures and approaches to cooperative ventures, with the result that no comprehensive, rigid, large-scale plan was desirable. Their report is the culmination of a long history of attempts to develop appropriate assignments and to designate responsibilities between the theoretical phase and the practical phase of teacher preparation.

The subcommittee analyzed special projects in teacher education involving various cooperative and partnership arrangements with the public schools by distributing 634 questionnaires to AACTE member institutions. To be included, a project had to fall within the definition of "those projects which have the additional dimensions of *equal partnership* and *actual cooperative school-college direction* of student teaching activities, internship programs, in-service teacher education, or research developments." Not falling within such a

definition were programs that completely delegated responsibility
for the supervision of interns to the public schools nor those that
established an off-campus student teaching center completely controlled by the college. In other words, only those operations that
were jointly planned and jointly executed fitted the definition of
the cooperative school-college activities. Of these 634 questionnaires,
354 were returned; 153 of the respondents indicated that their
institutions were involved in cooperative school-college activities
as defined above.

A classification of cooperative school-college activities revealed
the following categories:

    a. Statewide cooperative plans
    b. School-college councils and committees for cooperation in teacher
       education and/or research and development
    c. Regional inter-college and school centers
    d. Cooperative centers for teacher education
    e. Affiliated or associated schools
    f. Teacher internship and teacher aide programs
    g. Field centers for preparing teachers to work with the culturally de-
       prived or with children with special handicaps or talents
    h. Joint appointments and rotation of teachers between the school and
       college
    i. Cooperative supervision of teaching
    j. Joint selection and preparation of supervising teachers
    k. Cooperative observation programs
    l. Jointly developed student teaching guides and constitutions
    m. In-service teacher education centers. (Smith and Johnson, 1976, pp.
       6-56)

In summarizing the reports of scores of institutions as their programs
were classified in the above categories, the subcommittee stated that
"the controlling base for decision-making and instructional planning
in teacher education should be broadened quite extensively so that
school personnel are involved with college faculties in a partnership
of professional equals" (Smith and Johnson, 1965, p. 66).

Thus, the subcommittee added considerable weight to the
argument that the total profession should be involved in teacher
education decisions. The problem is deciding what governance responsibilities should be given to each segment of this phase of
teacher education. The subcommittee stated its position as follows:

On one side of the argument is the question of university autonomy in all matters regarding higher education. In a real sense the public already has placed the final responsibility with the college or university. It is under this designation of institutional role that teacher educators on university faculties have, until now, taken major responsibility for the education of teachers, even in bringing their influence to bear upon the state certifying agencies and national accrediting organizations. However, the practicing profession, feeling their rightful public responsibility as keepers of the school, has never quite accepted the university's domination over teacher education and has developed means for influencing local, state, and national groups to challenge the leadership of the colleges and universities. Thus, there had emerged a kind of cold war in many situations between university-oriented teacher educators and the school-oriented professionals. (Smith and Johnson, 1965, p. 61)

The issue appears to be one of power. Procedures for disbursing power on the basis of specified criteria are simply not available. For example, if a program should be built only on concepts from empirical trial-and-error studies of practices in teaching, then the school should decide the program for teacher preparation. But if it should be built either entirely on applied knowledge and theory from the disciplines, or at least in part on such knowledge, then the university should be the decision maker (Smith and Johnson, 1965, p. 62).

In its report, the subcommittee explored criteria by which an allocation of responsibilities might be made. It was suggested that specific autonomies be allotted in congruence with those general sovereignties already established: the school would be concerned largely with childhood education in the local community; the university would be concerned largely with higher education in the wider academic world. The subcommittee was even aware of the possibility that a new institution, created by both the local school system and the higher education institution, might now be necessary. Another potential criterion suggested by the subcommittee was to "let the schools, who know most about the everyday job of teaching children, be completely in charge of student teaching, methodology, and the supervision and improvement of instruction. Let the universities teach the psychology, the social foundations, the philosophy and the academic background for curriculum content" (Smith and Johnson, 1965, p. 63). This logical division of responsibilities is popular with the public and with liberal arts faculties, and was also hinted at in Conant's definition of the "clinical professor" (Conant, 1963).

So many good arguments can be made for controls and autonomy by both groups that the subcommittee was not able to reach a final conclusion on the assignment of responsibilities and the determination of administrative autonomies in student teaching and professional laboratory experiences, although there was general agreement that decisions should be reached cooperatively by representatives of both the teacher education unit of the institution and the local public schools. However, not until these issues of professional policy are clarified can the issue of administrative and instructional responsibility be resolved.

It was pointed out in Chapter II that one of the criteria in determining and assigning educational responsibilities is to make the assignment to that unit which can do it best but which is also closest to the people affected. If this criterion is followed, and cooperative procedures are used in the assignment of responsibilities and the determination of professional autonomies, then it is quite conceivable that the scores of activities carried on both by the institution and by the local schools could be divided equitably.

The search for structures that will appropriately allocate the responsibilities and hold accountable the various components of the professional laboratory phase of teacher education still continues. A conference held at Baltimore, Maryland, attempted to determine the role of the state education agency in the development of innovative programs in student teaching. It has been suggested that the state might be the coordinating or unifying agency determining the allocation of responsibilities to the institutions and to the local schools. A review of some of the innovative ideas in student teaching pointed out that the problem of transfer of learning from theory to practice is not unique to teacher education. Such other sources as the Job Corps, businesses that supply services to education, industrial training programs, management programs, government agencies, and the related professions of law and medicine were investigated to see if their preparation programs had merit for student teaching and the relationships between theory and practice in education. The investigation showed that the problems of transfer of learning from theory to practice in educational and non-educational interests were not comparable because of their differing motivations. Education programs concentrated on quantitatively organizing experiences that would prepare students for a variety of situations, whereas the non-education programs accepted the impossibility of educating students for specific situations and were willing to invest money in developing their trainees' unique assets. A review of the programs of some twenty-seven states and two regional laboratories did not really face up to the question of the governance of teacher education in the student teaching phase by the institutions and by the local schools (Edelfelt, 1969b, Ch. V).

In this connection Edelfelt summarized a review by Hess of state practices and trends in student teaching. Hess had devoted some attention to administrative and financial responsibilities of state departments of education in their role of supervision of student teaching. She indicated that what was needed in the future was more dynamic leadership and a coordinating and harmonizing of all the agencies, associations, and other groups and individuals involved in and potentially contributing to the continuous improvement of student teaching. Concerning the governance issue, her analysis showed that the role of the state was one of coordination (Edelfelt, 1969b, Ch. III).

In addition to the motivating forces of insufficient laboratory experiences in laboratory schools, large numbers of prospective teachers in universities, and the great demand for many new teachers, there is another motivating force that accounts for the movement in the development of student teaching centers. This is the demand for more realistic observational, participatory, and actual teaching experiences in the public schools. Demands for such experiences were being made by the teaching profession, the schools and colleges, local education agencies and the U.S. Office of Education, resulting in many real differences of opinion regarding the governance of teacher education and the appearance of many new and more sophisticated patterns of school-university partnerships on the professional scene. An analysis of this movement has been made by James F. Collins, who stated that

> While not entirely new, we see a strong and rapid insurgence of *student teaching centers*.
> Student teaching centers, as the name implies, typically are off-campus schools where, by mutual agreement, a college or university places a number of student teachers.
> Originally, while it was a tremendous step forward from the conventional pattern of assigning students to many widely scattered classrooms, throughout

a school system, it typically still perpetuated unilateral controls and unilateral decision-making. The university for the most part dictated policy, standards, and procedures, etc.

More recently, however, we have begun to see student teaching centers taking on a broader function with more extensive involvement. The Kenawha County Student Teaching Center in West Virginia is an example of this; where the state department of education plays a coordinating function, where there are a number of institutions of higher education feeding students into the center, and where the center is county-wide as opposed to one or two school buildings. (Collins, 1970)

The governance of these new arrangements was provided for by joint councils, with policy-making responsibility, including representatives from the state department of education, the participating institutions of higher education, and the school system. Controls, however, were "still heavily administratively and logistically oriented" (Collins, 1970, p. 5).

True cooperation in teacher education is a *sine qua non* if the profession is to advance. This cooperation implies joint decision-making, joint responsibility, and joint accountability. According to Collins, the distinguishing features of a teacher education center as opposed to a student teaching center are:

a. The teacher education center has for its focus *all* of teacher education, not just student teaching.
b. The public school assumes earlier and more essential responsibility for the pre-service program.
c. The college assumes increased responsibility for the in-service program by its remaining visibly and actively present in the schools.
d. The center is a laboratory for pre-student teaching experiences, student teaching experiences and graduate practice and internships.
e. All personnel in the center, professional as well as pre-professional, are students of teaching.
f. In-service and pre-service come together on a continuum.
g. Methods and practice are brought together in one place at one time which also brings together the theoretical (on campus) faculty with the clinic (off-campus) faculty—in a continuing working relationship.
h. Pre-service and in-service programs are individualized according to the needs of the individual.
i. Supervision of professional staff development, pre-service and/or in-service, is done by a team of people drawn from the school system, the university and possibly from the state department of education.
j. A full time coordinator is employed equally by the university and the school system to coordinate the staff development program for both the pre-service professionals and in-service professionals. (Collins, 1970, p. 4)

What is being developed here is essentially a new unit, an independent federation composed of the college, the state education department, and the local school district. The council governing such a federation makes policies binding on each of its constituents. In most cases, the leadership for its organization and subsequent powers has come from the college of education or its equivalent.

Probably the most influential force for improvement in teacher education and therefore in its governance is the recognition by the teacher education profession that schools also need improving. As a result of this awareness several innovative suggestions are being developed that depart rather noticeably from past teacher education practices and structures for facilitating those practices. Reviewing statewide plans for student teaching, James C. Stone asserted that teacher education is really not taken very seriously by the colleges; it is only passively accepted by the schools; state departments of education only give it a passing reference as it grants certificates; and it is merely tolerated by the profession of education itself. As a result, he concluded, reform will be effective only if teacher education is removed from its present concrete-like fixation in schools, colleges, and state departments of education. He therefore proposed a new organizational structure called the "Educational Professions Institute (EPI)." Schools and colleges are arms of the state, Stone reasoned; teacher education is an arm of the state; therefore, state departments of education, through enabling acts of legislatures, should reinstitute and reactivate fairly complete control over teacher education (Stone, 1969). He described the structure and the advantages of such an institute as follows:

> At either the local or regional level, the EPI would be operated under a joint-powers agreement. The "powers" brought together to organize the EPI and to formulate policy for it (within broad state guidelines) would be (a) a local community; (b) a college, (c) a school system, and (d) the state department of education. The four powers would establish an independent local institute board of control which would have fiscal and administrative authority to operate the institute with funds provided by state and federal sources. Each "power" on the governing board would appoint one representative, and these four would choose three others.
>
> The joint-powers arrangement has the advantage of local control within a state system, and it brings together on an equal basis the chief resources needed in effective teacher training—the colleges, the schools, the state, and the local community. A joint-powers agreement is particularly appropriate for the

education of teachers of the disadvantaged and for the most effective coordination and integration of student teaching. (Stone, 1969, p. 142)

Such reallocation of power bases is not easy to accomplish. Edward T. Ladd has documented three sources of tension that he felt were endemic to any interorganizational collaboration. The first source Ladd mentions includes constant exposure to each other, developing new learning habits, giving up old ways of doing things, and confronting differences that caused resentment. A second group of tensions arose from fundamental differences between the goals of the local school district on the one hand and of universities in general on the other. A third source of tensions was derived from nonessential differences between the two such as policy-making, daily activities, attitudes toward cooperation, expenditure of funds, personnel matters, relative professional status, and so on. This analysis dealt with fundamental individual differences among people and differences in institutional aims between local school personnel and higher education personnel. Until these are reconciled, Ladd concludes, governance mechanisms will be difficult to develop (Ladd, 1969).

Teacher Education Centers

Another analysis of school/university cooperation and the consequent search for new structures involves a clinical approach to teacher education. This clinical approach includes several procedures for determining responsibility for improving the continuity of the professional education sequence, for developing a team approach to professional education, for securing a variety of observational and practicing experiences for the student, for individualizing his preparation, and for providing for team teaching in this small group interaction (Travers, 1971).

If education and teacher education are to be reformed, then "reform must begin in several places, but it is particularly appropriate to move at the college and university level because that is where the responsibility for and control of teacher education now rest. It would be difficult—and indefensible—to call for a change in schools if there isn't substantial change in the institutions that educate teachers" (Edelfelt, 1972). The U.S. Office of Education attempted in 1972 to establish its so-called Educational Renewal Centers. These may be regarded as identical to teacher education schools; that is, they would be elementary and secondary schools or settings adjacent to schools where the education of teachers would take place concurrently with the education of children. These would be schools in which the community, the school, and the college would reach some mutual agreements about common purposes. Planning for these renewal centers or teacher education schools should involve teachers and include teacher organizations. The guidelines for these educational renewal centers should be developed for and by teacher education organizations, and teachers should have a central role in the governance of such centers (Edelfelt, 1972).

In Maryland, through the cooperative efforts of the public schools, several colleges, and the state department of education, the teacher education center has had a clear development. The center was defined as "a cluster of two or three geographically contiguous elementary schools, or one or two junior high schools (or middle schools), and a senior high school" (Behling, 1970, p. 7). The program has expanded from one elementary center involving one school system, one college, and the state department of education to include, in 1970, fifty public schools, seven colleges, and seven school systems. The limited number of quality student teaching stations, the need to prepare supervising teachers, the need to involve college and university personnel in public school programs, and the need to improve supervisory service all stimulated significant change. The need to combine in-service and pre-service programs into one continuous whole and the need to involve state departments of education more thoroughly in teacher education programs also were influential. By the spring of 1970 the University of Maryland maintained twelve of the teacher education centers, within which there were twenty-three elementary schools and twelve secondary schools. The teacher education center coordinator was jointly appointed by the state department of education, the cooperating university, and the local school system: he was both a local school and a university employee. (One responsibility of the university was to develop a preparation program designed to qualify personnel for that job.)

In the Maryland experience, the role of the state department of education was described as that of a partner in change, and adviser to planners, an arbitrator of regulations, an encourager of diversity, a silent partner when programs reached maturity, a financier, and a facilitator when change was needed (Behling, 1970). This experience suggests several ways in which power might be allocated and governance mechanisms developed.

Another center, sponsored by the City University of New York, Queens College, and the New York City Board of Education, developed a comprehensive training program for elementary school teachers for the inner city. This group developed an educational facility with a staff and a program responsive to community problems in an area where the population represented a cross-section of the economic and ethnic groups making up the city. The local school and the institutions involved developed a team comprising administrators of the school, the college coordinator, the local teachers, and the trainees, to develop innovations in the teacher education program, including parent workshops. Generally this was a voluntary cooperative arrangement where the question of governance was neither significant, studied, nor settled (Adair et al., 1967).

A somewhat similar cooperative program was developed between three elementary schools and the division of elementary education of the Oregon State University in a so-called model for an education complex. The purpose was to achieve the development of such new approaches to school practices as the multi-graded classroom, individualized instruction, and team teaching. A two-course in-service sequence in the instruction and supervision of cooperating teachers was available. An important factor in the success of the program was the two joint university-school appointments, one a classroom teacher and one a school of education staff member (Strowbridge, 1970).

In West Virginia the state department of education assumed the initiating leadership role by establishing six centers throughout the state. This was made possible by a legislative appropriation in 1971 enabling each of the seventeen teacher preparation institutions in the state to become a member of at least one of the six centers. The West Virginia experience had a reasonably clear definition of what was meant by the term "teacher education center":

A Teacher Education Center as defined in this model is a *concept* rather than a physical place. It recognizes the principle of *shared sovereignty*. Thus it involves public schools, communities, students, the state department of education and colleges in matters of teacher education. It is an acceptance of the principle of parity in the allocation of responsibility for educating teachers. It implies new administrative and financial relationships which involve joint appointments and shared budgets. Individuals who are involved in these new relationships accept the intrinsic worth of exchange programs for public school and college personnel. Individual, group, and institutional experiences at all levels of the education spectrum are viewed as avenues of expression and understanding, through which the student of teaching may build a positive self image and begin to relate to others in nondefensive ways. (Maddox, 1972, p. 1)

The idea of the teacher education center apparently first arose among British teachers:

Teacher centers are just what the term implies: Local physical facilities and self-improvement programs organized and run by the teachers themselves for purposes of upgrading educational performance. Their primary function is to make possible a review of existing curricula and other educational practices by groups of teachers and to encourage teacher attempts to bring about changes. (Bailey, 1971, p. 146)

A question has been raised as to whether or not, just because we have language in common, the British institution will work here. "To the extent that teacher centers make a statement about who controls what goes on in schools, the issues are political. To the extent that establishing teacher centers involves a redistribution of that power, the issues become those of political change and the strategies for achieving that change" (Pilcher, 1973, p. 340). In England, national coordination and planning has tended to be supplementary and largely after the fact, because the teacher centers there have been created and controlled by local teachers. The setting is thus not comparable to the setting in the United States, and the power relationships are therefore considerably different from the power of controls on American public schools. These pose questions that, as Paul Pilcher has stated, "have gone largely unexamined in the current rush to jump on the teacher center bandwagon." In the place of such an examination there is a disquietingly naive acceptance of the idea by American educators. The establishment of these centers by the schools of education at Harvard and the University of Massachusetts is an illustration of the bandwagon effect. Pilcher indicated that $15,000 planning grants for twenty teacher center sites had suddenly materialized from the U.S. Office of Education. In addition, three state departments of education had received federal funding of

$250,000 each to set up centers. In Houston, Texas, there were projects receiving USOE funds in the million dollar category for teacher training programs including teacher centers. It was rather amazing, Pilcher commented, to find that within six to eight months of the appearance of Bailey's article some seventy-five to one hundred teacher centers were reportedly *in operation* in the United States. Pilcher felt that this growth explosion could be a real threat to the survival of the teacher center concept, because these reformers were in so much of a hurry that they could not take time to consider the thorny and multi-faceted problems of power redistribution implied by the British model. He showed that there were three sets of power relationships involved in the establishment of teacher centers: the relationships of teachers with university and other outside Research and Development (R and D) experts; the relationship of teachers with school administrators; and the relationship of teachers with local community. Pilcher made a plea for the inclusion of class-room teachers in the power structure in order to avoid domination of that concept by state departments of education, by institutions of higher learning, and by local school administrators (Pilcher, 1972).

In 1972, James Collins made an analysis of the "state of the art" in the development of teacher centers based on conference papers delivered at Syracuse University by distinguished scholars and practitioners from the United States and England. Although data were admittedly limited at that time, it appeared that three general kinds of teacher education centers were emerging:

1. The teacher centers model, fashioned after the British model, wherein teachers assume the initiative and responsibility completely.

2. The school-based model, in which a school system directly or indirectly provides the support and initiative for developing various in-service centers for teachers in that school system.

3. The collaborative model, in which the initiative and re-sponsibility are shared by a school system, a teacher training institu-tion, the state education department, and possibly also by the com-munity and professional association for teachers. This model typically addresses both pre-service and in-service training.

From the foregoing analysis it appears that the general purpose of the teacher education center has been to achieve a joint sovereignty over teacher education that will be shared by the colleges, state departments of education, schools, and teachers' associations (Collins,

1972). Some distinction should be made between those centers that are primarily pre-service, those that are primarily in-service, and those that are both.

Summary

From this discussion of the impact of the local school system upon the governance of teacher education, one point emerges with reasonable clarity. Throughout the nation there seem to be developing a number of governance structures having in common the college or university that prepares teachers and grants the degree, the state department of education, which has the legal responsibility for licensing teachers, and the local school district, which constitutes the laboratory for a significant part of the preparation of teachers and which ultimately employs them, and the organized teaching profession as represented by a local teachers association. To the extent that this four-partner structure is based on the cooperation of individuals with mutual respect, it appears to be extremely successful and surely much more meaningful than present practice as an experience for prospective teachers in colleges and universities.

However, still unanswered is the question of who is to initiate the development of such a four-power structure, who is to have the responsibility for its coordination, and who is ultimately going to evaluate it in order to determine who is to be held accountable for the total teacher education program. It is our contention that only one agency has the resources to initiate, to organize, to coordinate, and to evaluate the practicum component of teacher education—the teacher education units in the colleges and universities. If such units are granted full legal authority to perform these four tasks, as is true in other professions, then, and only then, can they be held truly accountable for the performance of their graduates. The development of such a partnership under the leadership of colleges of education in universities can go far toward preventing an "education war" between the organized teaching profession and the institutions of higher education.

X

Governance by the Profession
of Teacher Educators

The teacher education unit in a university (hence, its faculty) is related to its suprasystems. These suprasystems may include state governmental units, the local school systems, and the organized teaching profession. The subsystem designated for the moment as the profession of teacher educators makes its opinions felt in three ways: (1) through its national organizations, i.e., the American Association of Colleges for Teacher Education (AACTE) and similar associations, (2) through those learned societies in both academic and vocational disciplines where genuine interest in and contributions to teacher education are made, and (3) through accreditation of teacher education programs.

The Profession of Teacher Educators

Even the National Education Association includes in its membership those individuals whose primary professional responsibility is the preparation of teachers for the school systems of the nation. This group of American educators has become a profession in itself, even according to Schein's broad definition of a profession mentioned earlier. They are found in colleges and universities and in supporting organizations, and on the professional staffs of many regional and national associations whose primary responsibility is the preparation of other professionals. Like any organization, they are a definable group who agree to act collectively in the pursuit of their shared interests or objectives. They recognize that they are most effective not as individuals but as a voluntary organization with distinctive features, typically democratic in form. Their organizations are governed by a written constitution or bylaws stating their specific purposes and prescribing the means for their own operation.

The education directory of the U.S. Office of Education listed over six hundred national and regional' educational associations in 1969. This was more than a 25 percent increase over the number reported in 1965. By 1975 the number was nearly one thousand. The proliferation of these associations on such a large scale attests to a diversity of special interests and a realization that their members can achieve their objectives collectively. Many of these organizations began as close personal associations of executives, such as the principals of the early normal schools, the presidents of teachers colleges, and the deans of colleges of education. As the organizations developed, the executives generally assumed a background role and the practitioners, department chairmen, deans, and faculty members assumed the more dominant role.

Educational associations are of several different types. These include the research and teacher-oriented associations such as the American Physical Society (APS), and the Modern Language Association (MLA); occupationally oriented associations such as the American Association of University Professors (AAUP); special task associations such as the National Commission on Accreditation (NCA) and the College Entrance Examination Board (CEEB); and the social change associations such as the Students for Democratic Society (SDS).

The explanation for the development of these associations in recent years may be found in their changed orientation, their influence on the increasing complexity of American society, the difficulty of gaining a hearing before representative government, the need to explain the work of the organization to the citizens of the community, and the fact that they need to consult with each other to learn newer developments in a field whose knowledge is expanding in almost geometric proportions.

At the beginning of the 1970s, national education associations were growing rapidly in number, size, and complexity and in the breadth of tasks they were undertaking. Their relationships to each other and to the federal government were of a new scope and entity. In an educational world in which the national government elected to figure prominently in the next decade, the national associations organized by educators seem more than ever to be slated for an important role in relations between the educational community and the federal government. (Dershimer and Bloland, 1971, p. 369)

For a century and a half, the people in the business of teaching the children and youth of the nation have been struggling to establish themselves as a profession. Similarly, the agencies that prepare teachers have attempted to establish teacher education as a true profession. Those agencies have made the teacher educator an identifiable component of the total profession of education and have delineated their own roles in governance. (This subject is treated in depth in Charles A. Harper's *A Century of Public Teacher Education* [1939] and in a chapter of *Teacher Education for a Free People,* written by Charles W. Hunt, entitled, "Toward a Profession of Teaching" [1956].)

The organized teaching profession has long assumed primary responsibility for the professional improvement of its members. As noted in Chapter VIII, the Society of Associated Teachers, organized in New York City in 1794, examined persons who wished to teach, and those applicants they found worthy were certified. Normal schools, which began in July, 1839, with the first such school established at Lexington, Massachusetts, numbered 127 by 1900. Their presidents, then often called principals, organized the first association for the improvement of teacher education. In 1918 it and several other organizations joined to form a national organization. In 1917 the North-Central Association of Normal School Presidents and Principals expanded into a national organization. This expansion was formalized in 1918 under the leadership of the presidents of institutions from Iowa, Missouri, Michigan, and Ohio, as the first regular session of the American Association of Teachers Colleges. It was then a division of the National Education Association, but the Department of Normal Schools of the NEA was disbanded in 1925 and the American Association of Teachers Colleges became a department of the NEA.

However, cooperative study of teacher education had taken

place even before these developments. In 1912, the Department of Normal Schools of the NEA set forth seven principles that constituted goals for the normal schools. These included supplying teachers for the rural schools, elementary schools, and high schools; emphasizing scholarship; expanding the courses of instruction and practice to four years; encouraging professional experimentation and investigation; emphasizing practice teaching; emphasizing the adaptation of education to rural community life; and accepting the profession's responsibility to relate itself to the life of the people so it could become an important social force. This movement spawned standards for accreditation and the study of professional education itself.

The American Association of Teachers Colleges published its first yearbook in 1922, which related the story of the previous organizations and recorded its experience to date. In 1927 it adopted a set of standards for teachers colleges, defining provisions for admission, graduation, size of faculty, preparation of faculty, and size of faculty's teaching load. The standards included descriptions of a training school and student teaching, of the organization of the curriculum, of living conditions of students, of the library, and of laboratory and shop equipment. There were also standards for classification of students, for financial support, for the character of the curriculum, for the efficiency of instruction, for the standards for granting degrees, and for the general tone of the teachers college. The basic structure and some of the fundamental knowledge of teacher education in the direction of professionalizing teacher preparation was thus launched well before 1930.

Further emphasis upon the preparation of teachers as a professional discipline itself is evidenced by the National Survey of the Education of Teachers done in 1933 by the U.S. Office of Education. Under the direction of E. S. Evenden, the survey was made by the American Association of Teachers Colleges at the request of the Commission on Education. It was also endorsed by the National Council of State Superintendents and Commissioners of Education, by the Association of Deans of Schools of Education and by the North-Central Association of Colleges and Secondary Schools (Evenden, 1933).

The accrediting committee of the American Association of Teachers Colleges also noted rising standards for the approval of teacher education programs, and the association organized a Commission on Teacher Education just prior to World War II. It was felt that the association should seek a broadened membership because critics were disturbed by the growing strengths of the teachers colleges and the lack of initiative and participation in the preparation of teachers by the older, academically oriented colleges and universities. The commission's investigation was followed by a grant from the General Education Board to the American Council on Education for the purpose of helping local groups to experiment, to share experiences, to encourage discussion and publication, and to stimulate improvement of teacher preparation at the local level. The association itself continued to provide a means of keeping its members to date on the newer developments in teacher education by holding its first "school for executives" at Clear Lake, Michigan, in 1942.

Through the efforts of the association, an attempt was made in 1949 by a Committee on Coordination of Collegiate Problems in Teacher Education to secure integration of related organizations in order to represent the various interests in teacher education more effectively. For example, the Association for Student Teaching had interests almost identical with but at a different level than those of the administrators of the colleges. The Association of Schools of Music had developed its own list of accredited music schools. This is also true of the teacher education personnel group. These organizations became departments of the American Association of Teachers Colleges. Subsequently, other organizations joined the AATC: it included fifteen by 1949. A more thorough amalgamation of other organizations had taken place in 1948. In that year the National Association of Colleges and Departments of Education and the National Association of Teacher Education Institutions in Metropolitan Districts joined with the American Association of Teachers Colleges to form the new organization called the American Association of Colleges for Teacher Education (AACTE). The change in name and in constitution made it possible for other organizations involved in the preparation of teachers to join in this program of voluntary association for improving the preparation of teachers in all institutions.

The American Association of Colleges for Teacher Education has now worked for over a half a century to stimulate better teacher education, and has sought to increase the effectiveness of its member institutions as institutions. It has worked with individual professors and executive personnel to improve education in general and teacher education in particular. Today there are more than 860 member institutions in AACTE. Its best work has been done in the improvement of the competency of members through its publications, which are now grouped under thirteen general headings.

The executive secretary has summarized some of the goals of the association as follows:

The American Association of Colleges for Teacher Education is an organization of more than 860 colleges and universities joined together in a common interest: more effective ways of preparing educational personnel for our changing society. It is national in scope, institutional in structure, and voluntary. It has served teacher education for 55 years in professional tasks which no single institution, agency, organization, or enterprise can accomplish alone. . . .

Through conferences, study committees, commissions, task forces, publications, and projects, AACTE conducts a program relevant to the current needs of those concerned with better preparation programs for educational personnel. Major programmatic thrusts are carried out by commissions on international education, multicultural education, and accreditation standards. Other activities include government relations and a consultative service in teacher education.

A number of activities are carried on collaboratively. These include major fiscal support for the selection of higher education representatives on the National Council for Accreditation of Teacher Education—an activity sanctioned by the National Commission on Accrediting and a joint enterprise of higher education institutions represented by AACTE, organizations of school board members, classroom teachers, state certification officers, and chief state school officers. (Pomeroy, 1973)

The American Association of Colleges for Teacher Education was also one of the founders of the ERIC Clearinghouse on Teacher Education. Other cosponsors of this information center included the National Commission on Teacher Education and Professional Standards of the NEA, the U.S. Office of Education, and the Association for Student Teaching. Some years ago it pioneered the Teacher Education and Media Project and more recently has sponsored many studies and publications concerning the Performance Based Teacher Education movement (PBTE). The AACTE reaches its member institutions through the AACTE *Bulletin* and the *Yearbook*, both of which alert teacher educators to new developments in public school education and in teacher education. Membership in AACTE is institutional, and each institution is represented by three individuals appointed by its president—one from the central administration, one from the teaching fields, and one from professional education. Annual meetings are held each February and financial support is derived from the dues of member institutions. There is little doubt that AACTE has had enormous influence on teacher education in the United States.

Several other organizations of professional educators have developed with similar purposes: to improve curriculum, methods of instruction, and professional laboratory experiences for prospective teachers. The Association for Student Teaching, for example, was organized in 1920 and for many years held its national meeting in conjunction with AACTE. In more recent years it has joined with the group called the College Professors of Education into an organization now known as the Association of Teacher Educators (ATE). This group encourages experimentation in teacher education and disseminates the results of such experimentation through yearbooks and other publications. Another organization, the Deans of Schools and Colleges of Education in the National Association of State Universities and Land Grant Colleges, has for many years considered the unique problems in the preparation of all school personnel— elementary, secondary, and graduate—that characterize the large multipurpose state universities. This association meets in October of each year as well as at the annual meeting of the AACTE in February. It has its own constitution and bylaws and its own executive committee.

Other organizations primarily concerned with the programs in professional education include the Association of Early Childhood Education, the Association for the Education of Exceptional Children, and the International Reading Association. These organizations have annual meetings and publish either yearbooks or bulletins dealing with special subjects, usually through some subcommittee or other type of organization. Under the auspices of AACTE, the International Council for the Education of Teachers (ICET) acts as a coordinating agency and provides publications, more than a dozen to date, dealing with teacher education on an international level.

It now appears that the number of organizations in professional education has proliferated to the point that there is need again, as was true in 1948, for developing some other inclusive hierarchy. This was partly accomplished several years ago with the formation of the Associated Organizations for Teacher Education (AOTE), which now acts as a clearinghouse for its constituent organizations. Other constituent organizations of AOTE include the Student Personnel Association for Teacher Education and the National Institutional Teacher Placement Association. The former Department of Audio-Visual Instruction of the NEA and the Association of School Librarians, now organized into a single agency, should also be included because of their relationship to the profession.

In recent years teachers in the field have asked for better in-service teacher education programs from the colleges and universities. In many states this has been done through the typical land grant or state university's extension division, but in several institutions the college of education has fairly complete responsibility for its extension activities. The Teachers College Extension and Field Service Association grew out of the former teachers colleges, but anyone doing extension work in teacher education can now join this association.

All of these organizations have a great impact on the decision-making process regarding what is taught, who teaches it, who is selected to enter the teaching profession, what standards are required for the completion of the teacher preparation program, and all of the other aspects of the governance of teacher education. Obviously these organizations are all components of the teaching profession, a fact recognized by the NEA. By Howsam's standards they are in fact a subsystem of the teaching profession, and as such constitute a distinct professional entity.

Learned Societies and Their Influence on Teacher Education

Learned societies have had and will continue to have an impact upon the preparation of teachers in two ways. Individual scholars working in their respective disciplines on the local university campus function as a kind of all-institutional policy-forming agency governing the teacher education program. Through the professional association of learned societies they have been invited to participate under the banner of the Associated Organizations for Teacher Education (AOTE). These societies do effect the guidelines and standards governing the preparation of teachers in their respective academic and vocational disciplines. But first, who are these individuals and what organizations are represented?

The secretary of the Associated Organizations for Teacher Education (AOTE) has worked with a task force responsible for developing guidelines that would enable the learned societies to evolve supplements to the regular standards and guidelines of the NCATE. The task force committee's bulletin, *Developing Guidelines in Teacher Education*, defines the role of professional associations and learned societies in the process of accreditation in teacher education (Smith, 1969). The new standards for the NCATE proposed by the Evaluative Criteria Study Committee recognized the important contribution of professional associations and learned societies to the improvement of teacher education and required this group to participate in all phases of the development of the new proposals. The new NCATE standards require the institutions to examine critically the recommendations of professional organizations concerned with the preparation of teachers in their specialties, and thus provide such learned societies with a systematic way of bringing their concern to the attention of college and university faculties.

A mere listing of these organizations will show clearly that one of the long-recognized components of teacher education is the subject matter, the academic disciplines, the *what* of teaching; this constitutes the basic knowledge of any teacher. The alleged rivalry between the professors of education and the professors of academic subjects has been greatly exaggerated and was more evident in the national press than on any given campus, where more often than not, a congenial atmosphere prevailed between the professors of the academic subjects and the faculties in professional education. No matter what his background, anyone who has thought very much about teacher education would have to conclude that the *what* of teaching and the *methodology* of teaching are so intricately interwoven that they cannot be separated. One cannot teach what one does not know, but merely knowing does not guarantee success in teaching. As I have stated repeatedly, the word teaching itself must require both a direct and an indirect object. One cannot teach something without teaching it to someone, and one cannot teach someone without teaching him something. Hence the involvement of professional associations and learned societies in the development of guidelines for accreditation of teacher education and in the development of policies, procedures, and standards for the governance of teacher education must be a cooperative venture. The *what* of teaching can be divided into two major categories—the academic disciplines and the vocational subject matter fields. The former includes such subjects as mathematics, English, science, social studies, speech, and foreign language, and the latter includes such areas as business education, home economics, industrial arts, trade and industrial education, distributive education, technical education, health occupations, guidance, and agricultural education.

In each of these subject matter fields, there are national associations to which professors give their allegiance. The academic group includes such organizations as the American Association for the Advancement of Science, the American Chemical Society, the American Historical Association, the Association of American Geographers, the Philosophy of Education Society, the Music Educators National Conference, and the National Art Education Association. The vocational group includes such organizations as the American Association of Health, Physical Education and Recreation, the American Association of Teacher Educators in Agriculture, the American Home Economics Association, the American Industrial Arts Association, and the National Association of Business Teacher Education. This list may not include all of the organizations called upon by NCATE to develop supplementary guidelines for their respective disciplines, but it includes most of them.

Several organizations within the learned societies themselves are uniquely devoted to the improvement of teaching in their disciplines. For example, the American Association of Physics Teachers was organized as long ago as 1930 by a group of physicists. Incorporated under the laws of New York State in 1958, it had only 42 members in 1938 but had 12,000 by 1970. Its fundamental objective is the advancement of the teaching of physics and the furtherance of the role of physics in our culture. It acts as the spokesman for physics teachers at all levels—elementary, secondary, and higher (Zemansky, 1971). The American Chemical Society has similar aims for the field of chemistry. In the National Council of Teachers of English both college and high school teachers of English work together to improve the teaching of literature and the English language. The National Council of Teachers of Mathematics has similar objectives.

Not yet involved in the AOTE project is the American Council of Learned Societies, a private, nonprofit federation of thirty-three national scholarly organizations in the humanities and in the social sciences. Although it has had little influence on teacher education in these fields prior to 1968, in that year it became involved in an attempt, along with other learned societies, to develop first a structure and then a program for involving scholars in the better preparation of teachers. A report of the conference of these organizations held at Grove Park Institute near Asheville, North Carolina, in 1969 contained nine papers on methods of improving teaching and teacher education and the role of universities and professional societies in this effort. The speeches presented were divided into what Thomas Vogt termed "five sequential levels of incompetence" (Vogt, 1969, p. 22). The report included some final recommendations and proposals for action by representatives of each of the eleven professional societies represented at the conference.

In addition to those educators whose responsibility is to the academic and vocational subject matter being taught, there is another group of educators defined as "school service personnel." They are not teachers; their role is to serve the regular teachers and the pupils, and facilitate classroom learning. This group includes principals and superintendents, school librarians, guidance counselors, speech and hearing specialists, school nurses, psychologists, special education teachers, and several others. They usually have their own national association, such as the American Association of School Administrators, the American Association of School Librarians, the American Personnel and Guidance Association, the American Speech and Hearing Association, the Association for Childhood Education International, the Council for Exceptional Children, the National Council Commission on Safety Education, and the Speech Association of America.

Thus the teachers in the academic disciplines and in the vocational subject matter fields as well as certain supporting specialists are being brought into the decision-making process in teacher education through their respective national organizations, where accreditation guidelines are being developed, and through participation on the local campuses, where teacher education requires considerably more coordination than in the past.

The Influence of Accreditation on the
Governance of Teacher Education

In the governance of teacher education few positions are more powerful than control of the accreditation of teacher education programs and institutions. First of all, what is accreditation? In 1936, "accreditment" was described as the "recognition accorded to an educational institution in the United States by inclusion in a list of institutions issued by some agency or organization which sets up standards or requirements that must be complied with in order to secure approval" (Zook and Hagerty, 1936, p. 18). More recently, it was defined as "the process whereby an organization or agency recognizes a college or university or a program of study as having met certain predetermined qualifications or standards" (Selden, 1960, p. 6). A paper prepared for the National Commission on Accrediting in 1966 stated: "Accreditation is the embodiment of Social Institution that one cannot live comfortably with, and yet cannot live without. The history of accrediting reveals its periodic reversal of perceived needs and accepted customs. Nowhere is this swing of the pendulum clearer than in the relationship of accreditation to governance" (Cartter, 1966).

The National Council for the Accreditation of Teacher Education has defined accreditation as the process by which a program of professional preparation is examined and evaluated by a select group of professionals, with only those programs that meet established standards being accredited.

A long-time review of the history of accrediting programs in teacher education reveals a slowly evolving clarification of purposes. In general, there are two purposes that are now clearly discernible and generally accepted:

1. To identify for public purposes educational institutions and programs of study which meet established standards of educational quality

2. To stimulate improvement in educational standards and in educational institutions and programs of study by involving faculty and staff in required self-evaluation, research, and planning.

Secondary purposes of accreditation include such objectives as the development of processes and instruments to evaluate institutions, to facilitate transfer of credit among different types and levels of institutions, to assure society that practitioners will not harm public health and safety, to assure acceptance of ethical standards in relationships with students, to protect institutions against external interference by groups and individuals who have sought to control, distort, and divert the educational function for partisan purposes, and finally to identify for public purposes those institutions making efficient use of their resources to meet stated goals and objectives (Dickey and Miller, 1972, p. 36).

Today accrediting agencies must increasingly accept a social responsibility for their actions. Such responsibility can be achieved through self-governance, as is now the case for voluntary accreditation, or it can be achieved through control by government. The public is going to be more and more concerned with and involved in accreditation, particularly accreditation of professional programs, because it is a principal component of the governance of post-secondary education in the United States, and those who control accreditation exert control over that post-secondary education. A measure of stability is required in order to avoid the exploitation of the accreditation process by state or federal administrations seeking to achieve their own ends (Dickey and Miller, 1972).

One type of accreditation is that granted a total institution—its program, administration, faculty, and facilities—by its regional association. The other type is the accreditation of institutional preparation programs for a profession. For many years, professionals have sought to regulate entry into their professions through the control of entry into the preparation programs. The professions have maintained for years that such control is justified on the grounds that the participants in the profession are the guardians of esoteric and specialized knowledge. Thus, only members of the profession are qualified to make judgements regarding educational programs that prepare future members. Once a profession can substantiate such a claim, it can then use accreditation of educational programs as a method of "choosing colleagues and successors" (Dickey and Miller, 1972, p. 40).

Accreditation of teacher education had its beginnings in the informal meetings of the North-Central Association of Normal School Presidents and Principals as early as 1902. At this time the normal schools began requiring high school diplomas for admission, and some normal schools sought accreditation by the North-Central Association because it required high schools to employ only graduates of the colleges on its accredited list. By 1938 the American Association of Teachers Colleges had an accrediting committee, which noted, in its 1938 yearbook, evidence of significant progress: the number of institutions being accredited continuously increased and the number of warnings and conditions for accredited institutions declined.

Charles Hunt has noted that "the standards of the association were being continually improved, the objectives were better understood, and the application of the standards was more effective in producing change and in indicating to all institutions that good standards were both possible and necessary. Improvements on the campuses by 1940 became widely distributed, enabling the association to publish a list with reference to 'the ladder'" (Hunt, 1956, p. 38).

After the amalgamation of several teacher education organizations into the American Association of Colleges for Teacher Education in 1948, responsibility for accreditation was assumed by the inter-institutional visitation committees of that association. In 1954-55, however, the NCATE became the principal agency for the accreditation of teacher education. This council comprised five organizations, representing teachers, administrators, state departments of education, school boards, and colleges.

The first action of the council was to extend accreditation to the 284 institutions that had previously been accredited by the intervisitation program of the AACTE. By September 1, 1974, 540 of the more than 1400 institutions preparing teachers had been judged, both by educators who had visited them during the twenty-year period and by the approval of the council itself, as offering programs meeting national standards developed and adopted by the teaching profession during those years (NCATE, 1975). These institutions prepared approximately 85 percent of the teachers. Somewhat less than 900 non-accredited institutions prepared only 15 percent.

During the 1960s NCATE was subjected to considerable criticism for dozens of reasons, two of which were that it did not adequately represent the learned professions in the liberal arts and it did not adequately represent the organized teaching profession as embodied in the National Education Association. This criticism resulted in a series of studies, commission reports, regional and national meetings, surveys and a re-evaluation by the National

Commission on Accrediting (the organization that accredits accrediting associations), and the development of new standards and guides in the early 1970s.

A standard on governance appeared in the first NCATE publication in 1954. Minor revisions were made in 1958 and 1960, and the revision process has continued in the more recent standards, which were first published for use in January of 1970 after an experimental edition. I shall concern myself here only with those standards and the suggestions for their implementation that deal with the governance and controls of teacher education. The version of the 1960s reads as follows:

Standard II

The organization of an institution in which teachers are prepared should be such as to facilitate the planning, the administration, and the continuous improvement of a consistently unified program of teacher education. Because colleges and universities differ in overall organizational structures, no pattern of organization for teacher education applicable to all types of institutions is prescribed. Instead, three criteria for evaluating this factor are set forth as follows:

The organization: (1) should assure consistent policies and practices with reference to the different segments of the teacher education program regardless of the administrative units under which they operate, (2) should facilitate the continuous development and improvement of the teacher education program, and (3) should clearly fix responsibility for the administration of policies agreed upon.

Implications of Standard for Program

The statement which follows should not be regarded as a part of the Standard. Instead, it is meant to show how the Standard might be applied to this aspect of a teacher education program.

An organization will be regarded as acceptable for the development of policies when a single agency is made responsible for coordinating: (1) the planning of teacher education curricula, (2) the development of policies that govern the admission of students to teacher education curricula, (3) the development of a system of registration and enrollment which makes it easy to identify all students preparing to teach and can be understood by students and faculty, and (4) the development of policies and standards for the satisfactory completion of all teacher education curricula. Such an agency will be the unit (college, schools, division, department) of Education or an interdepartmental committee or council. If it is an interdepartmental committee, its membership will be representative of those divisions within the institution in proportion to their proper concerns for teacher education.

An organization that is effective in the continuous development and improvement of the total teacher education program will be typified by: (1)

a clear definition of objectives for the major aspects of the program, (2) a continuous evaluation of the effectiveness of curricula and procedures, and (3) a consistent policy of development and testing of new and promising procedures.

Responsibility for the total program will be regarded as clearly assigned when some one person is held responsible for the administration of the total program and when that person is in a position to speak authoritatively for the total program. This same person will normally be the one responsible for recommending students for teacher certification.

In the 1970 revision of the standards, this general governance concept was retained in the requirement that the unit "may take the form of a council, commission, committee, department, school, college, or other recognizable organizational entity." Again, faculty was to be composed of those "staff members who are significantly involved in teacher education." It was expected that this faculty would be "composed of persons who have experience in, and commitment to, the task of educating teachers."

The one significant difference between this control standard (Standard 1.5), and the earlier one (Standard II) is the omission of any reference to an administrator in the 1970 version. However, it is quite possible that the commission considered the requirement for a responsible administrator to be a basic assumption needing no reiteration.

In the 1970 version, the control of basic programs, Standard 1.5, was stated as follows:

Administrative structure exists primarily as a practical arrangement for formulating and achieving goals, fixing responsibility, utilizing resources, and facilitating continuous development and improvement. The standard assumes that this principle is applicable to administrative units responsible for the preparation of teachers. It is expected that the particular unit within the institution officially designated as responsible for teacher education is composed of persons who have experience in, and commitment to, the task of educating teachers.

The standard does not prescribe any particular organizational structure. A unit as referred to below may take the form of a council, commission, committee, department, school, college, or other recognizable organizational entity.

While major responsibility for designing, approving, evaluating, and developing teacher education programs is carried by an officially designated unit, it is assumed that teacher education faculty members are systematically involved in the decision-making process.

Standard 1.5: *The design, approval, and continuous evaluation and development of teacher education programs are the primary responsibility of an officially designated unit; the majority of the membership of this unit is composed of faculty and/or staff members who are significantly involved in teacher education.*

Another important difference between the old and the new standards is in their control mechanisms. The 1970 version contains a standard on the control of graduate programs, Standard G-1.7, which was stated as follows:

The quality of the graduate programs depends on the quality of the faculty and students as well as on the content and design of the several curricula. It follows that the institution needs a structure by which the faculty can control every phase of the advanced programs. Procedures for admitting students, planning programs, adding new courses, hiring staff, and determining requirements for degrees are carefully organized and systematized, and faculty members are involved in the formation and execution of both policy and procedures.

Schools or departments of education are sometimes expected to provide training for teachers and other professional school personnel through courses, seminars, and workshops that are offered primarily at the convenience of school personnel in the field. Frequently this training is applied toward meeting the requirements of a graduate certificate or degree. The institution ensures that such courses, seminars, and workshops—regardless of the location and time at which the instruction takes place—are taught by qualified faculty members and supported by essential learning resources. In addition, the institution ensures that the requirements for earning credit are comparable to those made in regular graduate offerings.

Standard: *The primary responsibility for initiation, development, and implementation of advanced programs lies with the education faculty.*

The council is very specific as to who shall control advanced (post-baccalaureate) programs for the preparation of teachers and school service personnel. It states that "the primary responsibility for initiation, development, and implementation of advanced programs lies with the education faculty." It may be presumed that such faculty would achieve its purposes through a graduate faculty or graduate committee or a dean who normally serves the whole university, but such graduate agencies are expected to grant a high degree of operational freedom to the education faculty if the requirements of the standard are to be met. In view of the findings of William McKenzie on the effectiveness of graduate faculties and deans in the governance of teacher education, the council's position appears to have been justified (McKenzie, 1965).

Many of the learned societies and professional associations have special subunits devoting considerable attention to the preparation of teachers for their respective academic disciplines. The NCATE standards note that the same potential exists for developing strong programs in teacher preparation, and require the institution (and presumably its unit responsible for teacher education) to "give due consideration to guidelines for teacher preparation developed by national learned societies and professional associations."

Such societies are not the real determiners of academic curricula, because "the unit" will still shape its own curricula and has fulfilled its obligation when "due consideration" Has been given. The purpose of including a standard concerning learned societies is (1) to make sure that academic disciplines have an opportunity for input into the curricula and (2) to suggest that such disciplines avoid making teacher accreditation standards on their own initiative. This procedure is in accord with the position taken by the National Commission on Accrediting when it approved the revised constitution for the National Council for the Accreditation of Teacher Education in 1974. It should be noted that the same stance should be taken with reference to all those vocational programs offered by most universities.

What has been the influence of the standards of the National Council for Accreditation of Teacher Education upon the governance of the whole teacher education enterprise? That is, do the standards mentioned above, Standard II in the earlier version, and Standards 1.5 and G-1.7 in the current set of standards and guides, really have an influence on the governance of teacher education, particularly in universities? Mayor, in his report to the National Commission on Accrediting, and to the profession in general, addressed himself to this question. With regard to the influence of structure and administration, he reviewed the impact of national accreditation, regional accrediting agencies, and state accreditation upon teacher education. He observed that "the effects of national accreditation were felt in four areas: (1) the all-institutional committee; (2) the department and school or college of education; (3) the fixing of individual administrative responsibility; and (4) the analysis of several paths to certification."

The effects of state accreditation on structure and administration (with each effect probably felt in more than half of the states) were three in number: (1) the designation of one person in each teacher education institution to be responsible for recommending students for certification; (2) the appointment of all-institutional committees for formulating and supervising teacher education policies and programs; and (3) discouraging, to some extent, malfeasance in higher educational institutions through the threat of a state investigation (Mayor, 1965, p. 211). The effects of regional accreditation were two in number: (1) bringing about (in some instances) a change in the administration of an institution of higher education; and (2) bringing about, through stimulation to improvement, structural and personnel changes in the administration of higher education (Mayor, 1965, p. 212). The effects of national accreditation were four in number. These effects included: (1) the establishment of an overall institution-wide committee or council to formulate and supervise teacher education policies and programs; (2) the designation of one person to be responsible for the administration of all teacher education programs in the institution; (3) the establishment of undergraduate departments of education and schools or colleges of education for graduate work; (4) defining the channels of responsibility in teacher education (Mayor and Swartz, 1965, pp. 212-213).

In summarizing their study of structure and administration, Mayor indicated that the NCATE had a significant influence on institutions that prepare teachers in several ways:

1. in establishment of an overall, institutional-wide committee or council to formulate and supervise teacher education policies;
2. in the designation of one person to be responsible for the administration of all teacher education programs;
3. in the re-examination by institutions of their policies in regard to permitting students to satisfy teacher certification requirements without being registered in an officially recognized teacher education program. (Mayor, 1965)

Mayor also noted the establishment of departments of education in four-year colleges and in institutions offering graduate work in colleges of education because such institutions believed that was what NCATE wanted.

The regional association's general scrutiny of an institution's administrative organization at the time of the initial appraisal of the school, or when the institution is threatened with a loss of accreditation, has had an influence on institutional administration.

The regional associations have also brought about changes through recommendations for improvement. The rare cases of investigation of an institution, in cases where "bad" administration of the school is widely publicized, have occasionally resulted in a change of administration.

The state's insistence that one person in these institutions be designated to recommend for certification students who have successfully completed an approved program of teacher education has brought about (or supported) the practice in states where the approved program approach is used. In some states, usually those following the NCATE pattern of accreditation, the state authorities have been instrumental in the appointment of all-institutional committees with the responsibility for teacher education in those institutions not accredited by NCATE. The rarely used threat of a state department or legislative investigation of an institution, in the event that the internal affairs of an institution seem to justify or require it, probably has been influential in preventing excesses in administrative malfeasance (Mayor, 1965, pp. 144-145).

Rolf Larson, in the NCATE training document reviewing the experiences of the two previous years with Standard 1.5, stated that the programs thus envisioned should be carefully conceptualized. The experience of the evaluation boards revealed that this expectation had not been very well met, apparently due to the inadequate operation of the procedures recommended in Standard 1.5 on governance. Larson summarized the experience as follows:

> It is the understanding of the NCATE staff, and an attempt is made to convey this understanding to institutional representatives, that the designers of the present Standards saw that conceptualization of teacher education programs needed to be a joint, concerted team task. They did not see Education professors as the only source of ideas about professional problems. They did not see "arts" professors as an only source of knowledge about appropriate teaching content. Their reference to the "profession" was an indication of their belief about the help which could be obtained from those who were on the firing line, but they did not intend teacher education to be only a reflection of everyday problems in the classroom. They wrote Standard 1.4 to be a direct reference to the help which could be obtained from professional associations and societies—groups of specialists in single fields who give full attention to the problems of that field—but they never intended for the societies to be the absolute or only sources of input, as can be seen from the language of the Standard. They wanted students to be a source of input—to be considered and to be heard—but they

did not consider that student reaction, in itself, should be any more dominant than the input from the practitioner or the society. (NCATE, 1972, p. 3)

Several institutions seemed to feel that the council was imposing a particular kind of organizational structure upon them, and they resented it. There was, and is, considerable question as to whether or not structure had much relationship to the performance of the educational function of the unit provided in the teacher education program. In the past, the council had seemed willing to criticize institutions on the basis of Standard 1.5, but it has recently seemed reluctant to impose a particular structure on institutions. Yet the literature in the field points to the conclusion that Standard 1.5 was in many instances critical to successful teacher education.

It becomes increasingly clear that the application of Standard 1.5 is difficult because of the varying nature of (a) the types of institutions that prepare teachers, (b) the desire of many institutions to preserve their unique character, and (c) the difficulty of describing not only what the structure is but how it operates to facilitate the governance of teacher education. The function of governance structure is to facilitate performance. This is one of the basic principles of educational administration. Where the structure is faulty, performance may be faulty.

The concept, widespread after 1954, that teacher education was an all-university function and/or responsibility led NCATE to sidestep the governance-structure issue. It followed the practice of accrediting the teacher education program of the institution. It did not follow the practice of accrediting the teacher education program of the college of education. The college of education was not approved as the institution's agency for facilitating the program. The council notified the president of the institution, not the dean of the college of education, of its decision; the dean usually received only a carbon copy of their letter. Yet it was the college of education faculty that had made the institutional self-survey, squired the visiting team around the campus, and was generally held accountable for the success of the program. Such a concept and such a practice tended to weaken the college of education both on and off the campus, and made adherence to Standards II, 1.5, and G-1.7 very difficult.

Another survey attempting to determine the effectiveness of

NCATE accreditation was undertaken by Ray Maul in April of 1969 under the auspices of the National Commission on Accrediting and the American Association of Colleges for Teacher Education. This survey of opinions of the chief administrative officers of the institutions and of the directors of teacher education (under whatever title they held) was commissioned by the coordinating board of NCATE and prompted by real concern on the part of the National Commission on Accrediting (as well as the usual critics) as to whether or not there should be accreditation of teacher education at all. Most of the information Maul elicited was concerned with the operational aspects of NCATE rather than with analysis of the effectiveness of the application of the standards to the programs of the institutions then undergoing accreditation. The first part of the questionnaire was filled out by the president, or a general administrative officer he designated, and the second part was completed by the principal education officer, who had the major responsibility for preparing the institutional report and making arrangements for the work of the visiting committee. Maul's research indicated that 94 percent of the 123 deans and department chairmen in professional education were opposed to the idea that control of teacher education programs should be completely in the hands of each institution without accrediting by an inter-institutional agency; that percentage favored some form of accreditation for teacher education.

More specifically, 89 percent of those queried stated that participation in NCATE accreditation tended to strengthen the status of the school or department of education within the institution. Eighty-five percent of the respondents agreed that this participation tended to encourage closer cooperation of efforts between the academic departments and the education department. In general, one must conclude that both the chief administrative officers of these 149 institutions who made responses and their directors of teacher education strongly favored accreditation by NCATE. They also favored the procedures used by the council: most thought that these procedures compared favorably with the accreditation procedures of the regional associations (Maul, 1969, pp. 1-31).

At the February, 1973, meeting of the American Association of Colleges for Teacher Education an examination was made of the balance of power in the accreditation of teacher education. Margaret Lindsey cited two modifications in NCATE that have become fundamental to the issue of accreditation. The first was the shift in the balance of power among the constituencies, especially the NEA and AACTE. The latter then had ten representatives on the council and the NEA only six. The second shift in the operation of NCATE occurred with the establishment of the NCATE coordinating board. Here again, according to Lindsey, there was an imbalance of voting privileges on the board in favor of AACTE. She pointed out that the NEA board of directors voted to reduce its financial support for NCATE and accompanied this with a demand for greater involvement of classroom teachers in every step of the accrediting process. Lindsey warned that achieving a balance of power between these two agencies would not automatically mean quality in teacher education. She indicated that improvement would occur when roles and responsibilities of agencies were more adequately redefined because these agencies would then have an extended and deepened involvement (Lindsey, 1973).

A new balance of power was effected in early 1974 with the approval of a new constitution by the NCATE coordinating board, by NCATE, and by the National Commission on Accrediting. The council is now composed of "19 to 24 voting members representing constituent organizations and from one to nine non-voting representatives of associate members for an overall total not to exceed 28 voting and non-voting representatives. The AACTE and the NEA will select eight representatives each and the Council of Chief State School Officers (CCSSO), the National Association of State Directors of Teacher Education and Certification (NASDTEC) and the National School Boards Association (NSBA), one each . . . and one representative of an associate member organization shall be from a learned society. . ." (NCATE, 1974). In this connection, one is again reminded of Baldridge's comment that the political process was probably a better framework for understanding what had happened than were either the bureaucratic or the collegial models. The same process is apparently involved in the struggle for control of teacher education through the accreditation mechanisms.

During the last several years the teaching profession has studied and attempted to implement the concept of "performance-based teacher education" (PBTE). Such implementation raises the question of governance and administration; i.e., "who does what?" The NCATE standards of 1970 specifically provide for experimentation in teacher education.

Since the concept is relatively new, its characteristics are still evolving. Most students of the movement would probably accept Allen Schmeider's definition of competency-based teacher education (the word "competency" is used interchangeably with "performance," although there are obvious differences in emphasis) which describes competency-based teacher education as:

a system of teacher education which has as its specific purpose the development of specifically described knowledge, skills, and behaviors that will enable a teacher to meet performance criteria for classroom teaching. Presumably, each competency attained by the pre-service teacher related to student learning can be assessed by the following criteria of competence.

1. Knowledge criteria that assess the cognitive understandings of the teacher education student;

2. Performance criteria that assess specific teaching behaviors;

3. Product criteria that assess the teacher's ability to examine and assess the achievement of his or her pupils. (Schmeider, 1973, p. 57)

The AACTE Committee on Performance-Based Teacher Education commissioned Michael Kirst to analyze the issue of PBTE's relationship to governance, that is, "the means by which the movement is nurtured, blunted, or otherwise controlled." Kirst's analysis clarified many issues but provided few solutions, although his suggestions for the future merit considerable thought. He noted that since PBTE was still in an embryonic state, its implementation by any agency would be most difficult. Kirst stressed the following points, which he thought would help resolve some of the crucial governance issues:

1. The evolution of influence in teacher preparation, certification, and promotion has favored the universities and to a lesser extent state government (particularly state departments).

2. Since the current system was institutionalized, several interest groups have gained in strength and will demand a larger share of influence - e.g. teacher organizations, parent groups, ethnic minorities, students, state legislators, and state board members. Consequently, some redistribution of existing influence is likely when PBTE is implemented.

3. These groups have different value perspectives between each other and within their own membership. PBTE is unlikely to have a research base that will resolve many value issues through empirical data. Consequently, value issues will become intensely political, engendering negotiations, bargaining, coalitions, and compromises.

4. The outcome of this political activity will vary according to the prior

political culture in a state, the structure of statewide interest groups, and other state factors. A new national NCATE-type mechanism is unlikely because professional educators will be split according to such indices as humanists vs. behaviorists, classroom teachers vs. professors, and ethnic minorities vs. state department of education professionals.

5. Political theory provides no precise prescriptive or normative solutions for the optimal governance structures or procedures. Partial theories such as representation do suggest some appropriate directions.

6. Given the pluralistic and contending interest groups and the lack of research on proven "competencies," PBTE could become a negotiating slogan rather than an integrated conceptual framework. The motives and skill of political brokers will be of prime importance in determining the outcome.

7. Major policy trends such as tenure revision, affirmative action for minority employment, and the declining number of new elementary/secondary pupils will "spill over" into the bargaining on PBTE. (Kirst, 1973)

Another role for the PBTE movement is in making NCATE accreditation more specific and objective. Much of the criticism of NCATE (and probably of other professional accreditation agencies) has been directed toward its conspicuous lack of valid criteria. After examining the relationship between the accreditation of teacher education institutions and performance-based teacher education, Larson focused on four basic accreditation problems: (a) the need to allow for institutional differences; (b) the need to base decisions on substance rather than on form; (c) the need to determine the actual qualifications of the graduate; and (d) the need to determine the focus or function of accreditation. Performance-based teacher education, which requires the explicit definition of expected competencies, could help to move accreditation toward foundation elements of substantive achievement and could encourage a rethinking of admissions criteria:

> To the degree that the performance-based movement is good for teacher education, it provides those involved in accreditation with the material they need for revising and improving standards. . . . PBTE does not operate with the idea of improving the accreditation of teacher education . . . it operates to improve teacher education, and in so doing, it provides help for the auxiliary services surrounding teacher education, one of which is accreditation. (Larson, 1974, p. 27)

Perhaps the true role of the university in teacher education is to act as a referee in the many rivalries between the agencies that Kirst listed. This role was noted by Denemark when he addressed the 1973 annual meeting of the AACTE:

Clearly, a central goal of teacher education today must be the resolution of the current controversy regarding its governance. Equitable roles for schools, colleges, communities, the organized profession, and state and national governmental agencies must be established. Each has a significant contribution to make, but the present ambiguities of governance, if unresolved, will result in the demise of higher education as a significant force in determining the nature of teacher education. Should the control of teacher education fall solely to employing school systems heavily burdened with local pressures and problems or to a teaching profession currently preoccupied with organizational rivalries, the consequences could be disastrous. (Denemark, 1973, p. 1)

Other scholars have also predicted such an outcome if teacher education policies are to be determined solely, or even largely, by practitioners. Local schools are primarily engaged in the preparation of the young for participation in and adaptation to the current society—not with the improvement of it. Schools, therefore, tend to be conservative. Although higher education is also considered to be conservative, it does conduct research and experimentation and therefore is probably a better source of innovation. Collaboration between local schools and higher education institutions would probably provide the best assurance for the progressive development of both.

Summary

That group of American educators responsible for the preparation of the nation's classroom teachers and school service personnel is a subsystem of the whole teaching profession. It is large enough, provides professional services important enough, is self-governing enough, and is capable enough to constitute a respectable profession in its own right. It therefore should be accorded the authority for the governance of its members in their work and the governance of the procedures and standards of practice that would enable the profession to be accountable to its clientele, the public schools and the American people.

The profession of teacher educators has had a long history: some of its organizations date back three-quarters of a century. Today there are several dozen subsystems of teacher educators among both administrators and teaching personnel. In the colleges and universities there are many such subsystems representing the substantive components of teacher education, which are classifiable into three major categories: the academic disciplines, the vocational fields, and school service specialists. In all of these subject matter areas are hundreds of faculty members whose loyalty is devoted both to research in their scholarly fields and to the teaching of them. Many of these fields have national organizations whose primary purpose is the preparation of teachers in their areas of specialization. In the last two decades they have had an increasing influence on this component of the governance of teacher education.

Accreditation of teacher education began in the days of the normal school at the turn of the century. Its development has been slow but methodical, moving toward increasing levels of both scope and complexity. The major problem now confronting accreditation is the extent of controls to be exercised by the institutions, by the organized teaching profession, by state licensing agencies, and by the federal government. The NCATE, recognized for many years by the National Commission on Accrediting, is the agency now responsible for assuring the public of the quality of teacher education and for stimulating improvements in the process of preparing all school personnel. It has been subjected to pressures from many sources in recent years, but there is little doubt that its influence in the improvement of teacher education in the higher education institutions of the nation has been great indeed. Among its standards is the requirement that an identifiable unit in the institution must have the responsibility, and the authority commensurate with that responsibility, for the institution-wide effort to prepare personnel for the nation's schools. It is my contention that accreditation should now become compulsory, and that those several hundred institutions that prepare only 15 percent of new teachers should either meet the higher requirements or get out of the business. Continued state certification of their graduates implies that they are as capable as graduates from accredited institutions and makes accreditation meaningless except as a stimulus to improvement. The emphasis must now shift from stimulation toward improvement to the assurance of a high level of quality, a change in which motivation for improvement would still not be lost.

XI

Internal Organization of the University Teacher Education Unit

The effectiveness of the teacher education unit within the university will depend to a considerable extent upon what subdivisions of organization and what subject matter fields are included within it. Thus, if there is a department of science education included in the college of education, it can be assumed that the college faculty would have more control over the preparation of science teachers than if such control resided in the departments of biology or chemistry. If there is a department of business education included in the college of education, it can be assumed that the college faculty would have more control over the preparation of business teachers than if such control resided in a department in the college of business. John Millett has emphasized the importance of clear definition (Millett, 1968, pp. 137-161).

The Search for a Rationale

Even a superficial review of a dozen university catalogues will reveal that no two colleges of education have the same, or even similar, types of internal organization. Some include most of the departments or other units necessary for the preparation of nearly all school personnel. Others include little more than a minimum of professional education components. Such variety is not unique to colleges of education; indeed, one would have difficulty in ascertaining the logic of organization for many other parts of a modern complex university. Observation reveals that strong personalities in a university's early history, availability of grant funds for financing some administrator's pet project, available space in some old building, and similar odd criteria are often the origins of a present illogical structure.

Presumably, the structuring of the curriculum of a college of education should be logically consistent, yet flexible and contemporary. Curricular organization requires the formulation of some underlying principle of organization. Historically, some of the organizational principles which have been used include:

1. The principle of compatibility (i.e., those faculty who could get along with each other formed their own degree specializations);
2. The principle of current topics (i.e., the "hot topic" of the moment became the object of inquiry for a degree specialization);
3. The principle of federal categories (i.e., the category of inquiry which could attract federal or extramural funding became a degree specialization);
4. The principle of occupations (i.e., the curriculum was structured around the kinds of occupations for which students prepared themselves in colleges of education);
5. The principle of levels of schooling (i.e., the curriculum was organized around elementary education, secondary education, and higher education). (Christensen, Fisher, and King, 1973, p. 2)

While the use of the word "principle" to explain the above-mentioned historical antecedents may be somewhat presumptuous, it does help to clarify the current scene in many institutions. Christensen et al. sought some organizational principle that had logical consistency, was not restricted by traditional biases and pressure groups, permitted professional individuality without individual exploitation, and assured the integrity of the college. They concluded that the "principle of knowledge" would satisfy most of these criteria. The existence of this principle was established by asking questions concerning the mission of, and the roles in, a college of education.

Another search for some rationale for organizing the teacher education program in a college of education was conducted at the

University of Alabama. This investigation was concerned with identifying the major advantages and disadvantages inherent in the transition from a discipline-based structure to a program-oriented organization. The investigator found twenty-one major advantages and twenty major problems in such a transition (Tack, 1973).

Knowledge Unique to Professional Education

One of the characteristics of a profession is the possession of esoteric knowledge needed by its practitioners and not possessed by the average layman. Does education possess such a unique body of knowledge?

An attempt was made in 1966 by Pi Lambda Theta, a professional organization for women in education, to answer this question. The investigators asked specialists in supporting disciplines to prepare papers, then convened a conference and published a report of the discussions on the position papers in psychology, philosophy, history, anthropology, sociology, and research. It was conceded that the body of knowledge unique or fundamental to education was probably modest, despite the vast amount of literature in the field. The knowledge that the contributors and participants sought to isolate was knowledge uniquely formulated and applicable to education, of special interest to educators, relevant to education, and unavailable to the average person. In conclusion, the members of the colloquy did, indeed, think that

there was a "body of knowledge unique to the profession of education." They thought this body of knowledge was derived from a number of different disciplines. They were keenly aware of the fact that this body of knowledge is dynamic and changing and that it will increase as new knowledge is developed. They agreed that educators need to select, integrate, and organize appropriate knowledge which will make it applicable to education in a manner consistent with educational philosophy, learning theory, and educational objectives, both cognitive and affective. They recognized, too, that education needs to develop knowledge in its own right. (Pi Lambda Theta, 1966, pp. xi-xii)

But the colloquy admitted that the participants had not done much toward defining that body of knowledge. They made a beginning by suggesting a rationale for determining the categories into which such knowledge might be put. One suggestion, for example, was to use

David Ryan's classification of the five major classes of teacher behavior: (1) motivating-reinforcing teacher behavior, (2) presenting-explaining-demonstrating teacher behavior, (3) organizing-planning-managing teacher behavior, (4) evaluating teacher behavior, (5) counseling-advising teacher behavior (Pi Lambda Theta, 1966, p. 193). It is difficult to visualize such a body of knowledge as being useful in either governance or administration.

The conference recognized that the body of knowledge utilized by the profession of education was voluminous and complex, but much of it was not unique to education. While the requisite information is rooted in the supporting disciplines listed above, a discipline-oriented classification would probably not be very useful as a way of structuring the preparation of practitioners in the profession. Another means of classification suggested was a problems approach, i.e., classification according to problems encountered by the teacher in the classroom. If the field of education were to be studied just to learn about it, a psychological structure might facilitate such learning. Much of the study about higher education is in this category. Since there may well be more than one logic of organization, there may therefore be more than one way to organize the internal structure of a college of education, especially if the logical organization of subject matter in the field of education is the criterion.

Still another possible method of classification may be obtained by asking experienced teachers to list and evaluate the dimensions of the knowledge they feel is essential to all prospective teachers. Such a survey was conducted in 1975 by the Teacher Programs and Services Group of the Educational Testing Service with the assistance of the American Association of Colleges for Teacher Education. The survey involved 1,500 experienced teachers enrolled in graduate summer school courses at twelve universities throughout the country. According to ETS, the dimensions of knowledge given the highest ratings related to teaching methods, development of the learner, and knowledge of certain basic skills. Thus, respondents acknowledged the existence of a body of knowledge, primarily but not exclusively in professional education, that is important for all teachers. They assigned little importance to certain general education objectives—namely, specific knowledge in science, literature, and the fine arts. Knowledge related to learning theory, instructional media, instructional methods, classroom management, school curriculum and administration, and testing and test construction received consistently high ratings. Most interesting is the apparent belief among these 1,500 experienced teachers that all teachers should have certain specific knowledge in most of the disciplines of general education, and they were reasonably specific in what this knowledge should include. This raises the question of whether or not the college of education should control this aspect of teacher education. Although few of the suggestions emerging from this study would be useful in organizing a college of education on the basis of knowledge unique to professional education, several conclusions were reached. Among them were the following:

1. There is an identifiable aggregate of knowledge, primarily but not exclusively in professional education, that is considered by teachers as important knowledge for teaching.

2. Teachers at various grade levels and with varying degrees of experience agree substantially on which knowledge is important for teaching.

3. Within this aggregate of theoretical and practical knowledge, knowledge more directly related to classroom practice is considered most important.

4. Teachers distinguish between evaluation and research, with a clear emphasis on the importance of evaluation.

5. Teachers consider knowledge related to multicultural education important for teachers.

6. Black teachers place greater emphasis than white teachers on the importance of knowledge for teaching.

7. Teachers identify certain specific knowledge in the social sciences as important.

8. Health, safety, and first aid are considered important knowledge areas for teachers.

9. Knowledge related to communication skills and the use of library resources is considered important for all teachers.

10. With the exception of knowledge objectives dealing with the environment and with basic arithmetic and mathematics, specific knowledge in science and mathematics is not perceived as important for all teachers.

11. Specific knowledge related to art, literature, drama, and music is not perceived as important for all teachers. (Humphrey and Elford, 1975, p. 10).

One significant finding arose from another study of doctoral programs. In the section of the study devoted to institutions, the areas of concentration for graduates of Ph.D. and Ed.D. programs were delineated. These data deal only with the areas of specialization for doctoral programs, which probably differ from those in undergraduate programs. Also, these data do not show what agency controls the programs. Governance could be by the graduate school alone, by the college of education alone, or by both in concert. Additionally, one set of structures could be used for policy formation (governance) and another set for policy implementation (administration).

With regard to controls, the study indicated that,

of the 89 Ph.D. programs, six, or 6.7 percent, were under the control of the College of Education; 47, or 52.8 percent, were under the control of the Graduate College; and 34, or 38.2 percent, were administered by dual arrangement. The 90 Ed.D. programs were distributed in the following manner: Nineteen, or 21.1 percent, of these programs were under the control of the College of Education; 34, or 37.8 percent, fell under the jurisdiction of the Graduate College; while dual control operated for 35 or 38.9 percent of Ed.D. programs. (Robertson and Sistler, 1971, p. 7)

The areas of concentration shown in Table 1 are indicative of the great variety in the doctoral programs offered by the 113 institutions responding to the questionnaire. There is no information concerning the number of these areas that were housed in identifiable departments and controlled by them. It is common knowledge, however, that there are, in many institutions, distinct departments of school administration, elementary education, secondary education, and many others. Table 1 demonstrates the relative importance of each specialty as shown by the number of doctoral degree recipients in each. The first five areas, school administration, guidance and counseling, educational psychology, higher education, and elementary education account for more than half of the total degrees granted in the thirty areas of concentration.

Under a plan proposed by Christensen, Fisher, and King there would be only one doctoral program, only one master's program, and only one bachelor's program. Using the principle of the logical organization of knowledge, specializations within these degree programs would still continue to be offered: for example, educational administration, elementary education, physical education, etc. There would be a distinction between *program* and *specialization.* "The program would be the number of credit (unit) hours, the number and duration of examinations, the foreign language and the thesis and/or dissertation which would be required in order to grant a degree. The specialization would be the specific courses in the curriculum which a student would study in order to fulfill the credit-hour requirements" (Christensen, Fisher, and King, 1973, p. 12).

Table 1

Areas of Concentration for Doctoral Degrees

Area of Concentration	Total Number of Graduates, Both Degrees
School administration	3095
Guidance and counseling	1617
Educational psychology	1419
Higher education	886
Elementary education	778
General curriculum	743
Secondary education	703
History and philosophy of education	547
Special education	555
Physical and health education	462
Science education	398
Vocational education	272
Math education	220
Business education	219
Teacher education	204
Educational measurements and statistics	203
Reading	219
Adult education	188
Social science education	187
English education	165
Audio-visual education	142
Music education	145
Education-general	126
Art education	114
Foreign language education	115
Agriculture education	91
Nursing education	81
Religious education	65
Home economics education	61
Speech education	56

SOURCE. Neville Robertson and Jack K. Sistler, *The Doctorate in Education: The Institutions* (Bloomington, Indiana: Phi Delta Kappa and The American Association of Colleges for Teacher Education, 1971), p. 27.

What would a college of education look like if it were organized according to this "principle of knowledge"? These authors have placed the analysis, implications, and suggestions together in an organizational chart (Table 2). The authors state that "it is our

Table 2
Organization of a College of Education According to the
Principle of Kinds of Knowledge

| | Academic Departments (Organized around the process of inquiry) | | | |
	1	2	3	4
Interdepartmental curriculum committees (examples: (Organized around objects of inquiry; flexible in size and number as interest and support dictate)	Analytical Educology	Empirical Educology I	Empirical Educology II	Empirical Educology III
	Department of history, philosophy, and jurisprudence of education	Department of science of education	Department of praxiology of education	Department of politics of education
Administration Adult education Career education Comparative education Counseling				
Curriculum Early childhood education Elementary education Health education Higher education				
Home economics education Instructional materials Occupational education Physical education Recreation				
Secondary education Special education Teacher education Etc.				

SOURCE. James E. Christensen et al., *A "Knowledgeable" Approach to Organizing a College of Education* (Carbondale, Illinois: College of Education, Southern Illinois University, 1973).

conclusion, after giving the matter of curriculum reorganization a good hard-headed look, that knowledge is the principle by which a college of education should be organized in order that a college can maximize its effectiveness and can elicit the best efforts from its staff" (Christensen, Fisher and King, 1973, pp. 12-13).

Personal Growth Orientation

Organization around content has several limitations. For example, whatever the content, it is generally not sequential, like mathematics, in its successive levels of logic or difficulty. Also, in more recent years the profession of teacher education has provided students with practical observational and participatory experiences simultaneous with study on the campus. In analyzing the inadequacy of organization around content, Arthurs Combs has noted that a sequential structure of courses made some sense when content was the essential matter to be dealt with. However, professional education is not a discipline in its own right, but relies upon a number of supporting disciplines for its content. Hence, no longer can the professional college be divided into such departments as educational psychology, history and philosophy of education, general and specialized methods of teaching, and student teaching. Emphasis has shifted from the content to the learner. Combs maintained that an efficient program must: (1) permit the movement of students at different speeds; (2) provide content and experience in response to student needs; (3) provide simultaneous, rather than sequential, experience for the learner; (4) place much more responsibility upon the student himself (Combs, 1965, p. 115).

If the prospective teacher is the center of the program, and if organization around subject matter and methods is no longer tenable, Combs suggests a problem-oriented, personal-growth oriented program. His suggestions for organization included a central seminar as a guidance and counseling type of "educational home" for students throughout their college attendance; classroom experiences where students use the community resources and the faculty to expose themselves to the world of ideas; a college-wide lecture series using the best local and visiting faculty; and limited group presentations. Other suggestions included special workshops, exhibits, and trips, a program of classroom observation and practice teaching, and involvement in non-school young peoples' groups, in professional affairs with local teachers' organizations, and in educational research. Combs was aware of the administrative problems involved, but maintained that it was possible to fit the peculiar talents and contributions of each faculty member into a smoothly operating team (Combs, 1965, pp. 112-30).

Another example of personal growth orientation as a rationale for the internal organization of a college of education may be seen in the areas of specialization in which the practitioners are prepared. For example, most colleges of education prepare some young people to be mathematics teachers. However, if the classification suggested by the NCATE were used, all personnel would be classified as either teachers or school service personnel. We shall be somewhat more arbitrary and classify teachers into two categories—elementary and secondary—and the areas of subject matter specialization into two categories—academic and vocational. On these bases the internal organization of a college of education could be into departments classified as follows:

1. Elementary education—Primary, kindergarten, early and later elementary.
2. Secondary education—Academic and Fine Arts

Art	Science
English	Social studies
Foreign language	Speech
Mathematics	Performing arts—music, drama

3. Secondary education—Vocational
   - Agriculture
   - Business education
   - Home economics
   - Industrial arts
   - Physical education, health, and recreation
   - Vocational education
4. School service
   - Audio-visual and library education
   - Counseling and guidance
   - Educational foundations—historical, philosophical, psychological, and sociological
   - Extension, continuing and adult education
   - Higher education
   - Psychology
   - School administration
   - Secondary education
   - Special education
   - Supervision and curriculum

Many of the areas of specialization in group 4 are graduate level fields. Every area in all four groups also has a national professional organization to which most faculty members turn for a "professional home" in their respective fields.

I stated earlier that structure—that is, the organization of a faculty into such units as departments, schools, institutes and committees—exists to facilitate the performance of function. As functions change, structures should also change. In most universities, tradition has made it difficult for an institution to alter its structure. It is quite possible that colleges of education, and perhaps other professional schools as well, have copied the liberal arts colleges and the departments of their academic disciplines in the organization of the professional subject matter in teacher education, though this may not have been the best way to proceed. The problem has become acute in teacher education because the profession is not in agreement as to what the content of professional education is or should be.

Organization for Innovation

During the sixties and early seventies more experimental programs and new ways of preparing teachers have been developed than in any other comparable period. Innovation has been the order of the day. Since 1965 the AACTE has encouraged this trend by establishing its annual program of Distinguished Achievement Awards for Excellence in Teacher Education. Almost none of these awards have been accorded institutions for innovations in the structure by which teacher education is governed and administered. It must be obvious, however, that any current or newly proposed internal organization of a college of education within a university must provide for adaptation to the changing times and increase the efficiency by which the college seeks to reach its objectives. Following, are several examples of internal reorganization suggested by using planning, programming and budgeting systems (PPBS) and competency-based teacher education (CBTE).

At the University of Alabama, Paul Orr suggested that one good way to effect change in the internal structure of the college of education was to relate programs more closely to their financing. He maintained that the procedures involved in PPBS could be useful.

Key elements in the new structure recommended by Orr included:

1. The abolition of all departments and department headships or chairmanships.

2. The creation of five areas to house all programs; each area with an Area Head, and each program with a program chairman: (Special Education, Counseling and Guidance and Vocational Education are designated in the Educational Services Area but will continue to operate separately for the present time.)

    A. Educational Administration and Higher Education
    B. Educational Services
    C. Curriculum and Instruction
    D. Foundations
    E. Health, Physical Education and Recreation

3. Area Heads are relatively permanent and have primary responsibility for budgets, scheduling and faculty load assignments, coordination and development of all programs in the area, including contracts and grants, and linking the area to other areas by serving as a member of the Executive Council of the College.

4. Programs and Program Chairmen will be subject to change as program demands and developments warrant. Program Chairmen have primary responsibility for curriculum development, improvement of instruction and serving as members of their Area's Coordination Committee.

5. The structure is the new vehicle which will be used to study further the organization of the College and to generate other developments and alternatives. Additional improvements are anticipated.

6. A phase-in process will begin with the Spring term (1971-72) and be implemented fully by 1972-73. Modified program budgeting will begin in 1972, particularly for assignment of faculty time to programs. (Orr, 1971, pp. 183-188)

Another attempt to evolve a usable structure based on the inter-disciplinary nature of teacher education was made at the University of Wisconsin at Madison. A department of continuing and vocational education was created with financing from three sources: the school of education, the school of family resources, and the college of agricultural and life sciences. It was designed to have one chairman, appointed by the three deans, who would administer six programs in continuing and vocational education. Hoped-for benefits included improved undergraduate and graduate teaching and research programs, more effective use of staff, more effective relations with the Wisconsin Vocational, Technical, and Adult Education Board, and increasing visibility of the program for potential students. It appears that the rationale for this new structure was the creation of a program oriented to the needs of students rather than the needs of administrators, or a program shaped by the logical organization of subject matter. It was to become operative with the 1974-75 budget (University of Wisconsin, 1973).

Ohio, too, has sought new designs for its teacher education programs. Hendrick Gideonse presented a paper to the Ohio Association of Colleges for Teacher Education implying that colleges of education should be organized so as to constitute an equal partner with the liberal arts constituency and the practicing profession in the field, if reforms such as PBTE were to be implemented (Gideonse, 1973).

A number of the functions of a college of education are on-going: for example, the program for the preparation of mathematics teachers. Other functions are a one-time-only type: for example, a project to upgrade the preparation of science teachers by bringing them to the campus in a summer institute. In the former, regular staff, regular curricula, and the usual budget are used to achieve the purpose. In the latter, a project manager (in the example given, the science institute director) is appointed, who in turn draws upon staff wherever they may be found (in science education or in the chemistry department), determines the curriculum with them, and finances the project with special funds (e.g., a NSF Science Institute grant). The internal structure of a college of education should be sufficiently flexible that it can accommodate such projects. (It will be recalled that Ikenberry felt that one explanation for the proliferation of institutes in higher education in the last 20 years was a lack of such flexibility.)

Performance-based teacher education is the means of preparing teachers who are capable of achieving the objectives of performance-based instruction (PBI). The interdependence of these two concepts has been noted by Robert Howsam:

> PBI in its comprehensive application also should be perceived as a complex educational system with a variety of subsystems, each of which must function if the system is to "go." It behooves those who undertake the implementation of PBI and performance-based teacher education (PBTE) to look with care at the total system required, to identify the subsystem elements, and to ensure that the critical elements are capable of delivering. Failure to do so risks both the undertaking, and in the larger sense, the movement. (Howsam, 1973, p. 213)

There is a certain similarity between PBTE and PPBS management systems. Howsam describes this similarity as follows:

Like PBTE, PPBS starts with the identification of goals and objectives. As a next step, alternative programs to achieve the objectives are formulated. Budgets are derived from the programs, using the most efficient means for achieving objectives. Programs are monitored to detect discrepancies between expected and actual outcomes, and corrective actions are taken. The impact of the approach is to ensure that programs and activities are initiated only if they are perceived as likely to work and are continued only as long as they do achieve their objectives. The bureaucratic continuance of activities and budgets, whether effective or not, is thus broken.

PPBS appears to be quite compatible with PBTE: It can be used within traditional or non-traditional structures. (Howsam, 1973, p. 215)

The problem, then, of the internal organization of a college of education is to provide both stability and flexibility. Howsam has suggested that a matrix organization might accomplish this.

Matrix organization represents a method for combining functional organization and project or program management into a single system. The organization continues its functional structure in the form of the traditional pyramid within which authority and responsibility follow the usual chain of command. This part of the system performs the continuing and stable functions, thereby bringing in the resources upon which survival depends. In addition, a project system is superimposed on the functional. Since the functional organization is essentially vertical in structure and since project organization is lateral—cutting across the traditional and drawing on a number of the functional departments for talent— the effect is a grid or matrix.

If a college of education were to be functionally organized, it would have a number of professionally specialized departments (i.e., administration, guidance, foundations, curriculum, and teaching). If it were to decide to develop a performance-based program for teacher preparation, it might establish a special program or project. A manager would be appointed and probably be directly responsible to the dean. Objectives would be established, programs developed and tested, evaluations made, and the objective of having a program on line within a fixed time frame met. In so doing PPBS would have been used. Talent would have been drawn from all or several of the departments. A special budget would have been involved. Both the on-going program and the special project would have been carried on simultaneously. (Howsam, 1973, pp. 215-216)

Howsam concludes that "it is necessary to find ways of at least modifying traditional structures if not replacing them. A matrix approach has emerged as the most promising" (Howsam, 1973, p. 218). The accompanying figure illustrates the matrix organization, which includes the existing departments but adds provision for any number of programs and projects to be operated outside of the department structure.

Figure 2.
Matrix Organizational Chart (Function and Task)

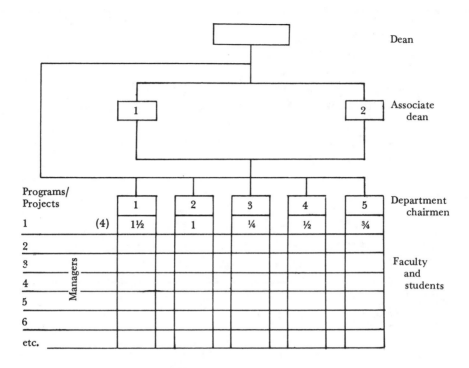

Source: Robert B. Howsam, "The Management of PBTE Programs," *Journal of Teacher Education* 24, no. 3 (Fall, 1973): 217.

Summary

In the search for a rationale for the internal organization of a professional teacher education unit in a university, several possible solutions have emerged. The unit may be organized around any of the following:

1. Areas of concentration for graduate study. (This basis would also include all areas at the undergraduate level, since the graduate level areas are more numerous.)

2. The personnel specializations required by the public schools for teachers and school service personnel.

3. Areas of specialization exemplified by national professional organizations.

4. The structure of knowledge unique to professional education and unique to the supporting disciplines: either empirical, analytical, or program oriented.

5. Classifications of teacher behavior with emphasis on problems the teacher encounters.

6. Partnership with other units of the university and the public schools.

7. Matrix organization involving both a faculty "home" and a temporary, revolving, changing structure to perform tasks as need arises.

Not until many institutions have experimented with these and other systems of organizing faculty and programs in teacher education, and evaluations have been made of such experimentation, can the profession know what systems are most productive in teacher education. It is very probable that several effective governance mechanisms will emerge in colleges of education in the near future. What is most needed at the present time is less dependence on current, traditional, rigid structures so that flexibility and experimentation can be given a chance to produce new models of governance. The best way to achieve this objective is to grant colleges of education authority commensurate with their responsibility.

XII

Politics of Control

Early in the history of American education, a system of education separate from and parallel to the system of civil government was established. State constitutions and state laws organized local school districts governed by elected local school boards, who were separate from local township, village, and city officials. The latter were expected to keep "hands off" school affairs. At the intermediate level, county superintendents of schools and usually some lay county boards were empowered to provide supervisory and administrative services to local districts—all separate from a county board of commissioners, who had civil powers and again were expected to leave school affairs alone. At the state level, the educational mechanisms usually consisted of a state board of education, a department of education, and a superintendent of public instruction or commissioner of education. All other state officials—treasurer, tax commissioner, auditor, and even the governor—were to have no part in policy formation or administration of public school education. In nearly every state this system of a three-level structure of school government parallel to and separate from civil government still prevails, although as we shall see considerable erosion has taken place.

Separation of Educational and Civil Government

The theory behind this arrangement was that the nature of education demanded that its purposes, content, and methods be nonpolitical—be completely incapable of tainting the next generation of pupils with partisan politics. This theory has long been taught in basic courses in school administration. For example, Moehlman has stated:

> The natural community organized as a school district makes possible the extension of the public school concept as a cultural clearinghouse, an impartial forum for the presentation and discussion of all points of view, and a means of reconciling social and economic differences. To meet this objective, the school district must be distinct from the partisan implications of local civil government.
>
> The maintenance of local school government independent of civil control demands budgetary independence and the direct non-partisan election of a legislative body which is held separately from civil elections.
>
> The appointment of the local education authority by the civil government invariably results in a bureaucratic and political control of the schools. This fact has been strikingly proved in New York, Chicago, St. Louis, Hoboken, and Jersey City. Even in Philadelphia, where the supposedly detached and non-partisan judges of probate appoint the board of education, members of the public schools are much too close to the city political machine. Appointment of school board members removes direct control of public education from the people to an officer or officers whose primary interest is not in education, and whose major responsibilities lie in other fields. (Moehlman, 1951, p. 81)

The justification for separation of educational government from civil government had its origin in the concept of local control as essential to a democracy. Mort maintained that political democracy demanded the exercise of control over policy or action be in the hands of the people as much as possible and that such placement should be legally assured. The strength of the principle seemed to lie in the anticipated results of close popular control of governmental enterprises. Three such results were predicted:

> 1. The system of control may be a channel for self-realization of the participants.
> 2. The system of control may contribute to safeguarding popular government at the more remote levels—state, national.
> 3. The system of control under home rule may make major contributions to the education of citizens at all levels of popular control—local, state, national. (Mort, 1946, p. 139)

Similarly, Wahlquist and his associates have explained the justification for separate governance mechanisms for education, particularly at the state level:

Some students of government have argued that education should be regarded as one of the state services, along with highways, police, and health. They have argued that it should be a part of the over-all state government, with the chief state school officer a member of what might be thought of as the governor's cabinet, much as the heads of the other departments would be. Under this arrangement, the state superintendent would, of course, preferably be an appointee of the governor. On the other hand, the idea has been developing for a long period in the United States that education must be regarded somewhat differently because of the significance which it has for the development of the people and of the state. Those accepting this point of view argue that the actual welfare of the state itself will be determined by the development of education, and that education, while encouraged and carried forward by the state, must not be in the interest of any one group which may be administering the state government at the time, nor too responsive to the administrative officers of the state. Rather they would seek a high measure of independence from state government in general for it, in order that it may stimulate the development of citizens who would achieve a state which would function in an ever improving manner. Today educators in very large part subscribe to the idea that education must, in this sense, stand apart from state government. This point of view, however, would not be accepted by a large number of political scientists or by many state administrators in departments other than education. (Wahlquist et al., 1952, p. 78)

Although education may be like other functions of government in that it makes possible through group action and group support services best provided through public rather than private efforts, it has been considered unique. Education has intrinsic features: personal growth for its recipients, the embracing of knowledge, training and aspiration, the practicing of the social arts, the promotion of the aspirations of the human race, the enrichment of life through the fine arts, and the inculcation of ethical responsibilities. In all countries and throughout all history, education has been the tool by which every society has perpetuated its system of values. It is this unique characteristic of education that led the Educational Policies Commission of the National Education Association to suggest the separation of education and civil government, a separation applying to colleges and universities no less than to local schools.

Taken in its fulness, education stands apart from the other public services, such as public works and public safety, and is distinguished by obligations of its own. It underlies and helps to sustain all public services. The schools furnish in the main the preliminary discipline upon which training for the services is based, and state universities provide technical instruction necessary for the discharge of professional duties. The schools and colleges disseminate knowledge pertaining to the sciences, arts, and crafts employed in every branch of administration. They distribute information and promote understanding respecting the services—information and understanding calculated to maintain the public support and cooperation which enable administrative division to function effectively. Education also supplies an ethical cement that helps to hold together the very civilization in which all services operate, upon which they depend for sustenance. American society could exist on some level of comfort and convenience without improved roads, electric lights, or sanitary codes; it did in the eighteenth century and at the same time demonstrated qualities of true greatness; but it cannot exist upon its present level or attain a higher level, with an illiterate and ignorant population dominated by low standards of taste, subsistence wants, and primitive concepts of life. (Beard, 1937, p. 101)

These views are not shared by many students of government. Mort and Reusser maintain that while educators have accepted education as unique and have ignored other governmental development, many political scientists have ignored the history of educational development as they seek generalizations that will apply to education along with other governmental functions. But these authors also note that even twenty-five years ago there were promising attempts by each to understand the other. "Students of school administration have been giving increasing attention to the work of the public administrators, and public administrators have sought occasionally to learn from the long experience in the education field" (Mort and Reusser, 1951, p. 22). Today, the "politics of education" has engaged the interest of many political scientists, sociologists, and professional educators. This must be understood as we view the attempts by many agencies to control one or more aspects of teacher education. Control of teacher education at the local level should be governed by the same principles of political democracy as is control of local school education. Control of teacher education by the university has the same base of academic freedom as does control of other aspects of higher education. Control of teacher education at state and national levels has the same theoretical dimension as control of all governmental functions—efficiency and economy.

But just as local education is regarded as unique by Beard and his colleagues, so too can higher education be regarded as unique. At least a word of caution must be expressed as we view the decision-making process in education as a political one. The human components of education may more properly be regarded as a family. Surely the first few grades in elementary school classrooms have long been so regarded. In secondary and higher education, however, the tendency has been to characterize the enterprise in quantitative terms and to ignore the fact that education and learning is a highly individual and uniquely human endeavor. Budgets, bureaus, sheer numbers of students, faculty, departments, buildings, and degrees hide the reality of what takes place, or ought to, between a teacher and his students. As Howard Bowen has observed, a useful analogy can be made between a college or university and a family:

> Like a college, a family is an environment in which people live, grow, and relate to one another. When we speak of efficiency for a family, we do not talk of credits earned, cost per person, ratio of parents to children, or index of space utilization. We judge the success of a family in terms of mutual affection, solidarity, helpfulness, willingness to sacrifice for one another, the aspirations and values of its members, its style of life, and the kinds of people it produces. The factors making for the success or failure of families are so subtle and intangible that they are almost indiscernible. We know a good family when we see one (though there may be differences of opinion in some cases), and we regard a good family more as a work of art than as the product of some standardized technology.
>
> From a narrow, pecuniary point of view, the typical American family is grossly inefficient. It wastes housing space. It provides specialized rooms for sleeping, eating, work, and recreation that are unused most of each day. It prepares food in inefficiently small quantities. It operates two cars that sit in the garage or on a parking lot most of the time. The mother may refrain from joining the paid labor force. It caters to the special needs of its individual members and loses many of the economies of scale. We not only condone these inefficiencies, we applaud them by calling them a high standard of living. We do make judgments as to what constitutes an acceptable minimal family income, but we regard this amount as a necessary but not sufficient condition for achieving the intangible qualities of a good family. We recognize that the performance of families cannot be measured by money alone, and that the concept of efficiency for families has little kinship with efficiency for factories or government bureaus.
>
> A college or university is very much like a family. It is a place where people are joined in common pursuits. It is designed for the personal development of people of all ages, for the preservation and advancement of learning and the arts, and directly and indirectly for the advancement of society. Production

in higher education is concerned with bringing about desired characteristics in people and facilitating scholarly endeavor. A college or university does its work through creating the right environment. The visible attributes of that environment are an aggregation of land, buildings, equipment, and supplies, and a group of people including students, faculty, staff, and governing groups. The invisible environment is the campus culture, consisting of the prevailing ways of doing things, the common values, expectations, standards, assumptions, traditions, behavioral patterns, and an ineffable quality called *atmosphere*. (Bowen, 1976, pp. 10-11)

Despite such an analogy, there is much to be said for regarding higher education as a political entity and considering its controls as subject to the methodology of political science. Anyone who has observed individuals and groups in educational settings from elementary school through the university must know that at times the nation's schools have been subjected to the spoils system, partisan squabbles, obvious struggles for power, and sensational journalism. Also, in this age of egalitarianism, with its court-promoted emphasis on the rights of minorities, great influence has been exerted by ethnic groups, the culturally deprived, the poor and unemployed, and even students. The result is an educational system that is so complex as to be almost ungovernable. Teacher education is only one of many educational responsibilities in the "ungovernable" category.

Regarding the governance of higher education and of teacher education as a political process, however, is not the same as involving the schools in politics—something that was feared by Moehlman, Beard, Mort, and Wahlquist, for the reasons noted above. The governance with which we are concerned is a dynamic, objective, political phenomenon that can be analyzed empirically.

Frederick Wirt and Michael Kirst have made such a scholarly analysis, and the following paragraphs are largely based on the first chapter of their book *Political and Social Foundations of Education.* This publication addressed two scholarly disciplines, education and political science, but was also concerned with developing "the reality of the politicalness of school policy making, which makes that institution's operations share much with other—more overtly recognized—political institutions that are also authorized to distribute resources and values in American society" (p. 3). The authors define the political act as "the struggle of men and groups to secure the authoritative support of government for their values" (p. 4).

Education as a Political System

Although the historical development noted above sketches the attempt to keep the school out of partisan politics, it cannot be concluded that schools are nonpolitical or apolitical. As Wirt and Kirst have noted, "Although elections and referenda concerning other policies were viewed as 'political,' these words did not connote 'politics' when used for educational policy. Two reasons for attempting to preserve the folklore that politics and education do not mix were the risk to the schoolmen who were overt players of politics and the relative benefits to schoolmen who preserved the image of the public schools as a unique, nonpolitical function of government" (p. 5). Although these authors maintain that the concept of schools as apolitical is a myth, they concede that the misunderstanding between educators and political scientists probably stems from differing conceptions of what constitutes a "political" act.

To begin their analysis, Wirt and Kirst employed Easton's heuristic scheme or framework for political analysis, first proposed in 1965, in developing the concepts and data around which their book was organized. Such a framework is also called systems analysis, a frame of reference we also used and described briefly in Chapter I and Chapter III. There we noted that in the systems analysis model there are three major components: input factors, throughput factors (the internal processes of operation), and output factors. Stimulants to activity are called interventions and outputs may also follow feedback loops to renew the process.

A similar simplified model of a political system was amplified by Wirt and Kirst to form the framework on which they placed their data. It was described in simple terms: "This relationship is one in which *stress* in other subsystems of the social environment generates *inputs* of *demands* and *supports* upon the *political system*, which then reduces or *converts* these inputs into public decisions or *outputs,* which in turn *feed back* allocated values into the society whence the process began" (p. 14). A brief sketch of this set of interactions is reproduced on page 228.

Among the inputs in the model are *demands* and *support*. Wirt and Kirst define *demands* as "the pressures upon the government, the requests for justice or help, for reward or recognition" (p. 15). In teacher education, *demands* have included the agitation

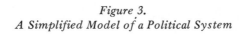

Figure 3.
A Simplified Model of a Political System

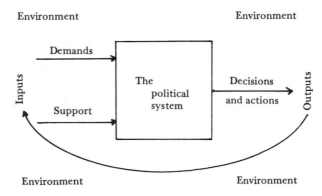

Source: David Easton, *A Systems Analysis of Political Life* (New York: Wiley, 1965), p. 32.

for specially trained teachers for the ghettos of the inner cities, the requirement by Spanish-speaking parents for Spanish-speaking teachers, and the pleas from humanists for teachers skilled in "open classroom" methods.

On the other hand, Wirt and Kirst state that *supports* "take the form of a willingness to accept the decisions of the system or the system itself." A steady flow of supports is necessary if any political system is long to maintain its legitimacy (the accepted sense that the system has the right to do what it is doing). In teacher education, *supports* would be exemplified by the university's insistence that it possess the major responsibility for the accreditation of the teacher education programs, by local school insistence on complete control of student teaching, or by liberal arts professors' insistence that they determine the content of the major for secondary school teachers.

The function of a political system is to provide a mechanism for the interaction of all these forces so that the outcome of such interaction will be socially desirable. The outcome of political activity is the "authoritative allocation of values."The process does not always stop with these outputs, because they can "generate another set of inputs to the political system through a *feedback loop.* This term designates one way in which the system copes with stress—that is, (1) dealing with stress causes a response in the system, (2) the response creates new stress, and (3) the new stress is communicated to the political authorities as a new round begins" (p. 17).

This sequence can be illustrated by a short review of the struggle between the National Education Association and the American Association of Colleges for Teacher Education for control of the accreditation process by the National Council for Accreditation of Teacher Education.

Accreditation as a political system had a fairly stable character from the founding of NCATE in 1954 until 1972, when the NEA proposed to withdraw its $45,000 annual support from NCATE operations. The reason given was insufficient NEA representation (only six members of twenty-two) on the NCATE council. Pressure was exerted on AACTE in 1971 by the NEA's espousal of "A Model Teacher Standards and Licensure Act" among its state organizations, each of which could attain certain controls over teacher education with the establishment of the state commission by the legislature. These were the interventions that removed the stability from the accreditation structure. The political process operated during the ensuing two or three years through many local and national meetings, passage of resolutions, studies and surveys, appeals to the National Commission on Accrediting (NCA), and conferences with the other constituent organizations of NCATE, namely the Council of Chief State School Officers (CCSSO), the National School Boards Association (NSBA), and the National Association of State Directors of Teacher Education and Certification (NASDTEC). Out of the process came the output—a new constitution for NCATE providing for a coordinating board of the constituent organizations whose representatives were chosen by each organization in the following numbers: AACTE, six members; NEA, six; CCSSO, one; NASDTEC, one; NSBA, one; and up to five associate members selected by the board. There were provisions for other adjustments after the constitution became effective in 1974. Thus NEA and AACTE each made one-third of the membership of the coordinating board. The council was to be composed of nineteen to twenty-four voting members from the constituent organizations with NEA and AACTE each selecting eight, the others one each at varying times. It is quite clear that the pendulum of control has swung to the side of the teachers, and NEA has agreed to contribute $51,000 to NCATE's

1973-74 budget. A new equilibrium has now been achieved—at least temporarily.

The essential elements of systems analysis on a somewhat more elaborate scale than the diagram above have been summarized by Wirt and Kirst in Figure 4. "This diagram bears a certain resemblance to a wide number of explanations of human behavior, such as tension reduction, conditioned responses, and information theory. More important, however, it offers a first approximation of a highly complex interrelationship of societal components. . . . This analytical framework presents the political system as something other than just an allocative process" (p. 17). Even so, there is great difficulty in placing within this framework the political process illustrated by my brief description of the power struggle between the NEA and AACTE. That struggle illustrates only a small part of the decision-reaching process in the governance of all the aspects of teacher education among the nineteen agencies involved in it, as will be shown in Chapter XIII.

In their book Wirt and Kirst pose the question, "How valid [is] such a general concept . . . in explaining the structure and processes of American public education in its time of increasing stress" (p. 20). We can say with confidence that, like most systems analysis models, it is useful—but that is not the same as saying it is valid. I believe its validity can be increased if the political entity can be divided into smaller, more comprehensible components. It would also be more useful if the strategies employed by individuals and groups within the system were clearly described so that they could be learned, refined, and replicated by others. Indeed, this should be our major purpose—not merely to describe but to control.

Techniques for control of the political process from input to output are sorely needed by administrators of teacher education. Their very position means they must control the wherewithal—budgets, buildings, equipment, faculty, program, associated colleagues both on and off the campus, and even the public—if teacher education is to produce the best teacher possible. They have the difficult task of reconciling all these conflicting interests, often in the face of hostility. To deal with confrontation one must anticipate the conflict but avoid assuming that all opposition must be eliminated. The ideal outcome is reconciliation and an amalgamation of the best of all ideas and proposed solutions. This is not only good political

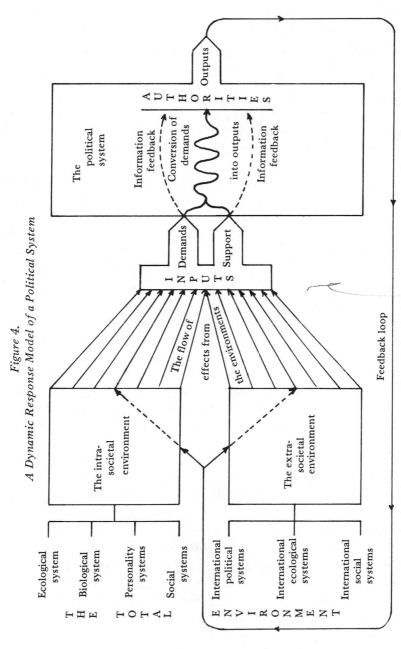

Figure 4.
A Dynamic Response Model of a Political System

Source: David Easton, *A Framework for Political Analysis* (Englewood Cliffs, N.J.: Prentice-Hall, 1965), p. 110.

strategy, it is also in the academic tradition of the search for truth—
or at least it is the best *modus operandi.*

Teacher Education as a Political System

The foregoing models by Wirt and Kirst are quite general
because they are applicable to the entire American educational
system, one of society's major institutions. One subsystem of this
institution is the professional preparation of teachers. It will be
recalled that in Chapter I we used the description of systems analysis
by Howsam as a point of departure for this book. In his brilliant
essay, Howsam described the further application of systems analysis
to the specifics of teacher education. Since that time, 1972, he has
condensed this part of his model for the recent publication by AACTE
"Educating a Profession." Because of its brevity, its importance, and
its applicability to analyzing the political aspects of the governance
of teacher education, that condensation is reproduced in its entirety
in an Appendix to this volume.

In this analysis of systems, Howsam shows that teacher education is a subsystem of the profession of education. His analysis is a
description of *structure,* whereas the analysis done by Wirt and Kirst
is a portrayal of a *process*—the political process. In his model of the
teacher education system, Howsam calls for efforts to decrease
state dominance and increase college and professional control of
teacher education. In political terms, the way for the teacher education unit to do this is to secure support from the organized teaching
profession and from its other suprasystem, the university in which it
is located. In Oregon and California, where the enactment of the
NEA's model law (with some variations) has provided for a powerful
professional practices commission, Howsam's question regarding the
desirability of decreasing the organized profession's dominance of
teacher education, with its legal power to control the institutional
program and the candidates' licensure, might profitably be raised.
If the teacher education unit and the university are to retain their
fair share of control, they will have to persuade legislatures to
provide legal definition of their proper role and responsibilities.

A number of "revolutions" have occurred in recent years that
may help teacher education to achieve such power. One such revolution is the "collaboration revolution," a term that means a

readjustment of power. The influence of money, as the NEA used it with AACTE in financing NCATE, is a powerful weapon in the acquisition of power. One explanation for the weaknesses of colleges of education is that their programs have nearly always been woefully underfinanced, especially when compared to other professional schools on a per-student cost basis. (This is a personal opinion, shared by few, but held stubbornly here.) The university will be required to share power in order to acquire the necessary funding. As William Smith has observed, "When we talk about collaboration, we now are talking about how we are going to have to share power differently. . . . A university is no longer able to sit back and say that they have the ivory tower that will allow them to sit and contemplate what is going to happen to children. For in the new power relationships, the necessary dollars will not necessarily be at that institution, and that institution is going to have to deliver services that it has not delivered before" (Smith, 1975, p. 39).

It is not my recommendation that the teacher education institution determine all policies in the governance process. I only ask that its authority to coordinate, to achieve collaboration, and to be held accountable for results be clearly assigned. To remain effective, the college of education must become political both on and off the campus. Its staff must divest itself of the notion that politics is dirty. As I have noted, that tradition of staying aloof from politics has long been prevalent not only in local public education but in work of scholars in higher education as well. Witness the reluctance of the NEA to use the strike as a political weapon before 1961 when the AFT won the election in New York City. The NEA at first called their efforts "withholding professional services," then "imposition of sanctions," a simple form of boycott. No apologies are made for teachers' strikes today. This syndrome is not being repeated in higher education, where both the NEA's Division of Higher Education and the AFT are competing for the loyalties of faculty members, while the American Association of University Professors (AAUP) remains little more than a spectator.

Structure for the Political Process

The development of changes in university-wide efforts to achieve better structure to facilitate teacher education is also a highly political endeavor. Universities differ amazingly in the units of teacher education they include and the assignment of teacher education functions to these units. The prestigious School of Education at the University of Michigan, even though it recommended 1123 persons for provisional teachers' certificates in 1973-74, had only 516 of these enrolled in the School of Education (Cohen, 1974, p. 9). One wonders how many lawyers were prepared at the University of Michigan outside its nationally reputed law school, or how many architects were graduated from schools other than the school of architecture. What is the rationale that in most institutions seems to single out teacher education from preparation of other professionals? Is it a lack of knowledge as to how to effect presumably desirable changes in the allocation of power? Or is it explained by a blindness to the use of political methods caused by the vestiges of the outdated belief that professionals must adhere to the academic tradition of acquisition of truth and use of persuasion to achieve innovations? The idea that political activity is the means to present and evaluate a variety of viewpoints so that an effective solution to a specific societal problem can be found has been well expressed by Michigan's Dean Wilbur Cohen, although his failure to mention the applicability of this idea to higher education's problem is noticeable:

> Education in a democracy is a vital matter upon which the whole principle of self-government depends. The determination of educational policy, therefore, must be sustained by the views, support, and criticism of everyone who participates in the system. We cannot expect politics to be divorced from educational policy; nor can we expect that the discussions will focus always on so-called "purely educational" concerns. Some would suggest that politics need not intrude on matters such as, for example, what subjects should be taught, how, and by whom. These people insist that mathematics or science or grammar have no political content.
>
> The political process is one of trying to reach some sort of workable agreement among various ideas. To demand that this process be eliminated from educational policymaking is to eliminate an element which is essential to improving programs: public discussion. Ellwood P. Cubberley, in his well-known *Public Education in the United States,* gives the flavor of the political context in which our schools evolved by his chapter headings referring to, "The Battle for Free State Schools," and "The Battle to Control the System." Politics usually implies a verbal "battle" of ideas.
>
> In fact, politics is and has been involved in education at every level. Local school board elections are the most political aspect of education. The well-accepted policy of "local control" of elementary and secondary schools is designed to insure that local politics remains in command of local schools.

In a society such as ours, political activity is the means used to present and evaluate a variety of viewpoints so that an effective solution can be found to a specific societal problem. An educational system must therefore be political in this sense or else it artificially limits the ways in which it serves the public. Never before in American education has the relationship between educational policy and politics been more encompassing than it is today.

Politics has clearly become important in determining educational policy at all levels of government. Some people regret this state of affairs; it does result in difficulties. I see it, however, as an opportunity for wider participation in the determination of educational goals, and this is, I believe, a truly desirable end in a free and democratic society. (Cohen, 1974, p. 11)

Of course, tradition and inertia explain in large part why universities have not organized themselves better to facilitate teacher education. What is needed is strong intervention to stimulate higher education faculties and administrators to action. Indeed, several such forms of intervention already loom menacingly on the horizon: (1) the NEA's state professional practices commissions, which, if fully empowered, will dictate the scope and nature of campus-based teacher education and will affect the liberal arts and other professional education unless they all join the battle together; (2) the determination of local schools to dictate policy for student teaching through professional negotiations with school boards; (3) the accreditation of programs by a body in which higher education has a minority voice; and (4) the demands by minority groups that teacher preparation be oriented toward their unique needs. Higher education must and will respond to these and other stimuli. What is still undetermined is the nature of that response. The purpose of this book is to provide some perspective so that the political process will result in desirable educational policy.

Illustrative Case Studies

Some perspective can be attained by a brief description of the current nature of institutional organization. Administrators and faculty members who have served on NCATE visiting teams have been acquiring a broadened view of each other's governance mechanisms and procedures, and the NCATE files contain a wealth of pertinent information. I myself have visited fourteen campuses in twelve states during the four years since this writing was undertaken.

These observational visits varied in length from a few days to a dozen weeks to two semesters, though I made little attempt at the sort of scientific research that characterized Charlesworth's effort a decade and a half earlier. But the picture, supplemented by some catalogue material, is revealing and even interesting. I shall not generalize from these case studies or extrapolate observations to other institutions, but my impressions do serve to throw some light on common problems. The states and institutions visited were as follows:

Arizona
       Arizona State University—Tempe
       University of Arizona—Tuscon
Colorado
       University of Denver—Denver
Florida
       University of Florida—Gainesville
Hawaii
       University of Hawaii—Honolulu
Illinois
       University of Illinois—Urbana-Champaign
       Southern Illinois University—Carbondale
Indiana
       Indiana University—Bloomington
Iowa
       Iowa State University—Ames
Kentucky
       University of Kentucky—Lexington
Michigan
       Western Michigan University—Kalamazoo
North Carolina
       University of North Carolina—Greensboro
North Dakota
       University of North Dakota—Grand Forks
Washington
       University of Washington—Seattle

The first question that arises is, "What are the major units having responsibilities for teacher education?" The College of Educa- at the University of Arizona contains the departments of counseling and guidance, educational administration, educational psychology, elementary education, reading, secondary education, and special education. Also in the college is a graduate library school, a rehabilitation center, and the Arizona Center for Educational Research and Development. All undergraduate students seeking teaching certificates other than vocational certificates in agriculture and in home economics and special certificates in art, music, and drama must be registered in the College of Education.

The College of Education at Arizona State University has seventeen subject fields organized in the following departments: elementary education, secondary education, educational administration and supervision, counselor education, educational psychology, special education, and educational technology and library science. Several bureaus have been established, including the University Testing Service, the Bureau of Educational Research and Services, Indian Education, Reading, Center for the Study of Higher Education, and several other laboratory facilities.

The University of Denver consists of the colleges of arts and sciences, business administration, engineering, and law. The School of Education is a part of the College of Arts and Sciences. While it is not organized into departments, the School of Education offers programs for elementary and secondary-school teachers and provides for a Bureau of Educational Research.

The College of Education at the University of Florida has departments of administration and supervision, childhood education, counselor education, foundations of education, special education, secondary education, vocational, technical and adult education and several cross-departmental general programs. Criteria used in considering students from the College of Arts and Sciences for the Teacher Education Program are the same as those used for admitting students into the College of Education.

At the University of Hawaii, the College of Education is an upper division college and a graduate professional school. It includes departments of curriculum and instruction (including industrial education), educational administration, educational communications and technology, educational foundations, educational psychology, health and physical education, special education, and field services.

The College of Education at the University of Illinois in Urbana-Champaign is composed of the departments of vocational and technical education, secondary and continuing education, special education, elementary and early childhood education, educational administration and supervision, educational psychology, higher education and history and philosophy of education. Also included is a Bureau of Educational Research and the Urbana Council on Teacher Education. In 1972-73 the faculty considered several proposals for internal reorganization.

At Southern Illinois University at Carbondale, the College of Education contains ten departments: educational administration and foundations, elementary education, guidance and educational psychology, health education, higher education, instructional materials, occupational education, physical education, secondary education, and special education. In 1974-75 this faculty also considered reorganization.

The School of Education at Indiana University is composed of four divisions: administration and administrative studies, social foundations and human behavior, instructional systems technology, and instruction and curriculum. Specific "Offices in the School of Education" include such specialties as elementary education, secondary education, art education, vocational education, English, science, social studies, mathematics, business, student teaching, speech and hearing therapy, special education, and urban education.

At Iowa State University, the College of Education, created only about a dozen years ago, encompasses elementary education, industrial education, physical education, professional studies, and secondary education. Although the College of Education recommends all candidates for teaching certificates, "each student is enrolled in the department in which he or she plans to major, and must meet the graduation requirements of that department and the college in which it is located."

At the University of Kentucky the catalogue does not list departments in the College of Education. The areas of preparation, however, are quite similar to those of other universities. College control of programs is evidenced by the following requirements: (a) certification recommendation is made by the College of Education, and all students expecting to receive teaching certificates must follow the general studies component of the College of Education; (b) students expecting to receive certificates as elementary or junior high school teachers are required to be enrolled in the College of Education; and (c) students expecting to receive certificates as senior high school teachers may be enrolled either in the College of Education or in some other but if enrolled in some other must meet the requirements of both colleges.

Western Michigan University is an example of a former single purpose teachers college that in the last quarter century has become a multi-purpose regional university. It has kept its focus on teacher education, however, by organizing a College of Education having the following departments: blind rehabilitation, counseling and personnel, directed teaching, educational leadership, physical education for men, physical education for women, special education, and teacher education, the last having several subdivisions.

The School of Education at the University of North Carolina at Greensboro offers a program in early childhood and intermediate education. According to the catalogue, the school "jointly directs, with departments in the College of Arts and Sciences, programs for secondary teacher certification in liberal arts fields. Recommendation for teaching certificates is completed through the office of the Registrar." The catalogue lists no departments for the College of Education.

The College of Education at the University of North Dakota was abolished in 1972. In that year the college consisted of the departments of business education, counseling and guidance, professional education, health, physical education, and recreation for men and women, home economics, industrial technology, and library science. The department of education was further divided into such areas of specialization as elementary education, secondary education and special education at the undergraduate level, and higher education, school administration, and teacher education at the graduate level. After July first, 1972, the college was combined with the "New School of Behavioral Studies in Education," a federally funded institute of the type described by Ikenberry. The chairmen and most faculty members in the departments other than education wanted no part of this arrangement and they formed their own unit designated as the "College for Human Resources Development." Only the department of education was left, and it was designated the "Center for Teaching and Learning." It has no departments.

At the University of Washington, the College of Education is organized into the departments of educational administration, educational curriculum and instruction, educational policy studies, educational psychology, higher education, special education, in-dependent study, research and field experiences, and a Bureau of School Services. The catalogue states that "all persons seeking certification at the University of Washington must be admitted to the Teacher Education Program. Requirements for teaching certif-icates shall be those prescribed by the College of Education at the time the certificate is to be granted."

The foregoing description of the structures for teacher education at fourteen institutions provides some basis for analysis of the political processes governing them, despite the limitations imposed by the brevity of most catalogues, which usually do not distinguish between departments (which are administrative structures) and programs (which are educational processes). Description of these institutional structures does not reveal which innovations have been developed or how they were established. We do not know, for example, the fates of the resurrected progressive-humanist approach at the University of Florida or the advisory approach to in-service training at the University of Illinois (Atkin and Raths, 1974). Perhaps these limitations partially explain why one has difficulty in determining the rationale of some of the structures. Why do some colleges of education have one department of physical educa-tion, others separate departments for men and women, and others none at all? Why aren't simple, direct names used to provide accurate descriptions? The name "Human Resources Development" does not reveal who is being prepared by what program for what career. Is not the whole university engaged in the "development of human resources?" The name "Center for Teaching and Learning" does not indicate that teachers are being prepared. Such a name could be as well applied to a college of engineering—one presumes that its faculty are teaching and its students are learning—but it would say nothing about preparing engineers. Why do several universities appear to apologize for preparing teachers, which is the attitude suggested by the fact that they permit teacher education students to enroll in many other schools and colleges on the campus instead of in the college of education only?

I suspect that one of the explanations for such irrational structures and assignment of functions is the lack of knowledge about and skill in using the political process to secure "authoritative support of government for their values" on the part of education professors and administrators. Or perhaps their values are not clear. One could at least begin to create a rational institutional structure by requiring all students in teacher education to fulfill the same requirements for recommendation for certification no matter where they are located and requiring them to fulfill the requirements of two degrees if they seek some other degree than that awarded by the College of Education. The University of Kentucky, as mentioned above, does make such a requirement.

Suggestions for Political Action

Every institution undergoes a political process in which the intensity of the interactions among the individuals and groups involved appears to be directly proportional to the strength and variation from the *status quo* of the interventions that stimulate the process. I mentioned in Chapter I the incidents that took place at the universities of Vermont, Illinois, and Montana. The national press suggested chaos and even corruption at the University of Massachusetts when many innovations in teacher education were undertaken there, but Donald Robinson found something quite different, even laudable, when he visited "the U. Mass. Mess" (Robinson, 1975). The College of Education at the University of Iowa has limped along for years with the distinction of being the only college of education in the country with no students and no graduates. Prospective teachers are enrolled in and graduate from other campus units. An analysis of the politics of internal struggles over the organization and administration of teacher education would make another book—and an interesting one.

The following summary of some of the procedures used by administrators and faculty groups to achieve their ends was derived from the experience of one of the above-named institutions.

1. Ignore the official governance structure of the university.

2. Ignore a faculty committee report that is at variance with your own proposal.

3. Suppress reports that are critical of new proposals.

4. Organize a new committee and place on it a majority favorable to the views you espouse.

5. Keep actions confidential until they are partially accomplished.

6. Issue press releases describing partial accomplishments as complete and final.

7. Overgeneralize on accomplishment of movement toward the final result.

8. Call a meeting of concerned faculty members to study a problem. If a majority of those present are on your side, rush the action through.

9. Eliminate from the decision-making process those individuals and groups known to oppose the proposed course of action.

The struggle for control of teacher education outside the university setting is also a political process and descriptions of it have in fact filled several books. That process almost defies analysis because of the large number of individuals and agencies involved, the complexity of the issues, and the vast sums of money used to achieve prescribed ends.

Edward C. Pomeroy alerted the profession to several of the more powerful outside interventions when he cited the agencies competing with higher education for the control of teacher education. Some local school administrators are proposing that teacher education be taken out of higher education and put into their schools (Spillane and Levenson, 1976). There is little doubt that the experience of student teaching in the schools contributes to competency in the classroom. But to turn over the whole teacher education program to local schools, when those schools are unable even to mount quality programs of in-service education for their own teachers and have almost no capacity to provide instruction in the supporting disciplines or the in-depth instruction required in subject-matter specializations, is to return to the apprenticeship system of the Middle Ages (Cushman and Steeves, 1976). Earlier, I noted the new laws in California and Oregon that have established teacher-dominated commissions to evaluate university programs and certify teachers. In Washington, D.C., the U.S. Office of Education is accrediting agencies, and it has recognized NCATE for only one year. These are indications, and there are many others, that control of teacher education is slipping from the hands of higher education. In the light of such indications, Pomeroy looked at some of the major issues facing teacher educators—governance, accreditation, collaboration, state and federal relations, continuing in-service education, and innovative program approaches—and concluded with the following suggestions:

1. We must test our ability to collaborate with other partners in the education enterprise, on a true parity basis.

2. We must strengthen our government relations. Let us move out into the public arenas with unified positions on governance, inservice education and other issues.

3. Let us lead in negotiations on the local and national levels.

4. Let us demonstrate our capacity to develop new programs.

5. Let us decide whether to institutionalize the inservice teacher center of the HETFIRE report, and the professional positions of the CEPT report.

6. But especially, let us guard our mutual interests together. (Pomeroy, 1975, p. 201)

From the point of view of improving the political power of AACTE, Pomeroy's suggestion for establishing strong state units may be no match for the state associations of the NEA. If state AACTE units can influence legislation by working with state education associations, higher education may retain some control over teacher education programs. But at his inauguration as Executive Secretary of the National Education Association in 1967, Sam Lambert set the tone for the new militancy of the NEA: "NEA will have more to say about how a teacher is educated, whether he should be admitted to the profession, and depending on his behavior and ability whether he should stay in the profession" (Lambert, 1967).

In the politics of control, appeals to the public must be accorded a high place. One of the problems of colleges of education is their remoteness from the citizens. University news bureaus usually carry the burden of publicity about the institution as a whole; its individual components and their accomplishments are frequently overlooked. Local schools, on the other hand, are not so isolated, because they are located among the people they serve. Colleges of education ought to learn from the many state and national organizations having public relations agencies. These vary from farm organizations, manufacturers' agencies, and labor unions to professional societies without number. Surely some use could be made of an organization such as the National Committee for Citizens in Education (NCCE), which in 1975 began a series of citizen's training institutes to help local lay leaders understand their schools better and seek greater control over the decision-making process. Each state governor was urged by NCCE to appoint a broadly representative task force "to revitalize the educational system as an accessible and responsive democratic institution" (NCCE, 1975). If the usual academic and public relations procedures do not produce results, someone may soon suggest that professors of education go on strike if professional negotiations with the Board of Higher Education fail to produce a contract that calls for enough faculty to provide at least one visit per week to every student teacher. It would be interesting to see a state's coterie of education deans wearing placards as they picket their legislature in behalf of equal representation on state professional practices commissions. The problem consists not so much of assigning more power to faculties in teacher education as of freeing them from present restraints, one of which is excessive reliance on the collegial model rather than the political model for getting things done.

In addition to their lack of political power, colleges have been faced with the public/private split, inadequate financial support in a period of declining economy, widely varying interests and capabilities among institutions, and the conceptual disarray of teacher education. Such explanations for the colleges' loss of influence led J. Myron Atkin to conclude that "the point is not that there are not good people or programs at universities, but rather that colleges of education as a group are unlikely to be influential in determining the course of their relationship with the organized profession because of lack of fundamental unity either politically or conceptually" (Atkin, 1976, p. 13).

The coordinating role played by the teacher education institution today is not the monopoly over programs exercised by the teachers colleges a half century ago or by university colleges of education in more recent times, although the latter hardly exercised a monopoly. A monopoly suggests control of general education and subject matter specialization as well as professional education—the hallmarks of a 1930's teachers college. No university ever had so autonomous a teachers college.

Summary

Believing in the principle of democracy, the American people from colonial times to the present have organized systems of government as locally based as possible consistent with reasonable economy, efficiency, and adequacy. Apparently our forebears felt that education was unique among all the services of government because it was a non-partisan, non-political, neutral search for and dissemination of truth. Accordingly, they developed a framework of governmental organization with its legislative and administrative functions separate from and parallel to the structure for civil government. Only in the judicial branch of government did the two systems overlap.

This historical development has led to the notion that educational organization and its management should be considered not just nonpolitical, but apolitical. Observation of events, however, suggests that elementary, secondary, and higher education are indeed very political, and political scientists have developed useful models to reveal the process whereby they are influenced. Using the systems analysis approach, Wirt and Kirst, Howsam, and others have clarified the ways in which it is possible to shape events so that men and groups may secure the authoritative support of government for their values.

The political process takes place within a structure. The achievements of the people and units within that structure are limited by the nature of the structure and the functions assigned to it. This is especially true in teacher education because of great differences in structure among institutions, the lack of agreement among teacher educators as to what a good teacher is and how to prepare one, and the need for the institution no matter how it is organized and empowered, to marshall appropriate resources both inside and outside itself.

This means that organizations and individuals who bear the primary responsibility for preparing the nation's educational personnel must agree on purposes and procedures and the mechanisms to achieve both if they are not to be shunted aside when vigorous proponents of other systems seek to replace them. In practical terms this means that all parts of a university must unite behind a strong teacher education unit if their authority is not to be usurped by forces outside the campus—powerful agencies on both national and local levels. It means that just as the National Education Association has been transformed from an agency designed to promote the professional competence of teachers into an agency designed primarily to protect their personal welfare, so too must the American Association of Colleges for Teacher Education be transformed from an agency to promote the professional competence of teacher educators into an agency designed to protect their personal welfare and the welfare of the institutions in which they work. And AACTE must also become just as militant.

The mechanisms are known. The purposes can be clarified. The political procedures are available for their employment. All that is needed is the will to act.

XIII

Evaluations and Models

The profession owes a great debt of gratitude to the many writers in the field of teacher education who have been conscious of the influences, real and potential, of the score or so of agencies having a stake in improving American education through better teacher preparation. The several hundred reports reviewed in this volume imply a need for objective research on the effectiveness of various patterns of control. During the last two decades, many programs have been tried and many structures for the development of new programs of teacher education have been experimented with, but frequently the justification for such changes has been simply that the proposals were new, appeared to be innovative, and therefore, *ipso facto*, must be good. Too often, programs have been new in name only.

This situation may be explained by the difficulty of evaluating the effectiveness of structures for decision-making in teacher education. The only sure way to evaluate such structures would be to determine the effect on programs of certain ways of forming policy, the effect on the teacher of the preparation he or she thus received, and the effect on the learning of the pupils in local school classrooms of what such a teacher did. The effectiveness of even the best governance policies for teacher preparation at the university might be too small to measure by the time they had filtered down to the pupils in the local classroom.

Discernible Trends

Despite these difficulties, there are some generalizations that seem to emerge from the mass of literature concerned with the governance of teacher education. The first striking fact is that there are almost two dozen agencies that have an influence in determining the nature of teacher education. About half of these are outside the university and about half of them are inside. Much of this diffusion of control mechanisms and policy-forming procedures can be explained by looking at the history of teacher education in the United States. The teaching profession has had a long struggle to achieve the status accorded other professions, and the preparation of practitioners for teaching has had a parallel struggle for status in institutions of higher learning. The development and growth of the high school level normal school, and the subsequent post-high school normal school, the teachers college, the popular land grant college, the chairs of pedagogy and later departments, schools, and colleges of education in universities were milestones on the march toward professional status for teacher education.

In large colleges and complex, multi-purpose universities teacher education has been subject to the same problems faced by the university as a whole. Especially during the sixties, higher education everywhere was under pressure: pressure from federal and state governments, who offered tempting funds to promote a governmental rather than an institutional purpose; pressure from the vast socio-economic changes taking place in American life; pressure from an increasingly tense international situation; and pressure from a new student and faculty militancy. Other difficulties arose from an almost exponential increase in knowledge, from demands by industry, business, and labor, from increasing costs, and demands from groups such as adults, women, and disadvantaged minorities who had not previously been included in the higher education process. There were pressures from other sources as well, but this list is enough to illustrate the point that teacher education, as a part of higher education, was caught up in the cross-currents of a host of problems it had never before known.

For the last twenty-five years, the profession of teacher educators and the administrators of preparation programs have become increasingly aware that they were operating under faulty governance structures. They believed that they were primarily responsible for the teachers and other school personnel they produced, but increasingly concluded that they had far too little control over many aspects of the program for which they were being held accountable. This seemed to be more true for teacher education than was the case for other professions such as law, medicine, and engineering. Professional sensitivity to this situation was evident in the reports by Evenden in 1932, McLure in 1948, Cushman in 1958, and Howsam in 1972 (see Chapter III).

During the 1950s, and to a greater degree in the 1960s, people began to raise questions about the effectiveness of their schools, particularly in the sciences, mathematics, and foreign languages, which led them to look more closely at the preparation programs that produced their teachers. This scrutiny led to a resurgence of the desire of liberal arts faculties for more emphasis on the academic disciplines in teacher preparation and to a myriad of problems in governance structures within the university. Everyone wanted a piece of the action—the college of arts and sciences, the president and his staff, the graduate school, the institutional governance structures such as senates and dean's councils, the vocational schools or departments, and student organizations. The college of education was buffeted from all sides.

But this was not all. Powerful forces outside the university also desired to influence the public schools by influencing the preparation programs for their teachers. Considerable influence was exerted by financial grants from foundations and from the federal government, by state governments through legislation and financing, by state boards of control, and by teacher certification requirements in state departments of education. The organized teaching profession increasingly demanded control of the profession by regulating the entrance to preparation programs, the nature of those programs, and the license to practice. Other outside forces included the organized professional teacher educators (represented by the American Association of Colleges for Teacher Education and its affiliates), a few knowledgeable scholars in the learned societies, and the members of the accreditation movement. The profession of teacher educators has probably led the way, however, in improving teacher education during the last twenty years. One evidence of their influence is the several hundred experimental programs and studies that have received distinguished achievement awards from the American Association of Colleges for Teacher Education. Very few of these innovations were initiated or completed by liberal arts faculties, graduate schools, state departments of education, or the teaching profession itself. Most of them were conceived and operated by professional teacher education specialists and administrators, although other groups were often involved. Many of these innovations were stimulated by foundation and federal financial support (American Association of Colleges for Teacher Education, 1965-1976).

These innovations and developments have produced several positive results. The qualities of a good teacher are being defined in behavioral terms, and programs that develop specific skills are being carefully nurtured. There is a move toward cooperative relationships between the profession of teacher educators and practicing teachers in both determining and implementing policy. Increasingly, the performance of teachers is being judged by both what they do and by what pupils learn.

A diagrammatic representation of the current teacher education governance scene is shown in Figure 5. The student enters at the feather end of the arrow, proceeds through four years of preparation, and emerges at the point of the arrow ready to teach. This model is also applicable to the preparation of school service personnel at the graduate level. The prospective superintendent, for example, would also enter at the feather end of the arrow and proceed to his specialist degree. Meanwhile, all the forces that have acted on his program from outside the university (below the arrow) and from inside the university (above the arrow) have determined the nature of his total preparation. The college of education is the inside or heart of the arrow itself. Clearly, *the major role of the college of education is to serve as a coordinating, reconciling, and arbitrating agency for all of the other governance agencies having a contribution to make to teacher education.*

Necessary Functions

The function of any college within a university, particularly a professional college, is much the same as that of the institution as

Figure 5.

A Model for the Governance of Teacher Education

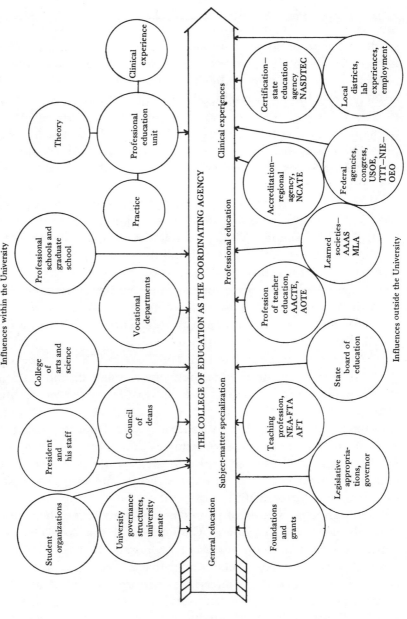

Influences within the University

Theory

Clinical experience

Professional education unit

Professional schools and graduate school

Practice

College of arts and science

Vocational departments

President and his staff

Council of deans

Student organizations

University governance structures, university senate

General education

Subject-matter specialization

THE COLLEGE OF EDUCATION AS THE COORDINATING AGENCY

Professional education

Clinical experiences

Certification—state education agency NASDTEC

Local districts, lab experiences, employment

Accreditation—regional agency, NCATE

Federal agencies, congress, USOE, TTT–NIE–OEO

Learned societies—AAAS MLA

Profession of teacher education, AACTE, AOTE

State board of education

Teaching profession, NEA-FTA AFT

Legislative appropriations, governor

Foundations and grants

Influences outside the University

a whole: teaching, research, and public service. The college of education must therefore be primarily a teaching agency. Its *raison d'être* is that students attend it—and students come first. The college must therefore either provide, or see to it that some other college or department provides, a broad basic general education—ideally, a liberal education. It must provide, or see to it that some other unit provides, the necessary subject matter specialization in both the academic and the vocational fields. Since its unique area of specialization is professional education, it must itself provide all the basic principles and theory necessary to the work of the teacher. It must provide, or see to it that some other agency provides, appropriate professional laboratory experiences. Its faculty should exemplify the principles of effective teaching embodied in its curriculum.

The second major function that the profession must perform is research. This can be of two kinds: research devoted to the problems of the public schools, and research devoted to the problems of teacher education. The former should be done by colleges of education to enable them to stay attuned to the market for their graduates. The latter should also be in the hands of teacher education programs in order to provide energy for self-renewal. Because the current state of the art in educational research leaves much to be desired, we shall devote considerable attention to it.

A survey was completed in 1967 of the 727 members of the AACTE in order to determine their involvement in and capacity for educational research. Such research was found to be limited by insufficient faculty time and a shortage of money, though the latter was ameliorated somewhat by federal grants. Only about half of the institutions studied were carrying on developmental research projects. Priorities assigned research topics by deans indicated major concern with teacher education, learning processes, and curriculum studies, in that order (Puffer, 1967).

Research on scores of problems confronting teacher education is sorely needed. The Studies Committee of the AACTE compiled a list of topics needing research, proposed them in the form of research titles, and listed them under five categories: scope, function, and objectives of teacher education; organization and administration; student personnel programs and services; curriculum and instruction; and relationships of teacher education institutions with other professional and public groups and agencies. Of the 574 suggested titles (some topics overlapped) 51 were concerned quite directly with the governance of teacher education. It is significant that this list was compiled twenty years ago, and despite all the research undertaken during these two decades it is quite probable that a similar committee could propose another five hundred topics worthy of serious investigation. From the list concerned with institutional patterns for the governance of teacher education one could suggest the following topics as needing investigation both then and now:

1. The function of institutional organization in the education of teachers.
2. Comparative patterns of institutional organization for teacher education in teachers colleges and liberal arts colleges.
3. Comparative analysis of types of institutional organization and their effect upon general faculty morale.
4. Comparative success in teacher education of a separate teachers college and a school of education in a large institution.
5. Investigation of the relationships of the school of education with the other professional schools in state universities. (AACTE, 1954)

I would suggest a number of other topics worth investigating. Charlesworth's study analyzing whether centralized controls make better teacher education programs available than do decentralized controls is worth repeating (Charlesworth, 1958). Performance-based teacher education (PBTE) should be logically subdivided and its components investigated to determine whether or not graduation from a PBTE program really contributes to more effective teaching and to more effective learning. The "alternative schools" movement needs a similar analysis. The concept of the "open classroom" also should have thorough evaluation. So much missionary zeal is exhibited by the proponents of these innovations that too few educators have thought to subject them to research that would justify more than experimental and temporary adoption. Many of the innovative programs described in the distinguished achievement awards of AACTE have not been systematically evaluated. Some of them have been periodically subjected to careful scrutiny, but the vast majority have not. One hopeful sign is the emphasis on research by the winner of the AACTE 1974 Distinguished Achievement Award, the Oregon College of Education, which made research an integral part of its CBTE program (AACTE, 1965-1976).

Conducting research about teaching and learning has long been an important function of colleges of education because they are the only agency equipped and motivated to conduct such research. The public schools do research, to be sure, but it is concerned largely with their own "in-house" problems. The National Education Association has an excellent research capability but this capacity has not generally been devoted to teacher education, particularly in recent years as the NEA has become more oriented toward unions and teacher welfare. Very little research on the problems of preparing teachers has been done by faculties in colleges of arts and sciences, although many individual faculty members have occasionally cooperated with their colleagues in education. Some research in teacher education has been stimulated by federal and foundation funds, but the colleges of education did most of the work.

There has never been a time in the history of teacher education when definitive research was more sorely needed nor when the opportunity for doing it was so clearly evident. Colleges of education in universities are in the best position to undertake such investigation as the case of PBTE illustrates. For example, Robert Travers has drawn upon ideas from social psychology and from the theater to suggest a model quite different from PBTE for teacher education. Bagley summarized this model by stating that "the teacher is seen as an international actor, not a system of molecular learnings; a minded player in human drama, not a robot carefully machined and ingeniously programmed with interchangeable modular compenents" (Travers, 1974, p. v). A hopeful sign that teacher educators are responding to this need is contained in Cyphert's analysis of eighty-three recent reports of research gathered by the ERIC Clearinghouse on Teacher Education, which showed that the amount of research done had increased over the past ten years.

The third major function to be performed in teacher education is service to society through the local schools. The value of research is greatly enhanced if its results are tested in the schools. In recent years *development* has probably had more emphasis than research, and "R and D centers" are not at all uncommon. Colleges of education have long been engaged in extension teaching, conducting in-service education for teachers and administrators, performing school surveys on such topics as design of school buildings, curriculum, finance, school administration, school district reorganization, and many others.

The final major function of the college of education is to

coordinate resources inside and outside the institution in order to develop unified, coherent, and rich teacher education programs for a wide variety of students preparing for a wide variety of positions. As noted above, there are eight agencies within the university and ten agencies outside the university with important contributions to make. During the sixties, influenced by NCATE accreditation standards and guidelines, many institutions developed an "all university teacher-education committee." Some of these committees were advisory and some were policy-making, but most exemplified the all-university approach to the governance of teacher education. There was considerable confusion about their roles. Some interpreted the concept of "teacher education as an all-university function" to be synonymous with "teacher education as an all-university responsibility." It was not and should not be an all-university responsibility. Responsibility rests with the colleges of education, and they should be held accountable to the public schools, their pupils, and society in general for the performance of their graduates. In many instances, however, the colleges could not be held responsible because they had insufficient control over the coordinating function. In the final analysis, though, only as the college can act as the final arbitrator of all the forces impinging on teacher education can it be held accountable to its suprasystem, the overall teaching profession.

The Future

Scattered throughout the literature on teacher education and its controls are numerous questions concerning the effectiveness and future viability of colleges of education as integral parts of universities. There are those who suspect they may have served their purpose well but that the time for them has gone. Several critics maintain that colleges of education are going the way of the single-purpose teachers colleges of 1920-50. It will be recalled that Woodring thought that the teachers college had disappeared when he observed these institutions taking on new functions and new names during this period, forgetting that they continued to produce many thousands of teachers then and now (Woodring, 1963). Colleges of education, like all social institutions, will survive only if they serve a useful social purpose.

Using PBTE as a vehicle for speculation concerning the future,

Harry S. Broudy has stated that the NEA, imitating the unions, will try teacher education centered in local schools, and it will largely fail. State departments of education will also try to center teacher education in state capitals but will ultimately not certify teachers on the basis of behavioral objectives and acceptable performance. Schools of education will not turn out replacements for two and one-half million teachers on a really professional basis because the public is not willing to pay the required cost. (By a really professional basis Broudy meant general education for two college years, followed by three years of professional work including subject matter specialization, learning and teaching theory, and practicum and internships with the awarding of the bachelor's and then the master's degrees.) Colleges of education in a university setting might conceivably turn out 15 percent of the required total of such teachers and persuade local districts and the unions to hire them. Let other schools produce the other 85 percent, most of whom would be paraprofessionals (Broudy, 1973).

A somewhat more optimistic view of the future of teacher education, at least in Canada, was presented by S. C. T. Clark and H. T. Coutts. Their study used the Delphi technique to determine the degree of consensus on the future of teacher education among a panel comprised of forty chief administrative officers in Canadian English-language teacher education institutions. Panelists were given a list of projective statements and asked at what date they thought each statement would be descriptive of teacher education. A large majority judged that the most probable date when teacher education would be the responsibility of universities, or university-related institutions, was 1975. Between 80 and 89 percent believed that "never (but certainly not before the year 2000) will institutions devoted to the preparation of teachers disappear." Between 70 and 79 percent believed that "by 1980 teachers and teachers' organizations will share control of teacher education about equally with teacher education institutions in determining the overall goals of teacher education." Between 60 to 69 percent agreed that "by 1980 teachers and teachers' organizations will share control of teacher education about equally with teacher education institutions in recruitment and selection of candidates." There was a similar consensus on the notion that "teachers and teachers' organizations will share control of teacher education about equally with teacher education institutions (a) by 1990 in determining the curriculum and procedures used in teacher education institutions and (b) by 1980 in determining which candidates have successfully completed the program and warrant certification" (Clark and Coutts, 1971). It would be interesting to find out if a replication of this study in the United States would produce similar results.

With some fascination, Seymour Lemeshaw permitted himself to dream a bit on the future prospects of teacher education. Regarding colleges and resources of higher education, as he looked back from the year 2015 he saw

the designations, "teachers college," "school of education" and other identifying stigmata dropped fifty years earlier as the result of pressures of those who were prepared to negate the worth of the discipline of education will once again be re-established. An enhanced professional self-image and status will emerge. The intensity and depth of teacher education will render the status of institutions comparable to that of the schools of medicine fifty years earlier and to that of contemporary schools of space engineering. Unlike the practice of 1965, educational and curriculum leadership will be drawn from those qualified to lead. Such qualifications will be based on professional education in a bonafide school of education and not on merits earned in related sciences and arts. Not only will it be respectable for professionally trained educators to look to other professionally trained educators for leadership; it will be incumbent on them to do so. (Lemeshaw, 1965, p. 230)

In making similar projections for the future organization of teacher education, Robert N. Bush looked briefly at the changes that have occurred during the last decade in education as a whole in order to discern the future shape of teacher education. He recommended development of a "special school for teacher education," which was to be "an individual school that is part of a local school system. . . . This major unit in teacher education, the 'Special School,' is made up of several major partners: the school system, the community of the school site, one or more institutions of higher education, members of the professions who are in local, state and national professional associations, state government and federal government. Each will have an authentic and vigorous voice in the enterprise" (Bush, 1975, p. 149).

Bush left unanswered the question of who would be designated to coordinate this complex and to preside over the agency that would develop policies for its governance. The answer has been suggested by Atkin and Raths, who predicted that while there will be continuing pressures to shift the locus of responsibility to either local school districts or to the organized profession or to both, and while legislatures and the courts will influence the system, it is unlikely as far as organization of teacher education is concerned that these pressures will do more than increase the number of cooperative relationships among teacher education institutions, local education authorities, and units of the organized profession. While it is true that local authorities and the organized profession have begun experimenting with teacher centers (somewhat after the British model) as focal points for inservice teacher education, it is likely that even continuing education never will be separated completely from universities. Rather, existing colleges of education will likely share in the total effort cooperatively with the new groups demanding a larger role. The results, as past practice and present trends portend, probably will be non-uniform and diffuse. (Atkin and Raths, 1974, p. 7)

Model Development

If colleges of education are to survive in the twenty-first century, as Lemeshaw, Clark, and Coutts imply they will, their structure, functions, and authorities must be more clearly defined than is now the case. Their relationships and responsibilities to the internal governance mechanisms of the university must be specifically set forth. The ways by which they relate to all those agencies outside the university must also be clearly delineated. In short, what is needed is a very clear model.

There is a difference between a model college of education and a college of education model. The former implies an example worthy of emulation, something approaching the ideal. The latter suggests a form, a system, an organization in which the parts are organized into appropriate relationships with each other, in which the processes have meaning and logic. It is the latter with which we are here concerned. Such a model must be complete, reflect an operational reality, be understandable, encourage analysis, and encourage feedback (Le Baron and Klatt, 1971). A college of education model having these characteristics would have the energy for internal self renewal. Such a model must be capable of meshing with the present system, particularly with the realities of institutions of higher education, and also be capable of simultaneously responding and looking forward to a changing society, while not losing track of the identity of the teacher in the process (Le Baron, 1969).

A model for a college of education must be derived from the

teacher preparation program it is meant to implement. This is axiomatic. Several teacher preparation models have already been reported. In their 1967 study, John R. Verduin, Jr., and his associates developed several aspects of a program model (Verduin, 1967). J. Zeb Wright's suggested models for revising teacher education took into account the total professional education of teachers and was divided into four quadrants: the learner, quest areas, teaching-learning ecology, and the profession (Wright, 1971).

Some characteristics of a viable model for a college of education have been suggested by Ralph Tyler:

A college of education cannot, and should not, try to assume the total university responsibility for helping professionals and laymen understand what is going on in the important enterprise of education. The college can, however, be the antenna of the university in finding crucial problems and can encourage university scholars to collaborate in solving them. Much emphasis in this paper is placed upon gaining a better picture of educational situations and problems because the rapid changes in our society are creating the need for new educational tasks. Two major functions for a college of education are 1) to bring the relevant scholarship of the university to bear on the practices and problems of education, and 2) to play a major role in the preparation of educational personnel. Four areas which could benefit from systematic studies by groups of university scholars are 1) dissatisfaction about the education of teachers brought about by confusion over the rapid changes in social conditions, curriculum outlines, and the characteristics of teacher recruitees; 2) a need for involving a variety of university scholars; 3) the learning students require for acquiring and using appropriately the knowledge, skills, and emotional responses, and controls representing the important resources of a given subject; and 4) the kinds of constructive roles available for teachers. (Tyler, 1971)

One of the characteristics of a college of education is that it should have scholars on its faculty, professors who could extend the boundaries of knowledge about education as well as scholars in the supporting disciplines.

But we need scholars of educational practice as much as we need those whose preparations have been closely related to basic disciplines. Scholars of educational practice are concerned with curriculum, administration, counseling, and higher education; they may have strength in a particular discipline, such as social psychology or philosophy, but they should also have sensitivity about an institution or a body of practice within an institution. Frequently their studies deal with these educational phenomena, but such studies should not ignore relevant knowledge in related disciplines. These students of practice will probably become the necessary link between the. disciplinary scholar and those who actually teach and administer the schools. (Campbell, 1968, p. 500)

If colleges of education are not to become obsolete they must have viable self-renewal mechanisms built into their governance structure. In effect, this is what Tyler and Campbell were pleading for. The need for self-renewal is also evident in the experience of several thousand institutes noted in Chapter II. The lesson to be learned from these structures is that if an existing structure is capable of doing a project for which an independent, semi-autonomous institute is being considered, then assign the project to the existing structure. If it is not capable, or if its capability is questioned, then before a separate institute is created, the existing structure should be given the opportunity to make whatever modifications are necessary. Only after this has been done can the organization of a separate institute be justified.

A college of education model ought to have several characteristics required by the definition of what a model is from the general concepts of systems analysis. A system must have objectives or purposes; it must have some kind of internal action, some processes; and it must have some internal mechanisms, or components. Other corollary attributes or subsystems include inputs, energizing forces, products, and feedback. A college of education model would therefore include objectives for the college; it would include processes by which the people in it could work to achieve its purposes; and it would include components, that is, some internal organization by which people in it could operate in order to develop the final product which, in this case, is the development of governance policy for teacher education. Other desirable characteristics of a model were suggested by Donald Haefele when he derived some lessons from the Comprehensive Elementary Teacher Education Models (CETEM). These include completeness, operational reality, understandability, encouragement of analysis, and encouragement of feedback (Haefele, 1971, pp. 95-100).

Any model must also account for interventions. All of the agencies inside and outside the university that must be coordinated in teacher education are, in one sense, interventions. They are change agents, and they have a heavy impact on the college of education. Changes in all the activities of a college of education are almost inevitable when student organizations, university governance structures, the institution's administration, other colleges and departments, and the relevant supporting disciplines have all had their say. Innovation in the program of a college of education is also almost inevitable when outside funding sources, the organized teaching profession, governmental supports and constraints, learned societies, and the profession of teacher educators have all had their impact on that college. Such multiple interventions in the system should assure the continued viability of the college.

A model must also have feedback. The college of education will receive feedback by evaluating its graduates, as required by accreditation standards. It will receive feedback from other units within the university. It will receive feedback in no uncertain terms from the practitioners in the teaching profession. It will receive feedback from the local communities that employ its graduates, and it will get feedback as no other component of the teacher education process can—from its own research.

In short, if the college of education is the authorized coordinator of all the forces concerned with teacher education, it will inevitably be subject to so much intervention and get so much feedback that no one need have misgivings about a balance between stability and innovation in teacher education.

Every institution will have to develop its own model for its college of education. The faculty of the teacher education unit will have to define its objectives, determine its internal organization, and develop its own policy for the governance of teacher education. There may very well be some common elements in its structure irrespective of the institutional locale, but a comprehensive college of education should be organized and administered so it is able to prepare every kind of teacher, elementary and secondary, and every kind of school service specialist needed by the public schools. Its structure should include all the potential contributors to the teacher education program from inside and from outside the university as set forth in Figure 5. It should either contain these units or control the units' contribution to teacher education. It should derive its legal power from the state. In short, the comprehensive college of education should contain the elements which Edgar H. Schein says should characterize all professional schools:

We have defined some elements of what may be regarded as a utopian concept—a professional school organized around modules which integrate basic, applied, and skill components; run by an innovative, largely part-time faculty who are expert in learning theory, teamwork, and interpersonal skills; administered flexibly with heavy involvement from students, faculty, and future employers; constantly evaluating itself, its output, and the effectiveness of the profession itself through perpetual self-diagnosis and evaluation research. Such a school should at least be tried out—if it has the characteristics we have specified, it can easily go back to some version of the old system. It is our conviction that in a rapidly changing, turbulent world, it will be the adaptive type of system such as we have described that will be both the cheapest and the most effective way of educating tomorrow's professionals. (Schein, 1972, p. 149)

Required Action

Schein's description of the professional school of the future appears to lodge the final decision-making role with the professional school. The growing militance of classroom teachers and the need to base more of the teacher's preparation in the field have led to demands by the National Education Association for a greater voice in the governance process. The NEA does not and cannot speak for the entire teaching profession because it does not represent too many important constituencies—the school administrators, the American Federation of Teachers with its several hundred thousand members, and most of the professionals in higher education. As a result, the subsystem of teacher education specialists has moved in the direction of suggesting a partnership to control the development of educational policy. That is the gist of a recent report by the Higher Education Task Force on Improvement and Reform in American Education (HETFIRE), sponsored jointly by the AACTE and the USOE:

The Task Force's conception of educational improvement grows out of three basic assertions: that educational improvement can come about only through accelerated reform; that this reform can come about only through significant changes in teacher education; and that these changes can be effected only through a real partnership of all those concerned.

Focusing thus on the preparation of education personnel, the Task Force describes in its report those important structures and processes in governance, management and operation, staffing, curriculum, and financing of education personnel development programs.

To provide a matrix in which to deal with these various dimensions, the Task Force created and utilizes the construct "Personnel Development Center," which it defines as a complex of persons working together in the interest of teacher education. The Personnel Development Center is not to be construed as a new place, but as a new set of interrelationships among people that would operate in an existing or combination of existing locations. The Task Force believes that partnership as effected in Personnel Development Centers, and manifested in different ways in various activities, is a key element in teacher education. . . .

In this new cooperative framework, education personnel development programs are a lifelong process beginning at the time an individual starts to become a teacher and continuing until he retires from the profession. These programs are characterized by the integration of practice and theory in teaching and learning; by the development of measurable performance and instruction; by experiences and learning in school-related areas such as the community and its social agencies, the business world and politics; and by the application and continuous assessment of research findings as conditions of professional competency. In short, the Task Force believes that neither higher education nor the public schools alone can train teachers effectively. (Denemark and Yff, 1974, pp. 39-40)

The notion that governance can be and should be a cooperative venture among the constituent groups having an interest in teacher education and a contribution to make to it has gained considerable attention in very recent years. The HETFIRE Task Force is a good example. A report on alternative models for the cooperative governance of teacher education programs by a dean's committee reviewed the characteristics of bureaucratic governance, collaborative governance, and systems analysis in governance. The report was clarified by the inclusion of twenty figures illustrating the various possibilities of both the process and the product which could be developed by cooperative procedures among university personnel, local school personnel, the public, and other constituencies. Despite their tendency to over-generalize from the responses to a questionnaire by a dozen deans, Edgar Sagan and Barbara Smith have provided many useful suggestions for a faculty to follow in developing its own governance objectives, processes, and mechanisms. Their summary follows.

The implementation of a new teacher education system and restructured governance model is a complex experience requiring the integration of a number of techniques and resources. If the proposed organization is to resemble a predetermined model, and if its attainment is to proceed in an orderly and scheduled manner, many of the planning and project management procedures discussed previously will need to be utilized. It is hoped that this discussion will stimulate further thinking, planning, and action relative to the programs and governance of teacher preparation. Planners will have to determine the needs of prospective participating groups, develop objectives for the new system, establish timetables for accomplishment of planning and organizing activities, accommodate the needs and autonomy of the different groups, and monitor the progress of the planning and organizing activities. Participants may have to make significant financial commitments, provide personnel for the planning tasks, and make adjustments to compensate for the time these planners are away from their administrative or teaching duties.

Many approaches to the revision of the governance of teacher education programs tend to be so general that it is difficult to conceptualize the practical implications of what is being proposed. Educators will talk about the desirability of teacher education graduates being free from racial prejudice, sensitive to the needs of children from non-mainstream cultures, and competent in subject matter and classroom management. However, there is very little agreement on how specific changes in governance and program can accomplish these ends. Perhaps by suggesting some concrete models and guidelines, this paper can help educators work toward operationalizing some of their good thoughts and intentions, in order to produce the best possible teachers for the nation's schools. (Sagan and Smith, 1973, pp. 87-88)

Both of these reports raise several serious questions. What does sociology say about group behavior in these situations? Is it possible to have a *troika*? (It didn't last very long in the Soviet Union.) Is there a similarity between policy formation in education and policy formation in industry? A corporation is able to proceed, to get its work done, and to reach decisions precisely because everyone knows who owns 51 percent of the stock. Is it possible to bring "warring factions" together by the sheer force of leadership? Until more colleges of education have developed new models of governance for teacher education and subjected these processes to objective research we shall not know much about the effectiveness of such models in helping pupils in classrooms reach their educational potential.

Several reports provide guidelines for institutions showing how they might move toward the future with deliberation and planning rather than by drifting—or by having structure and governance mechanisms and power imposed by forces from outside the college of education and even from outside the university.

Although we would like the governance of higher education to be explained by the collegial model, the reality of what happens is better explained by the bureaucratic model and best explained by the political model. Hence faculties and administrators of teacher education programs must use the political devices used by other groups to acquire or retain control over the teacher education programs for whose success they are held responsible. Such devices include stacked committees, organized student support, alumni contributions, widespread journalistic publicity, assistance by the state department of education, consortia with other institutions, old-fashioned horse trading, cooperative relationships with other professional schools, and many other procedures—some too devious to mention.

Institutions might bring about innovations by developing a clearcut statement of mission. Colleges of education should enable an institution to develop and fulfill its mission by having a supporting one of their own. The single-purpose teachers colleges of the 1920s and 1930s had such a mission, and it gave them status in the eyes of the public and the profession at a time when such prestige was very much needed. This mission might even be expanded to become a "saga," as described by Burton R. Clark in his analysis of the distinctive character of Antioch, Reed, and Swarthmore colleges (Clark, 1970 and 1971). Clark has observed that on the large campus, especially if that campus is to become an administratable political system encompassing factions of divergent beliefs, solutions to problems of governance must tend basically in one of two directions: first, toward acceptance of the general nature of the system and an attempt to devise the best machinery for the formal representation of factions and the formal resolution of conflicts; or second, toward more unified self-belief and a reduction rather than an explication and formalization of factions; that is, toward centralization. At this point I would urge colleges of education to take the second alternative, to enlist support through the dean, faculty, students, and alumni, to build pride in the college, to be autonomous, and to exemplify the fact that a true university is a unified collection of semi-autonomous, self-governing colleges. A strong college of education possessing a "saga" will be an invaluable aid to the university in achieving its broader social purposes.

Several proposals have been made showing how the structure of college and university governance might be modified. John J. Corson has suggested that one broad goal is to place authority where the required competency exists. Noting the diminution of power and authority in the president and the board of trustees in recent years, he suggested that their leadership must be strengthened if the college or university is to remain a viable institution. At the same time he advised that those who are given authority to make decisions be required to consult continuously with those affected by the decisions (Corson, 1971). If the real nature of a college presidency is that of a political leader, then the real nature of the deanship is also that of a political leader.

This notion is further amplified by Haberman, who developed a brief checklist for evaluating deans as a guide to assessment of leadership in schools of education. (This list might also be used to evaluate department chairmen and other administrative officers.) The checklist includes evaluation of the administrator's capacity for decision-making, communication, relationships with the faculty, his professional values and his effectiveness as a change agent (Haberman, 1972). More detailed suggestions for developing models for the governance of teacher education, with emphasis on cooperative structures, have been proposed to colleges of education by Sagan and Smith (Sagan and Smith, 1973).

Attributes of the Good Professional Life

When one summarizes all that must be done to prepare professional personnel for the nation's schools, whether such efforts are in teaching, supervising clinical experiences, conducting research, extending service to the public and to the teachers in service, or creating a collegial atmosphere so that such services are possible, one must conclude that if colleges of education did not exist, it would be necessary to create them. One must also conclude that such a college would have to possess the following seven attributes if it were to perform its service to the institution of which it is a part and to the public which it serves and which in the final analysis sustains it:

1. A distinct and unified *faculty*
2. A *program* of teacher education developed cooperatively by all constituents
3. A centralized *locale*, or building, to encourage interaction among faculty and students
4. A body of *students* registered in, advised by, and graduating from the college

5. A *degree* that it alone awards to all graduates of the university who become qualified for service in the schools

6. A *budget* that it alone controls

7. A *dean* who serves it by exemplary leadership made possible by the requisite assignment of authority.

Of these seven attributes, the most important is the faculty. I have recommended that all professional education faculty members have an academic or vocational subject matter specialization equivalent to the competency required for teaching at least freshman and sophomore level courses in these subjects in any university. Many such teacher educators now have such preparation and most have had experience teaching their subjects in the public schools. Although such a group of faculty members should constitute the core of the professional education personnel, they should be supplemented by other specialists as the "mission" of the college requires, probably on a part-time basis, as suggested by Schein. Such a faculty serving teacher education in a college having the seven attributes noted above could be trusted to discharge the teacher education function of any university. There are enough outstanding colleges of education in the National Association of State Universities and Land Grant Colleges, in the American Association of State Colleges and Universities, in many municipal universities, and in many of the large privately endowed universities to assure the American people that they and their schools have been better served than is generally appreciated. The paths they have lighted are clear for others to follow.

It is about time teacher education ceased to be the whipping boy for all the weaknesses of the public schools and for the ills of society in general. It is time for the top echelon of university administrators to accord the same managerial autonomy to their colleges of education that they accord to their other professional schools. It is time for all those who have only a peripheral interest in teacher education to accept the reduced role to which they are entitled in determining programs. It is time for all concerned to realize that teacher education involves a planned, unified program of liberal education, subject matter specialization, professional theory, and practice that builds requisite competencies, not just any four-year degree with a few courses in education tacked on as an afterthought. It is time to broaden the concept of what a college of education can become. It is time to eliminate teacher education from an institution of whatever type—public, private, liberal arts, junior college, or municipal—that can provide only a two- or three-man department of education. It is about as ridiculous for an institution to prepare, at best, only a few elementary or secondary teachers as it would be for a dental school to train dentists who can only extract teeth or a medical school to train physicians who can only treat broken bones.

A truly comprehensive college of education should provide a program and a faculty capable of preparing almost any specialized teaching and school service personnel needed by the public schools from pre-school levels to college. The areas of staff specialization and the number of faculty members needed to implement them might be as shown in Table 3.

What is important here is not the suggestion that a modern college of education should have a faculty of 114 members. What is important is the method of arriving at the appropriate number: (1) decide what personnel the schools should employ; (2) propose the educational program needed to prepare such personnel; and (3) determine the number of faculty members required to produce such a program.

Some critics may retort that it is dangerous to propose so specific a program. But note several modifying factors. Only land grant institutions possessing a college of agriculture could produce agriculture teachers. Many of the personnel listed in Table 3 would be supplied by the public schools. Many would be supplied, if qualified, by other colleges and departments on the campus. Most of the faculty members in elementary and secondary education would be specialists in the teaching of their subjects and would not be expected to provide depth and breadth of subject matter specialization. Most of them would supervise the student teachers in their fields and would change positions with teachers in the local schools in order to become the "clinical professors" envisioned by Conant. Subjects might be combined: counseling and guidance with psychological foundations and educational psychology, for example. Every college of education can become comprehensive only by using its current faculty resources, and it can be said with some assurance that a truly comprehensive college of education should have a minimum of at least one hundred faculty members. Such a comprehensive college could also prepare educational personnel for

Table 3.
Suggested Faculty for a Comprehensive College of Education

UNDERGRADUATE		GRADUATE	
Elementary Education		School administration (including principals and supervisors)	7
Specialty	*Number of Faculty*		
Early childhood education	3	Counseling and guidance	5
Reading and language arts	3	Educational psychology	2
Mathematics	3	Educational foundations (historical, sociological, philosophical, political, psychological, anthropological and economic)	7
Social studies	3		
Sciences	3		
Student teaching	4		
Total	**19**	Special education (speech and hearing, psychological handicaps, physical handicaps)	6
Secondary Education			
Mathematics	2	Research methodology	2
English (literature and composition)	3	Higher education	7
		Teacher education	2
Sciences (life, physical and earth)	3	Adult education	1
Speech and dramatics	2	Media (library and audio-visual aids)	5
Social studies (economics, history, political science, etc.)	3	**Total**	**44**
Foreign languages (French, German, Spanish)	3		
Health, physical education, and recreation (men and women)	4		
Home economics education	2		
Industrial arts education	2	**Administrative Staff**	
Agricultural education	2		
Business education	3	Dean, associate dean and assistant dean	3
Music education	2	Department chairmen	8
Art education	1		
Student teaching	8	**Total**	**11**
Total	**40**	**GRAND TOTAL**	**114**

professions related to teaching but not requiring teacher certification. It is estimated that nearly half the colleges of education in the National Association of State Universities and Land Grant Colleges now provide programs of preparation for several careers in which education is a strong component but which do not lead to teacher certification. Several institutions have a "College of Education and Human Resources" to encompass this broadened concept. New York University is probably the most comprehensive institution. In 1975 it completed its first year under an administrative structure entitled

"School of Education, Health, Nursing, and Arts Professions" (NYU *Quarterly*, Fall, 1975).

Let this view of a broadened concept of what a college of education should be not be construed as a conservative one. It is in fact a liberal view, if the word "liberal" means forward-looking, new, constructive, progressive, innovative, and truly free. It is the direction toward which the best two hundred colleges of education have been moving, despite many obstacles, for the last twenty years. The conservative view, in contrast, would hold that colleges of education should be subservient rather than independent, that they should be governed by the university's administrative hierarchy rather than by their own faculty, that they should surrender the control of their clinical practice to others, and that they should take orders from the governors of an overarching and nebulous profession instead of standing on their own. The progressive view assumes that there is probably as much wisdom concerning how teachers should be prepared to be found among those on university campuses who have devoted a lifetime to the business as resides in Washington.

The broadened, comprehensive college should have the necessary adaptability and innovative foresight to develop new practices with promise, to discard the old as it becomes obsolete, and acquire a balance between the two so as not to become overly conservative on the one hand or to jump on every bandwagon labeled "innovation" on the other. With practices tempered by research and with roots planted firmly in the realities of practice in the schools, such a balance is possible.

One cannot be assured that colleges of education will be continued; they are, after all, human institutions. Fred Harcleroad reminds us that on September 18, 1936, Abbot Lawrence adjourned the meeting of the Harvard tercentenary until September 18, 2036, with the following words:

> If I read history aright, human institutions have rarely been killed while they retain vitality. They commit suicide or die from lack of vigor, and then the adversary comes and buries them. So long as an institution is conducive to human welfare, so long as the university gives to youth strong active methods of life, so long as its scholarship does not degenerate into pedantry, nothing can prevent its going on to greater prosperity. (Harcleroad et al., 1969, p. 117)

To paraphrase some of Lawrence's concluding words, we would

note that the colleges of education in the institutions of this country have a rare opportunity in the next decade to go on to "greater prosperity" providing they are "conducive to human welfare," aware of and responsive to the needs of the society, and giving to our youth the "strong, active methods of life."

The American colleges and universities exemplify much of what mankind must regard as the good life. All who teach and learn in them are engaged in two of mankind's noblest aspirations—to work for people and to work with ideas. There are few human endeavors more challenging, and as John Masefield has said, there are few earthly things more beautiful than a university. *What one would wish for a university he should wish no less for a college of education whose responsibility is to prepare teachers whose pupils will in the future sustain them both.*

Appendix

A Conceptual Framework for Analysis
of Collaborative Efforts in Governance

An Analysis and a Model

In the following model, the simple notions of suprasystem, system, and subsystem are used. In systems terms, everything is composed of parts. If the

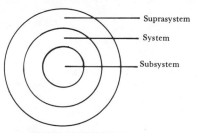

LEVELS OF SYSTEMS

object is called the system, then its parts are subsystems of it. The object, however, is a part of a larger system which is its suprasystem.

The model also makes use of a concept of accountability as it relates to systems. Two concepts are used, namely, *accountability* and *responsiveness*.

Note: This appendix, written by Robert B. Howsam, originally appeared in *Educating a Profession: The Report of the Bicentennial Commission on Education for the Profession of Teaching of the AACTE*. It is reprinted by permission of the AACTE.

1. *Accountability* is to the suprasystem only. It is never to another element or subsystem of the same suprasystem. It is never to a subsystem. A child (subsystem) is accountable to his father and mother (larger system) but not to a brother or sister (other subsystems of the same larger system).

2. A system must be *responsive* to other systems in its environment to which it relates. Though the children in a family are not accountable to each other, they are expected to be considerate of or responsive to the others' situation or need.

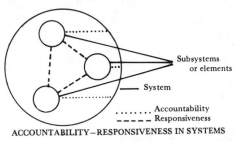

ACCOUNTABILITY—RESPONSIVENESS IN SYSTEMS

The Teacher Education System

Education is a complex system serving society by providing learning opportunities. The system is made up of many parts, each of which is itself a system.

Teacher education in this report is held to be the preparation arm of the teaching profession.

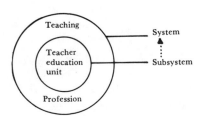

As such, it is a subsystem of the teaching profession, and so it is accountable to the profession for what it does. Additionally, it is subject to control by the profession. Systems can be simultaneously elements or subsystems of more than one suprasystem. A child is a member of a family social system but at the same time may play with a

group of other children, be in a
school class, and play ball with
a team.

Teacher education is a unit of
a college or university which is
also its suprasystem. By changing
the shape of the suprasystems the
drawings can be combined to
show the two suprasystems of
teacher education.

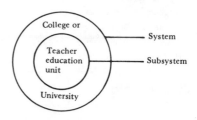

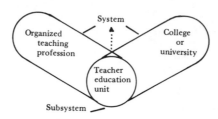

Here teacher education is shown as responsible for a teacher program and
accountable to both the university and the teaching profession. This is a representation of how the governance of teacher education ideally should be. However, at the present time, the state unit of government exercises the dominant
role in controlling what goes on in teacher education.

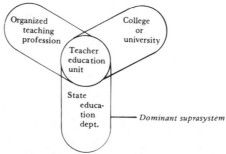

In accordance with principles of professionalization, every effort should
be made to decrease state dominance and increase college and professional
control of teacher education.

The Public School System

As was indicated earlier
in this discussion, education
is a function of the state;
and school systems are
created by and accountable
to the state.

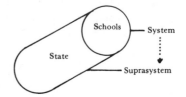

States have, however, delegated substantial control of the schools to the local education authority.

Once again there are two major partners.

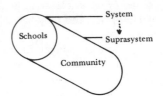

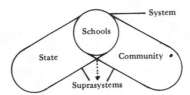

The Larger Education System

It will be observed that there now are two sets of system-suprasystem, both of which are part of the larger education system.

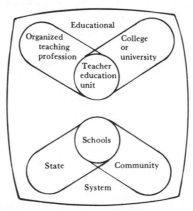

EDUCATIONAL SYSTEM

The teacher preparation system and the public school system, each with its own function, exist side by side within the larger educational system. Each is accountable to the larger system; they are not accountable to each other. Since they live together within a larger system and since they have necessary relationships with each other, they need to be *responsive*. This is to say that they must consider each other as they act. They will both do better if they act together. Thus a collaborative relationship is indicated.

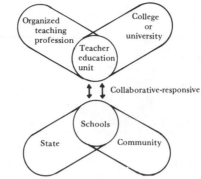

COLLABORATIVE-RESPONSIVE RELATIONSHIP

It should be observed that there are six partners in the operation of a teacher center:
1. Teacher education unit
2. The schools
3. The teacher organization(s)
4. The university outside the teacher education unit
5. The school board and the community
6. The state or intermediate agency of the state

TEACHER CENTER PARTNERSHIP

Teacher centers are governance mechanisms; they are not places. They can, however, establish places where teacher education takes place. These too are called Teacher Centers or Teachers Centers (National Education Association). In such centers, an array of preservice, inservice, and continuing education can take place as each of the major partners assumes responsibilities that fall within its jurisdiction.

Bibliography

Adair, Thelma, et al. "School-University Teacher Education Center." *The National Elementary School Principal* 46, no. 4 (February, 1967): 6-13. (ED-033-060)

American Academy of Arts and Sciences. *A First Report: The Assembly on University Goals and Governance.* Washington, D.C.: The Academy, 1971.*

American Association of Colleges for Teacher Education. *Excellence in Teacher Education: The Distinguished Achievement Awards Program.* Washington, D.C.: The Association, 1965-1976.

——. *Liberal Arts Colleges and Teacher Education.* Washington, D.C.: The Association, 1963.*

——. *Power and Decision-Making in Teacher Education, Yearbook 1971.* Washington, D.C.: The Association, 1971.

——, Committee on Studies and Standards. *Needed Research in Teacher Education.* Washington, D.C.: The Association, 1954.*

——, Special Study Commission. *Crisis in Teacher Education: A Dynamic Response to AACTE's Future Role.* Washington, D.C.: The Association, January, 1971.*

American Association of Teachers Colleges. *Yearbook.* Oneonta, N.Y.: The Association, 1922.*

American Association of University Professors. *Statement on Government of*

Note. Entries followed by an asterisk are supplemental readings.

Colleges and Universities. In *A.A.U.P. Bulletin*, Winter, 1966. Washington, D.C.: The Association, 1966.

American Council on Education. *The Improvement of Teacher Education.* A final report of the Commission on Teacher Education. Washington, D.C.: The American Council on Education, 1946.*

Armstrong, W. Earl, Hollis, Ernest V., and Davis, Helen B. *The College and Teacher Education.* Prepared for the Commission on Teacher Education. Washington, D.C.: The American Council on Education, 1944.*

Atkin, J. Myron. "Colleges of Education and the Organized Teaching Profession: A Troubled Relationship." *New York University Education Quarterly* 7, no. 4 (Summer, 1976): 8-13.

Atkin, J. Myron, and Raths, James D. "Changing Patterns of Teacher Education in the United States." A report prepared for the Directorate for Scientific Affairs: Organization for Economic Cooperation and Development. Urbana-Champaign: University of Illinois, 1974. (Mimeographed)

Axelrod, Joseph. "New Patterns of Internal Organization." In *Emerging Patterns in American Higher Education*, ed. Logan Wilson. Washington, D.C.: The American Council on Education, 1965.*

Ayers, Archie R., and Russell, John H. *Internal Structure, Organization and Administration of Institutions of Higher Education.* Bulletin 1962, no. 9, U.S. Office of Education. Washington, D.C.: Government Printing Office, 1962.

Bail, Milo. "Summary of a Questionnaire Survey of Teacher Education in Multi-Purpose Institutions." Omaha, Nebraska: University of Omaha, 1958. (Mimeographed)*

Bailey, Steven K. "Teachers' Centers: A British First." *Phi Delta Kappan* 53, no. 3 (November, 1971): 146-149.

Bain, Helen. "Self-Governance Must Come First, Then Accountability." *Phi Delta Kappan* 51, no. 8 (April, 1970): 413.

Baldridge, J. Victor. (ed.) *Academic Governance: Research on Institutional Politics and Decision-Making.* Berkeley, California: McCutchan Publishing Corp., 1971.

Banghart, Frank W. *Educational Systems Analysis.* New York: MacMillan Co., 1969.

Battle, J.A. "What is the Task of A College of Education?" *The Journal of Teacher Education* 12, no. 2 (Fall, 1961): 362-365.*

Beard, Charles A. *The Unique Function of Education in American Democracy.* Washington, D.C.: Educational Policies Commission, National Education Association, 1937.

Becker, James. *Accountability.* Washington, D.C.: National Education Association, 1972.

Beggs, Walter K. "Teacher Education in a Multi-Purpose State University." Lecture given at the University of North Dakota, July 16, 1970. Grand Forks, North Dakota: College of Education, 1970. (Mimeographed)

Behling, Herman E., Jr. *Toward a Partnership in Teacher Education.* Denver Colorado: Improving State Leadership in Education, 1970. (Mimeographed)

Bigelow, Donald N. (ed.) *The Liberal Arts and Teacher Education: A Confrontation.* Lincoln: University of Nebraska Press, 1971.

Bigelow, Karl W. "The Control of Teacher Education in the United States." *The International Review of Education* 1, no. 3 (1955): 289-299.*

Blau, Peter M., and Margulies, Rebecca Z. "Preliminary report on *A Study of American Professional Schools.*" New York: Columbia University, Comparative Organization Research Program, 1973. (Mimeographed)*

Blocker, Clyde E., and Hastings, Chester. *The Informal Organization in a State College.* Austin, Texas: Texas College of Education, 1964.*

——. *The Liberal and Technical in Teacher Education.* New York: Teachers College Press, Columbia University, 1956.*

——. (ed.) *Teacher Education in America: A Documentary History.* New York: Teachers College Press, 1965.

——. "History of Teacher Education." In *Encyclopedia of Education*, ed. Lee C. Deighton. New York: Macmillan Co. and The Free Press, 1971. Vol. 9, pp. 71-79.

Bowen, Howard R. "Where Numbers Fail." In *Individualizing the System: Current Issues in Higher Education*, ed. D. W. Vermilye. San Francisco: Jossey-Bass, 1976. Pp. 8-17.

Bowman, James, et al. *Of Education and Human Community.* Lincoln, Nebraska: Nebraska Curriculum Development Center, University of Nebraska, 1972.

Broudy, Harry S. "The Future of Colleges of Education." Interview with the author, April 25, 1973.

——. *The Real World of Public Schools.* New York: Harcourt, Brace, Jovanovich, 1972.

Brown, Leiba. *Educational Research and the Liberal Arts.* New York: Bureau of Applied Social Research, Columbia University, 1966. (Mimeographed) (ED-011-055)

Brubacher, John S., and Rudy, Willis. *Higher Education in Transition: A History of American Colleges and Universities, 1636-1976.* Rev. ed. New York: Harper and Row, 1968.

Bulger, Paul. *Education as a Profession.* Washington, D.C.: ERIC Clearinghouse on Teacher Education, 1972. (ED-059-148)*

Bush, Robert N. "Teacher Education for the Future: Focus upon an Entire School." *Journal of Teacher Education* 26, no. 2 (Summer, 1975): 148-149.

Butts, R. Freeman. *A Cultural History of Western Education.* 2d ed. New York: McGraw-Hill, 1955.

Campbell, Roald F. "The Professional School of Education and Its Relevance." *Journal of Teacher Education* 19, no. 4 (Winter, 1968): 499-506.

Carnegie Commission on Higher Education. *College Graduates and Jobs.* Hightstown, New Jersey: McGraw-Hill, 1973. (a)*

——. *Governance of Higher Education.* New York: McGraw-Hill, 1973. (b)*

Cartter, Allan M. *The Role and Function of the National Commission on Accrediting.* Washington, D.C.: National Commission on Accrediting, 1966.

Cartwright, William H. "The Liberal Arts College and the Preparation of Teachers." *Journal of Teacher Education* 18, no. 1, (Spring, 1957): 104-108.*

Case, Charles W. "The University Reorganizes for Human Services." Burlington, Vermont: The University of Vermont, 1972. (Mimeographed)

Case, Charles W., and Olson, Paul A. (eds.) *The Future: Create or Inherit.* Lincoln, Nebraska: Nebraska Curriculum Development Center, University of Nebraska, 1974.*

Charlesworth, George H. "The Relationship Between Varying Degrees of Centralized Control and Organizational Patterns for Selected Aspects of Teacher Education in Multiple Purpose Institutions." Ph.D. diss., The George Washington University, 1958.

Christensen, James E., Fisher, James E., and King, John E. "A 'Knowledgeable' Approach to Organizing a College of Education." Carbondale, Illinois: College of Education, Southern Illinois University, 1973. (Mimeographed)

Clark, Burton R. "Belief and Loyalty in College Organization." *Journal of Higher Education* 42, no. 6 (June, 1971): 499-515.

——. "The Making of An Organizational Saga." In *The Distinctive College*, ch. 10. Chicago: Aldine Publishing Co. 1970. Pp. 233-262.

Clark, S. C. T., and Coutts, H. T. *The Future of Teacher Education.* 1971. Edmondton, Alberta: Faculty of Education, University of Alberta (ED-054-065)

Cohen, Wilbur J. "Reflections on our Fiftieth Anniversary." *The Innovator* 3, no. 6 (December, 1971). Ann Arbor, Michigan: The University of Michigan School of Education.

——. "Report to the President of the University for the Year 1973-74." *The Innovator* 6, no. 5 (December, 1974). Ann Arbor, Michigan: The University of Michigan School of Education.

Cole, Luella. *A History of Education: Socrates to Montessori.* New York: Rinehart and Co., 1950.

Collins, Evan R. "Intra-Guild Renewals: Examples and their Principles." In *To Be A Phoenix: The Education Professoriate*, ed. James Steve Counelis. Bloomington, Indiana: Phi Delta Kappa, Inc., 1969. Pp. 77-89.

——. *The Impossible Imperatives: Power, Authority and Decision-Making in Teacher Education.* The twelfth Charles W. Hunt Lecture. Washington, D.C.: The American Association of Colleges for Teacher Education, 1971.

Collins, James F. *Identifying New and Emerging Patterns of School-University Partnerships in Teacher Education and Implications for Research.* Syracuse, New York: School of Education, Syracuse University, 1970. (ED-042-692)

——. "Teacher Centers: State of the Art." *Update*, Spring, 1972. Syracuse, New York: School of Education, Syracuse University. Pp. 1-2.

Combs, Arthur W. *The Professional Education of Teachers.* Boston: Allyn and Bacon, Inc., 1965.

Commager, Henry Steele. "Our Schools Have Kept Us Free." *Life*, October 16, 1950.

Commission on University Governance. *Departmental Governance: Interim Report.* Durham, N.C.: Duke University, May 29, 1970. (ED-041-553)

Conant, James B. "The Certification of Teachers: The Restricted State-Approved Program Approach." In *A Decade of Thought on Teacher*

Education: The Charles W. Hunt Lectures. Washington: The American Association of Colleges for Teacher Education, 1969.

——— . *The Education of American Teachers.* New York: McGraw-Hill, 1963.

Corson, John J. *Governance of Colleges and Universities.* New York: McGraw-Hill, 1960.

——— . *The Governance of Colleges and Universities: Modernizing Structure and Processes.* Rev. ed. New York: McGraw-Hill, 1975.*

——— . "New Developments in Governance." In *New Teaching, New Learning.* Ed. G. Kerry Smith. San Francisco: Jossey-Bass, 1971. Pp. 179-185.

Cottrell, Donald P. "A Review of J. R. Mayor's *Accreditation in Teacher Education: Its Influence on Higher Education.*" *Journal of Teacher Education* 16, no 3 (September, 1965): 366-369.*

——— . *National Policy for the Improvement of the Quality of Teacher Education.* A statement by the National Association of Colleges and Schools of Education in State Universities and Land-Grant Colleges. Washington, D.C.: The American Association of Colleges for Teacher Education, 1970. (a)

——— . *Selected Bibliography on the Accreditation of Teacher Education.* Washington, D.C.: ERIC Clearinghouse on Teacher Education, 1970. (b) (ED-036-467)*

——— . (ed.) *Teacher Education for a Free People.* Washington, D.C.: The American Association of Colleges for Teacher Education, 1956.

Counts, George S. "What is a School of Education?" *Teachers College Record* 30 (1929): 647-655.*

Cremin, Lawrence A. "The Heritage of American Teacher Education" (part I). *Journal of Teacher Education* 4, no. 2 (June, 1953): 163-170. (a)*

——— . "The Heritage of American Teacher Education" (part II). *Journal of Teacher Education* 4, no. 3 (September, 1953): 246-250. (b)*

Cubberley, Ellwood P. *Public Education in the United States.* Rev. ed. Boston: Houghton Mifflin Co. 1947.*

——— . *Readings in Public Education in the United States.* Boston: Houghton Mifflin Co. 1934.*

Cushman, M. L. "Organization and Administration of Teacher Education." In *The Education of Teachers: New Perspectives.* Washington, D.C.: National Education Association, 1958.

——— , and Steeves, Frank. "In Defense of the Comprehensive College of Education." *Phi Delta Kappan* 57, no. 10 (June 1976): 684-688.

Cyphert, Frederick R. "An Analysis of Research in Teacher Education." *Journal of Teacher Education* 23 (Summer, 1972): 145-151.

Darland, D. D. "The Profession's Quest for Responsibility and Accountability." In *Unfinished Business of the Teaching Profession in the 1970s,* ed. T. M. Stinnett. Bloomington, Indiana: Phi Delta Kappa, Inc., 1971.

Davies, Don. *The Education Professions, Annual Report.* A report for the U.S. Office of Education. Washington, D.C.: Government Printing Office, 1970. (OE-58032-70)

Davies, Don. "The Relevance of Accountability." Address before the Dean's

Conference on Teacher Education, sponsored by the University of Minnesota College of Education, 1969. Minneapolis, Minn.: College of Education, University of Minnesota, 1969. (Mimeographed)* (ED-036-479)

Dehner, W. Joseph, Jr. "Creative Tension and Home Rule." In *New Teaching, New Learning: Current Issues in Higher Education, 1971*, ed. G. Kerry Smith, San Francisco: Jossey-Bass, 1971. Pp. 156-162.

Deighton, Lee C. "Federal Education Activities, Summary by Agencies." *The Encyclopedia of Education*, ed. Lee C. Deighton. New York: Macmillan Co. and The Free Press, 1971. Vol. 3, pp. 523-544.

Denemark, George W. "Goals for Teacher Education: A Time for Decision." In *Time for Decision in Teacher Education*. AACTE yearbook, 1973. Washington, D.C.: The American Association of Colleges for Teacher Education, 1973. Pp. 1-13.

——, and Yff, Joost. *Obligation for Reform*. Final report of the Higher Education Task Force on Improvement and Reform in American Education. Washington, D.C.: The American Association of Colleges for Teacher Education, 1974.

Department of Health, Education, and Welfare, USOE. *Progress of Public Education in the United States of America 1963-64*. Washington, D.C.: U.S. Office of Education. Superintendent of Documents. Catalogue No. FS 5.210: 10005-64-A. (ED-019-304)

Dershimer, Richard, and Bloland, Harland. "Associations, Educational." *The Encyclopedia of Education*, ed. Lee C. Deighton. New York: Macmillan Co. and The Free Press, 1971. Vol. 1, pp. 364-369.

Dibden, Arthur J. (ed.) *The Academic Deanship in American Colleges and Universities*. Carbondale, Illinois: Southern Illinois University Press, 1968.*

Dickey, Frank C., and Miller, Jerry W. *A Current Perspective on Accreditation*. Washington, D.C.: The American Association for Higher Education, 1972.

Dill, David. *Case Studies in University Governance*. Washington, D.C. The National Association of State Universities and Land Grant Colleges, 1971.*

Edelfelt, Roy. (ed.) *Innovative Programs in Student Teaching*. Report of a conference held at Baltimore, Maryland, October 21-23, 1968. Baltimore, Maryland: Maryland State Department of Education, 1969. (a)

——. *Redesigning the Education Profession*. Washington, D.C.: The National Education Association, 1969. (b)

——. *Remaking the World of the Career Teacher*. The record of the teacher education and professional standards regional conferences, 1965-66. Washington, D.C.: The National Education Association, 1966.

——. "The Reform of Education and Teacher Education: A Complex Task." *Journal of Teacher Education* 23, no. 2 (Summer, 1972): 117-125.

Elam, Stanley. (ed.) *Improving Teacher Education in the United States*. Bloomington, Indiana: Phi Delta Kappa, Inc., 1967.

——. "Oregon Teachers Take Control of Teacher Preparation, and Licensing." *Phi Delta Kappan* 55, no. 9 (May, 1974): 646.

Epstein, Leon D. *Governing the University*. San Francisco, Ca.: Jossey-Bass, 1974.*

Evenden, E. S. *National Survey of the Education of Teachers.* Bulletin, 1933, no. 10. Washington, D.C.: U.S. Office of Education, 1933.

Ewing, John C., and Stickler, W. Hugh. "Progress in the Development of Higher Education as a Field of Professional Graduate Study and Research." *Journal of Teacher Education* 15, no. 4 (December, 1964): 397-403.*

Fasold, Jesse. *Educational Personnel Development: A Planning Statement.* Salem, Oregon: Department of Public Instruction, 1974.*

Feaster, E. K. "Analysis of Responses to an Inquiry into the Organization, Administration, Scope and Functions of Colleges, Schools, Divisions and Departments of Education in Representative Land-Grant Universities." Morgantown, West Virginia, 1956. (Mimeographed)

Ford Foundation. *Decade of Experiment: The Fund for the Advancement of Education, 1951-1961.* New York: The Fund for the Advancement of Education, 1961.

Foundation Center, Columbia University. *Foundation Directory: American Foundations and Their Fields.* New York: Columbia University Press, 1971.

Full, Harold. (ed.) *Controversy in American Education.* Part 4, "The Profession and the Teacher: Complacency and Confusion." New York: Macmillan Co., 1972. Pp. 253-373.

Gallup, George H. "Fourth Annual Gallup Poll of Public Attitudes Toward Education." *Phi Delta Kappan* 45, no. 1 (September, 1972): 33-46.

Gideonse, Hendrick D. "Redesigning Teacher Education." Unpublished paper. Cincinnati, Ohio: College of Education and Home Economics, University of Cincinnati, 1973.

Gould, John W. *The Academic Deanship.* New York: Teachers College Press, 1964.

Government of the University: The Study of Education at Stanford. Report to the University. The Steering Committee, Herbert L. Packer, Chairman. Palo Alto, California: Stanford University, 1969. (ED-032-851)*

Haberman, Martin. "Evaluating Deans: A Guide to Assessment of Leadership in Schools of Education." *Journal of Teacher Education* 23, no. 2 (Summer, 1972): 126-128.*

Haefele, Donald. *Systems and Modeling: Self-Renewal Approaches to Teacher Education.* Washington, D.C.: The American Association of Colleges for Teacher Education 1971.

Hansen, John H. "Status of Teacher Education in Land-Grant Institutions." *Journal of Teacher Education* 17, no. 2 (Summer, 1966): 210-217.

Harcleroad, Fred F., Sagen, H. Bradley, and Molen, C. Theodore, Jr. *The Developing State Colleges and Universities: Historical Background, Current Status, and Future Plans.* Iowa City, Iowa: The American College Testing Program, 1969.

Harper, Charles A. *A Century of Public Teacher Education.* Trenton, New Jersey: State Teachers College (for the American Association of Teachers Colleges), 1939.

Haskew, Laurence D. *Renewal of the Administration for Education.* West Lafayette, Indiana: Kappa Delta Pi, 1965.*

Hazard, William R. (ed.) *The Clinical Professorship in Teacher Education.* Evanston, Illinois: Northwestern University Press, 1967.*

Henderson, Kenneth B., and Brown, Edward. "Student Participation in Determining College Policy." *Journal of Teacher Education* 1, no. 4 (December 1950): 299-301.

Hodenfeld, G. K., and Stinnett, T. M. *The Education of Teachers.* Englewood Cliffs, New Jersey: Prentice-Hall, 1961.

Hodgkinson, Harold L. "Governance and Factions—Who Decides Who Decides?" *The Research Reporter* 3, no. 3, 1968. Berkeley, California: University of California, Center for Research and Development in Higher Education. (ED-025-208)

——, and Meeth, Richard. (eds.) *Power and Authority: Transformation of Campus Governance.* San Francisco: Jossey-Bass, 1971.

Howsam, Robert B. "Management of PBTE Programs." *Journal of Teacher Education* 24, no. 3 (Fall, 1973): 213-220.

——. "Teacher Education and Systems." In *Systems and Modeling: Self-Renewal Approaches to Teacher Education*, ed. Donald Haefele. Washington, D.C.: The American Association of Colleges for Teacher Education, 1971. Pp. 11-18.

——. *The Governance of Teacher Education.* Washington, D.C.: ERIC Clearinghouse on Teacher Education, 1972. (ED-062-270)

——, et al. *Educating a Profession.* Report of the Bicentennial Commission on Education for the Profession of Teaching. Washington, D.C.: The American Association of Colleges for Teacher Education, 1976.

Hubbell, Leigh G. *The Development of University Departments of Education.* Washington, D.C.: Catholic University Press, 1924.*

Humphrey, Betty J., and Elford, George. "ETS-AACTE Pilot Study: Teacher Ratings of Knowledge Objectives of Undergraduate Teacher Education." Princeton, New Jersey: Educational Testing Service, 1975. (Mimeographed)

Hunt, Charles W. "Toward a Profession of Teaching." In *Teacher Education for a Free People*, ed. Donald P. Cottrell. Oneonta, New York: The American Association of Colleges for Teacher Education, 1956, Pp. 18-25.

Hutson, P. W. "Who Shall Control the Content?" *Journal of Teacher Education* 11, no. 4 (December, 1960): 479-482.*

Ikenberry, Stanley O. *A Profile of Proliferating Institutes: A Study of Selected Characteristics of Institutes and Centers in 51 Land-Grant Universities.* Report no. 6, Center for the Study of Higher Education. University Park, Pennsylvania: The Pennsylvania State University, 1970.

——. "Restructuring College and University Organization and Governance: An Introduction." *Journal of Higher Education* 42, no. 6 (June, 1971): 421-429.

——. *Roles and Structures for Participation in Higher Education Governance: A Rationale.* Report no. 5. University Park, Pennsylvania: Center for the Study of Higher Education, 1970. (ED-045-023)*

——, and Friedman, Renee C. *Beyond Academic Departments: The Story of Institutes and Centers.* San Francisco, Ca. Jossey-Bass, 1972.

Isenberg, Robert. *The Community School and the Intermediate Unit.* Yearbook of the Department of Rural Education. Washington, D.C.: The National Education Association, 1954.

Joyce, Bruce R., and Weil, Marsha. *Concepts of Teacher Centers.* Washington, D.C.: ERIC Clearinghouse on Teacher Education, 1973.*

Keeton, Morris. "The Disenfranchised on Campus." G. Kerry Smith (ed.) *The Troubled Campus.* San Francisco, Ca.: Jossey-Bass, 1970. (a)*

———. *Shared Authority on Campus.* Washington, D.C.: American Association for Higher Education, 1970. (b)*

———. "Symposium on the Conant Report." *Journal of Teacher Education* 15, no. 1 (March, 1964): 11-15.*

King, Edgar A. "Can Professional Education Survive in the Traditional Liberal Arts College?" *Journal of Teacher Education* 20, no. 1 (Spring, 1969): 15-16.*

King, James H., and Ellis, Joseph R. "A Survey of the Characteristics Judged to Contribute to the Ineffectiveness of College Teacher Educators." *Journal of Teacher Education* 23, no. 3 (Fall, 1971): 331-334.

Kirst, Michael W. *Issues in Governance for Performance-Based Teacher Education.* Washington, D.C.: American Association of Colleges for Teacher Education, October, 1973.*

———. "The Future Federal Role in Education: Parties, Candidates, and the 1976 Elections." *Phi Delta Kappan* 58, no. 2 (October, 1976): 155-158.

Knight, Edgar W. *Education in the United States.* 3d ed. Boston: Ginn and Company, 1951.

Koerner, James D. *The Miseducation of American Teachers.* Baltimore, Maryland: Penguin Books, 1963.*

———. *Who Controls American Education?* Boston: Beacon Press, 1968.*

Koontz, David E., and Flaherty, Joseph E. *The Legitimate Role of the Professions in Teacher Preparation.* Washington, D.C.: The National Education Association, 1970.

Krug, Edward A. *Salient Dates in American Education, 1635-1964.* New York: Harper and Row, 1964.

Ladd, Edward T. *Sources of Tension in School-University Collaboration.* Atlanta, Georgia: Urban Laboratory in Education, 1969. (ED-031-434)

La Grone, Herbert F. *A Proposal for the Revision of the Pre-Service Professional Component of a Program of Teacher Education.* Washington, D.C.: The American Association of Colleges for Teacher Education, 1964.*

Lambert, Sam. *Inaugural Speech, October 20, 1967.* Washington, D.C.: The National Education Association, 1967.

Landini, Richard G. "The Future Structure of the University." Intra-campus Memorandum. Missoula, Montana: The University of Montana, 1973. (Mimeographed)

Larson, Rolf W. *Accreditation Problems and the Promise of P.B.T.E.* Washington, D.C.: The American Association of Colleges for Teacher Education and ERIC Clearinghouse on Teacher Education, 1974.

Lasher, William F. "Academic Governance in University Professional Schools."

The Innovator 7, no. 4 (December, 1975): 11-12. Ann Arbor: School of Education, University of Michigan.*

Le Baron, Walt. *A Systems Approach to the Organization of Teacher Training Experiences.* Santa Monica, California: Systems Development Corporation, 1969. (ED-035-587)

——, and Klatt, Judith. "A Scenario of Models, Systems Analyses, and Learning Systems." In *Systems and Modeling: Self-Renewal in Teacher Education.* Washington, D.C.: The American Association of Colleges for Teacher Education, 1971.

Lee, Edwin Augustus. *The Development of Professional Programs in Education.* New York, 1925.*

Lee, Eugene C., and Bowen, Frank M. *The Multi-Campus University: A Study of Academic Governance.* A Report of the Carnegie Commission on Higher Education. New York: McGraw-Hill, 1973.

Lemeshaw, Seymour. "Teacher Education in 2015: A Projected Outline." *Journal of Teacher Education* 16, no. 2 (June, 1965): 229-231.

Lierheimer, Alvin P. "Give Up the Ship: A New Basis for State Certification." *English Record* 20, no. 1 (October, 1969): 64-70. (ED-035-646)

Lindsey, Margaret. "Accreditation of Teacher Education." *Time for Decision in Teacher Education, AACTE Yearbook 1973.* Washington, D.C.: The American Association of Colleges for Teacher Education, 1973. Pp. 29-37.

Lucky, G. W. A. *The Professional Training of Secondary School Teachers in the United States.* New York: Macmillan, 1903.*

Maaske, Roben J., Wright, Wendell W., and Cottrell, Donald P. "The Role of Administration in Teacher Education." Ch. 10 in *Teacher Education for a Free People* ed. Donald P. Cottrell. Washington, D.C.: The American Association of Colleges for Teacher Education, 1956.*

Maddox, Kathryn (ed.) *In West Virginia It Is Working.* Washington, D.C.: The American Association of Colleges for Teacher Education, 1972.

Margulies, Rebecca Zames. "A Study of American Professional Schools: Preliminary Report." New York: Comparative Organization Research Program, Columbia University, 1973. (Mimeographed)*

Marian, Bert. "How to Research the Power Structure of your University or College." Lincoln, Nebraska: Nebraska Curriculum Development Center, University of Nebraska. 1974. (Mimeographed)*

Masoner, Paul H. *An Imperative: A National Policy for Teacher Education.* An address presented at the sixteenth annual convention of the International Reading Association, Atlantic City, April 22, 1971. Washington, D.C.: American Association of Colleges for Teacher Education, 1972.

Massanari, Karl (ed.) *Evaluative Criteria for Accrediting Teacher Education, A Source Book on Selected Issues.* Washington, D.C.: The American Association of Colleges for Teacher Education (Evaluative Criteria Study Committee), 1967.*

Mathieson, Moira. "What Do They Mean by Parity?" *Journal of Teacher Education* 23, no. 4 (Winter, 1972): 500-507.*

Maul, Ray C. *Accreditation of Teacher Education by NCATE: A Survey of Opinions Commissioned by the Coordinating Board of the National Council for Teacher Education.* Washington, D.C.: The American Association of Colleges for Teacher Education, 1969.

Mayhew, Lewis B. "Comment." *Journal of Higher Education* 42, no. 6 (June, 1971): 495-498.

Mayhew, Lewis B., and Ford, Patrick F. *Reform in Graduate and Professional Education.* San Francisco, Ca.: Jossey-Bass, 1974.*

Mayor, John R. *Accreditation in Teacher Education: Its Influence on Higher Education.* Washington, D.C.: National Commission on Accrediting, 1965.

McConnell, Thomas R. *The Redistribution of Power in Higher Education: Changing Patterns in Internal Governance.* Berkeley, California: University of California, Center for Research and Development in Higher Education, 1971. (ED-048-842)*

McKenzie, William R. "Elements of Graduate Organization in Ten Universities." Carbondale, Illinois: Southern Illinois University, Graduate School and College of Education, 1965. (Mimeographed)

McLure, John R. "Organization and Administration of the Teacher Education Institution." In *The Education of Teachers as Viewed by the Profession.* Washington, D.C.: The National Education Association, 1948.

McPhie, Walter E., and Kinney, Lucien B. "Professional Autonomy in Education." *Journal of Teacher Education* 10, no. 3 (September, 1959): 285-290.*

Miedl, George Thomas. "Relationship Between Organizational Control Structure for Teacher Education and Institutional Practice in Texas Colleges and Universities." Ph.D. diss., University of Texas, 1964-65.*

Miller, G. Tyler. "College Organization for Teacher Education." In *Eighth Yearbook.* Oneonta, New York: American Association of Colleges for Teacher Education, 1955. Pp. 60-70.

Millett, John D. *Decision-Making and Administration in Higher Education.* Kent, Ohio: Kent State University Press, 1968.

——. *The Academic Community.* New York: McGraw-Hill, 1962.

——. *An Outline of Concepts of Organization, Operation and Administration for Colleges and Universities.* Washington, D.C.: Management Division, Academy for Educational Development, Inc., February, 1974.*

Moehlman, Arthur B. *School Administration: Its Development, Principles, and Function in the United States.* Boston: Houghton Mifflin, 1951.

Morphet, Edgar L., and Ryan, Charles O. "Designing Education for the Future: An Eight-State Project." In *The Educational Program,* ed. Clifford F. S. Bebell. 1362 Lincoln Street, Denver, Colorado, 1967.

Mort, Paul R. *Principles of School Administration: A Synthesis of Basic Concepts.* New York: McGraw-Hill, 1951.

——, and Reusser, Walter C. *Public School Finance.* New York: McGraw-Hill, 1951.

Mortimer, Kenneth P., Ikenberry, Stanley O., and Anderson, G. Lester. *Governance and Emerging Values in Higher Education.* Report no. 12, Center for the Study of Higher Education. University Park, Pennsylvania: The Pennsylvania State University, 1971.

Nachtigal, Paul. *A Foundation Goes to School: The Ford Foundation Comprehensive School Improvement Program, 1960-1970.* New York: The Ford Foundation, 1972.

Nash, Robert J., and Ducharme, Edward R. "The University Can Prepare Teachers." *Educational Forum* 39, no. 1 (November, 1974): 99-109.*

National Association of State Directors of Teacher Education and Certification. "Revisions of 1971 Edition, Standards for State Approval of Teacher Education." Salt Lake City, Utah: Utah State Board of Education, 1972. (Mimeographed)

National Committee for Citizens in Education, Commission on Educational Governance. *Public Testimony on Public Schools.* Berkeley, California: McCutchan Publishing Corp., 1975.

National Council for Accreditation of Teacher Education. *Constitution.* Washington, D.C.: The Council, 1974.

——. *Twenty-First Annual List, 1974-75.* Washington, D.C.: The Council, 1975.*

——. *Standards for Accreditation of Teacher Education.* Washington, D.C.: The Council, 1954, 1958, 1960 and January, 1970. (Reprinted 1972)

——. *Training Document.* Washington, D.C.: The Council, 1972.*

National Education Association. "What Does Governance Mean?" *Today's Education,* December, 1971.*

——, Council on Instruction and Professional Development. *NEA Report on Practitioner Involvement in Teacher Education, 1973-74.* Appendix. Washington, D.C.: The Association, 1974. Pp. 87-89.

——, National Commission on Teacher Education and Professional Standards. *A Model Teacher Standards and Licensure Act.* Washington, D.C.: The Association, 1971.

——, National Commission on Teacher Education and Professional Standards. *Governance for the Teaching Profession,* Working paper no. 1. Washington, D.C.: The Association, 1970.

——, National Commission on Teacher Education and Professional Standards. *Guidelines for Establishing Greater Student Voice in Teacher Education Through a Student-Faculty Committee.* Washington, D.C.: The Association, 1968. (ED-028-132)

——, National Commission on Teacher Education and Professional Standards. *Self-Governance for the Teaching Profession: Why?* Washington, D.C.: The Association, 1970.* (ED-045-578)

——, National Commission on Teacher Education and Professional Standards. *The Education of Teachers: Curriculum Programs. A Guide for Follow-up Studies of the Kansas TEPS Conference.* Washington, D.C.: The Commission, National Education Association, 1959.*

——. *Teachers Can Change Teacher Education.* Washington, D.C.: The Association, 1976. P. 42. (a)

——. *Resolutions, New Business, and Other Actions, 1976-1977.* Washington, D.C.: The National Education Association, 1976, p. 75. (b)

——, National Commission on Teacher Education and Professional Standards. *The Education of Teachers: Considerations in Planning Institutional Programs.* 1960 Regional TEPS Conferences. Washington, D.C.: The Commission, National Education Association, 1960.

"Number of Doctoral Granting Institutions in the United States." *The Chronicle of Higher Education,* February 19, 1974, p. 8.*

O'Hanlon, James. "Organizing a College of Education." *Journal of Teacher Education* 27, no. 2 (Summer, 1976): 132-135.*

Oliver, Kenneth H., Jr., and Miller, Kathryn J. *Organizational Patterns of Certain Colleges and Universities in the United States Enrolling 5,000 to 10,000 Students.* Springfield, Missouri: Southwest Missouri State College, 1966.*

Olson, Paul. "Articles Based on Correspondence and Official Reports." In *Undergraduate Preparation of Educational Personhel Program.* Lincoln, Nebraska: Study Commission on Undergraduate Education and the Education of Teachers, March, 1973.*

——. "Guidelines for UPEP Program." In *Undergraduate Preparation of Educational Personnel Program.* Lincoln, Nebraska: Study Commission on Undergraduate Education and the Education of Teachers, February 1, 1973.*

——. "Manpower Information Issue Includes Data on Teachers, Sampling of States, History, Research, Policy Concerns." *Newsletter of the Study Commission on Undergraduate Education and the Education of Teachers.* Lincoln, Nebraska: The Commission, University of Nebraska, December, 1973.

——, Freeman, Larry, and Bowman, James. *Education for 1984 and After.* Lincoln, Nebraska: Directorate of the Study Commission on Undergraduate Education and the Education of Teachers, 1971.

——, et al. *The University Can't Train Teachers.* Lincoln, Nebraska: Directorate of the Study Commission on Undergraduate Education and the Education of Teachers, 1971.

Oncken, Gerald R. *Organizational Control in University Departments.* Seattle: University of Washington, Department of Psychology, 1971. (ED-057-758: Mimeographed)*

O'Neil, Robert M. "Paradoxes of Campus Power." In *New Teaching, New Learning: Current Issues in Higher Education,* ed. G. Kerry Smith. San Francisco, Ca.: Jossey-Bass, 1971. Pp. 172-178.

Orr, Paul G. "Reorganizing the College of Education." In *Education for 1984 and After,* ed. Paul A. Olson, Larry Freeman, and James Bowman. Lincoln, Nebraska: The Study Commission on Undergraduate Education and the Education of Teachers, 1972. Pp. 181-188. (a)*

——. "Restructuring University Organization Through Program Budgeting." In *Education for 1984 and After,* ed. Paul A. Olson, Larry Freeman, and James Bowman. Lincoln, Nebraska: Study Commission on Undergraduate Education and the Education of Teachers, University of Nebraska, 1972. (b)

Pangborn, Jesse M. *The Evolution of the American Teachers College.* Contributions to Education no. 500. New York: Teachers College, Columbia University Bureau of Publications, 1932.

Partridge, Arthur Ray. "The Rise of the University School of Education as a Professional Institution." Ed. D. diss., Stanford University, 1957.

Perkins, James A. (ed.) *The University as an Organization.* A report for the Carnegie Commission on Higher Education. New York: McGraw-Hill, 1973.*

Peterson, Marvin W. "Decentralization: A Strategic Approach." *Journal of Higher Education.* 42, no. 6 (June, 1971): 521-539.

Pi Lambda Theta. *The Body of Knowledge Unique to the Profession of Education.* Washington, D.C.: Pi Lambda Theta, 1966.

Pilcher, Paul S. "Teacher Centers: Can They Work Here?" *Phi Delta Kappan* 54, no. 5 (January, 1973): 340-343.

Pilecki, Francis J. *The Interrelations of Systems: A Systems Look at Where Teacher Education Fits into the Whole of Education, University and Society.* Washington, D.C.: ERIC Clearinghouse on Teacher Education, 1972.

Pino, Lewis N. *Nothing But Praise.* Lincoln, Nebraska: Nebraska Curriculum Development Center, University of Nebraska, 1972.

Poliakoff, Lorraine. "Teacher Centers: An Outline of Current Information." *Journal of Teacher Education* 23, no. 1 (Fall, 1972): 389-397.*

Pomeroy, Edward C. "About AACTE." In *Issues in Governance for Performance-Based Teacher Education,* ed. Michael W. Kirst. Washington, D.C.: American Association of Colleges for Teacher Education, 1973. Pp. 28-29.

——— . "American Association of Colleges for Teacher Education." In *The Encyclopedia of Education,* ed. Lee C. Deighton. New York: Macmillan and The Free Press, 1971. Vol. 1, pp. 177-178.*

——— . *Beyond the Upheaval.* Thirteenth Charles W. Hunt Lecture. Washington, D.C.: American Association of Colleges for Teacher Education, 1972.

——— . "What's Going on in Teacher Education—The View from Washington." *Journal of Teacher Education* 26, no. 3 (Fall, 1975): 196-201.*

Price, James L. *Organizational Effectiveness.* Homewood, Illinois: Richard D. Irwin, Inc., 1968.*

Prorus, Malcolm M. *The Grand Experiment: The Life and Death of the TTT Program as Seen through the Eyes of its Evaluators.* Ed. Bonnie Herndon. Berkeley, Ca.: McCutchan Publishing Corporation, 1975.*

Puffer, Richard J. *The Educational Research Involvement and Capabilities of Institutions for Teacher Education.* Evanston, Illinois: Northwestern University, 1967. (ED-013-250)

Purpel, David E. "Teacher Educators: Followers or Leaders?" *Journal of Teacher Education* 20, no. 1 (Spring, 1969): 111-115.*

Rackley, J. R. "University Organization for Teacher Education." In *Eighth Yearbook.* Oneonta, New York: American Association of Colleges for Teacher Education, 1955. Pp. 73-83.

Robb, Felix C. "Teachers: The Need and the Task." In *A Decade of Thought on Teacher Education: The Charles W. Hunt Lectures.* Washington, D.C.: The American Association of Colleges for Teacher Education, 1969.

Robert, E. B. "Statement on Teacher Education and Professional Standards and Summary of Response to an Inquiry Dated October 10, 1957." Baton Rouge, Louisiana: Louisiana State University, 1957. (Mimeographed)

Robertson, Neville, and Sistler, Jack K. *The Doctorate in Education: The Institutions.* Bloomington, Indiana: Phi Delta Kappa and the American Association of Colleges for Teacher Education, 1971.

Robinson, Donald W. "One View of the U. Mass Mess." *Phi Delta Kappan* 56, no. 8 (April, 1975): 532-534.

Rogers, James F. *Higher Education as a Field of Study at the Doctoral Level.* Washington, D.C.: American Association for Higher Education, 1969.

Rourke, Francis E., and Brooks, Glenn E. "The Managerial Revolution in Higher Education." In *Academic Governance*, ed. J. Victor Baldridge. Berkeley, California: McCutchan Publishing Corp., 1971.*

Rudolph, Frederick. *The American College and University.* New York: Random House, Vintage Books, 1962.

Rummel, J. Francis. "The Future Structure of the University." Intra-campus memorandum. Missoula, Montana: The University of Montana School of Education, 1973. (Mimeographed)

Russell, James Earl. "A Summary of Some of the Difficulties Connected with the Making of a Teachers College." In *Yearbook, 1924.* Oneonta, New York: The American Association of Teachers Colleges. Pp. 23-28.

Rutkowski, Edward. "A Study of the Various Viewpoints Expressed Concerning the Establishment of University Schools of Education During Their Formative Years, 1890-1905." Ph.D. diss., Michigan State University of Agriculture and Applied Science. 1964.*

Ryan, Kevin A. (ed.) *Teacher Education in 1975.* Yearbook, Part II. Chicago: The National Society for the Study of Education, The University of Chicago Press, 1975.*

Sagan, Edgar L., and Smith, Barbara G. *Alternative Models for the Cooperative Governance of Teacher Education Programs.* Lincoln, Nebraska: The Nebraska Curriculum Development Center, University of Nebraska, 1973.

Schein, Edgar H. *Professional Education—Some New Directions.* A report of the Carnegie Commission on Higher Education. New York: McGraw-Hill, 1972.

Schmieder, Allen A. "A Glossary of Educational Reform." *Journal of Teacher Education* 24, no. 1 (Spring, 1973): 55-62.

Selden, William K. *Accreditation: A Struggle over Standards in Higher Education.* New York: Harper and Brothers, 1960.

Sharp, Paul F. What Might Be Done through Associations, University Structures, and Career Patterns to Increase Involvement of the Scholar. Paper presented at the Park Grove Institute, June, 1969. (In ED-052-148, *Five Levels of Incompetence*)

Shipman, M. D. *Participation and Staff-Student Relations. A Seven Year Study of Social Changes in an Expanding College of Education.* Research into

Higher Education Monographs, no. 6. London, England: The Society for Research into Higher Education, Ltd., 1969. (ED-029-611)

Silberman, Charles E. *Crisis in the Classroom.* New York: Random House, 1970.

Smith, B. Othanel. "A Joint Task: The Preparation of Teachers." *Journal of Teacher Education* 10, no. 2 (June, 1959): 189-198.*

——, Cohen, S. B., and Cohen, Pearl A. *Teachers for the Real World.* Washington, D.C.: The American Association of Colleges for Teacher Education, 1969.*

Smith, E. Brooks, and Johnson, Patrick. *Cooperative Structures in School-College Relationships for Teacher Education.* Washington, D.C.: The American Association of Colleges for Teacher Education, 1965.

——, and Johnson, Patrick (eds.) *School-College Relationships in Teacher Education: Report of a National Survey of Cooperative Ventures.* Washington, D.C.: The American Association of Colleges for Teacher Education, 1964.*

——, et al. *Partnership in Teacher Education.* American Association of Colleges for Teacher Education. Washington, D.C.: Association for Student Teaching, 1968. (ED-022-726)*

Smith, G. Kerry (ed.) *New Teaching, New Learning: Current Issues in Higher Education, 1971.* San Francisco, Ca.: Jossey-Bass. 1971.*

——. *The Troubled Campus: Current Issues in Higher Education, 1970.* San Francisco, Ca.: Jossey-Bass, 1970.

Smith, Mark. *Developing Guidelines in Teacher Education.* Washington, D.C.: Associated Organizations for Teacher Education, 1969.*

Smith, William L. "Government's Responsibility in Improving Education Outcomes." *Journal of Teacher Education* 26, no. 1 (Spring, 1975): 35-40.

Snedden, David. "What is a School of Education?" *Teachers College Record* 30 (1929): 656-660.*

Southern Regional Education Board. *The Organization of Higher Education.* Atlanta, Georgia: The Board, 1967.*

Southworth, Horton C. "Needed: A Revolution in Teacher Education." *Pennsylvania School Journal* 117 (September, 1968): 6-8 (Summary from ERIC document ED-025-454)

Spillane, Robert R., and Levenson, Dorothy. "Teacher Training: A Question of Control, Not Content." *Phi Delta Kappan* 57, no. 7 (March, 1976): 435-439.

Statler, Ellsworth S. "Some Principles for Teacher Education." *Journal of Teacher Education* 13, no. 1 (March, 1962): 12-18.*

Stiles, Lindley J., et al. *Teacher Education in the United States.* New York: The Ronald Press, 1960.*

Stinnett, T. M. "The Accreditation of Teacher Education Institutions and Agencies." *Phi Delta Kappan* 52, no. 1 (1970): 25-31.*

——. (ed.) *Unfinished Business of the Teaching Profession in the 1970's.* Bloomington, Indiana: Phi Delta Kappa Inc., 1971.*

Stone, James C. "Breakthrough in Teacher Education?" In *Improving Teacher Education in the United States,* ed. Stanley Elam. Bloomington, Indiana: Phi Delta Kappa, Inc., 1967. Pp. 165-190.

——. "One Step Further." In *Innovative Programs in Student Teaching,* ed. Roy Edelfelt. Baltimore, Maryland: Maryland State Department of Education, 1969. Pp. 135-144.

Strowbridge, E. D. *Cooperative Program in Teacher Education: Model for an Educational Complex.* Corvallis, Oregon: Corvallis School District 509J, 1970. (ED-053-082)

Subcommittee on School-College Relationships in Teacher Education of the Committee on Studies. *Cooperative Structures in School-College Relationships for Teacher Education.* Washington, D.C.: The American Association of Colleges for Teacher Education, 1965.*

Tack, Martha W. "Program-Based Organization in Colleges of Education." Ph.D. diss., University of Alabama, 1973.

Taylor, Harold. *The World and the American Teacher.* Washington, D.C.: The American Association of Colleges for Teacher Education, 1968.*

Teacher Education in the United States: The Responsibility Gap. A Report by the Study Commission on Undergraduate Education and the Education of Teachers. Lincoln, Nebraska: University of Nebraska Press, 1976.

"Teaching Centers." *The Journal of Teacher Education,* Special Issue, Vol. XXV, No. 1, Spring, 1974.

Thompson, James D. (ed.) *Approaches to Organizational Design.* Pittsburgh: The University of Pittsburgh Press, 1966.*

Travers, Kenneth J. "School-University Cooperation: A Search for New Structures in Teacher Education." A paper presented at the 1971 annual meeting of the National Council of Teachers of Mathematics, Anaheim, California. (Revised, October, 1971) Urbana, Illinois: University of Illinois, 1971. (Mimeographed)

Travers, Robert M. W. *Empirically Based Teacher Education.* A paper presented to the Society of Professors of Education at its annual meeting in Chicago, February 22, 1974. Minneapolis, Minnesota: The College of Education, University of Minnesota, 1974.

Tyler, Ralph. *A Viable Model for a College of Education.* An address presented at the inauguration of Dean Doi, University of Rochester, October 30, 1971. Rochester, N.Y.: University of Rochester, 1971. (ED-059-961)

Tyson, James C., and Carroll, Mary Ann. "Will Schools of Education Survive?" *Journal of Teacher Education* 23, no. 4 (Winter, 1972): 438-441.

U.S., Congress. *An Act to Amend and Extend the National Defense Act of 1958.* Public law 88-665. 88th Cong., October 16, 1964.

U.S., Congress. *Economic Opportunity Act of 1964.* Public law 88-452. 88th Cong., August 20, 1964.

U.S., Congress. *Education Amendments of 1972.* 92d Cong., 2d sess., Report no. 92-798. Title III, sec. 405. The National Institute of Education.

U.S., Congress. *National Defense Education Act of 1958.* Public law 85-8642. 85th Cong., September 2, 1958.

U.S. Office of Education, Bureau of Educational Personnel Development. *Education Professions Development Act: Facts about Programs for 1971-72,* parts B, C, D, and F. Washington, D.C.: The U.S. Office of Education, 1971. (OE-58030-72)

U.S. Office of Education. *Proposed Minimum Standards for State Approval of Teacher Preparing Institutions.* Circular no. 351. Washington, D.C.: U.S. Office of Education, 1952, 1966.

U.S. Office of Education. *Education Directory,* 1968-69 and 1975. Washington, D.C.: U.S. Office of Education. DHEW publ. no. (10E) 75-01040.

University of Illinois, College of Education. *A Report to the National Council for the Accreditation of Teacher Education.* Urbana: University of Illinois, College of Education, 1971.*

University of Wisconsin. *School of Education Newsletter.* "New Department in Vocational Education." Madison, Wisconsin: University of Wisconsin School of Education, 1973. P. 4.

Verduin, John R., Jr. *Conceptual Models in Teacher Education.* Washington, D.C.: The American Association of Colleges for Teacher Education, 1967.

Vogt, Thomas. *Five Levels of Incompetence, Higher Education, Teaching and the Education of Teachers.* Report of the Park Grove Institute, June 10-15, 1969. Washington, D.C.: U.S. Office of Education, 1969. (ED-052-148)*

Wahlquist, John T., et al. *The Administration of Public Education.* New York: The Ronald Press, 1952.

Wesley, Edgar B. "American Education, 1945-1973." *Notes and Abstracts in American International Education,* no. 42 (Spring, 1973): 1-6. Ann Arbor, Michigan, School of Education.

Wesley, Edgar B. *N.E.A.: The First Hundred Years.* New York: Harper and Brothers, 1957.

Whitney, Allen S. *History of the Professional Training of Teachers: At the University of Michigan for the First Half Century, 1879-1929.* Ann Arbor, Michigan, Wahr Bookstor, Inc., Publisher, 1931.*

Wiggins, Sam P. "The American Teachers College Revisited." *Journal of Teacher Education* 28, no. 2 (Summer, 1967): 227-232.

Williams, Robert L. *The Administration of Academic Affairs in Higher Education.* Ann Arbor, Michigan: University of Michigan Press, 1965.*

Wilson, Logan. (ed.) *Emerging Patterns in American Higher Education.* Washington, D.C.: American Council on Education, 1965.*

Wirt, Frederick, and Kirst, Michael W. *Political and Social Foundations of Education.* Berkeley, California: McCutchan Publishing Corp., 1972.

Woodring, Paul. *Investment in Innovation: An Historical Appraisal of the Fund for the Advancement of Education.* Boston: Little, Brown and Co., 1970.*

——— . "The Short, Happy Life of the Teachers College." In *American Education Today,* ed. Paul Woodring and John Scanlon. New York: McGraw-Hill, 1963.

Wright, J. Zeb. *Models for Revising Teacher Education.* Charleston, West Virginia: The West Virginia State Department of Education, 1971. (ED-054-081)

Zemansky, Mark W. "Learned Societies: The American Association of Physics Teachers." In *The Encyclopedia of Education,* ed. by Lee C. Deighton. New York: Macmillan and The Free Press, 1971. Vol. 1, pp. 182-183.

Zook, George F., and Hagerty, M. E. *Principles of Accrediting Higher Institutions.* Chicago: The University of Chicago Press, 1942.